ALARMS AND EXCURSIONS

Alarms and Excursions

THIRTY YEARS
IN ISRAEL

NAOMI SHEPHERD

COLLINS
8 Grafton Street, London W1
1990

William Collins Sons & Co. Ltd
London · Glasgow · Sydney · Auckland
Toronto · Johannesburg

BRITISH LIBRARY CATALOGUING IN PUBLICATION DATA

Shepherd, Naomi
Alarms and excursions: thirty years in Israel.
1. Israel. Social life, 1948–. Biographies
I. Title
956.9405092

ISBN 0 00 215333–5

First pubished in 1990
Copyright © Naomi Shepherd 1990

Map by Martin Gilbert

Photoset in Linotron Ehrhardt at The Spartan Press Ltd
Lymington, Hampshire
Printed and bound in Great Britain by
T.J. Press (Padstow) Ltd, Padstow, Cornwall

For Josh

Acknowledgement

I should like to thank Carol O'Brien, my editor at Collins, for her critical advice and guidance during the writing of this memoir.

Contents

1 A 'British' Girlhood   1

2 Terminus   12

3 On the Road   43

4 Matters of Life and Death   67

5 Intermezzo   100

6 War   130

7 Upheaval   145

8 The Children of the Intifada   179

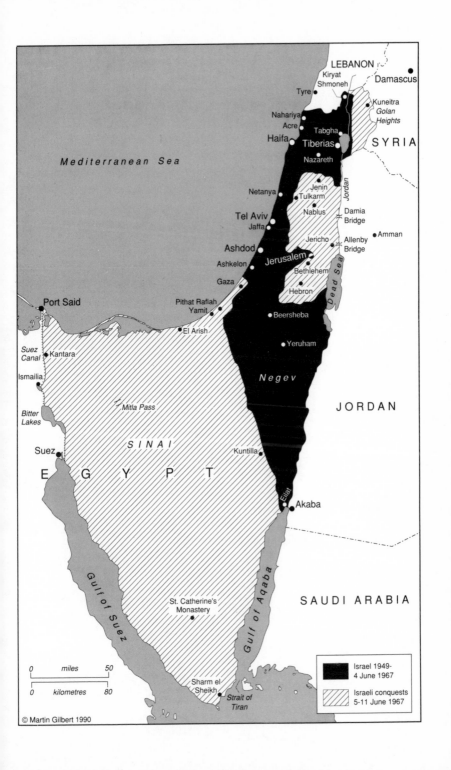

LEBANON
Damascus
Kiryat Shmoneh
Tyre
Kuneitra
Golan Heights
Nahariya
Acre
Tabgha
Haifa
Tiberias
SYRIA
Nazareth
Netanya
Jenin
Tulkarm
Nablus
Jordan
Damia Bridge
Tel Aviv
Jaffa
Jericho
Allenby Bridge
Amman
Ashdod
Jerusalem
Ashkelon
Bethlehem
Dead Sea
Gaza
Hebron
Pithat Rafiah
Yamit
Beersheba
Port Said
El Arish
Yeruham
Suez Canal
Kantara
Mediterranean Sea
Ismailia
Negev
Bitter Lakes
Mitla Pass
JORDAN
S I N A I
Kuntilla
Suez
E G Y P T
Eilat
Akaba
Gulf of Suez
Gulf of Aqaba
SAUDI ARABIA
St. Catherine's Monastery

0   miles   50
0   kilometres   80

Sharm el Sheikh
Strait of Tiran

© Martin Gilbert 1990

■ Israel 1949–4 June 1967

▨ Israeli conquests 5–11 June 1967

I

A 'British' Girlhood

EVERY GARDEN in our road had a lawn surrounded by flower-beds with nasturtiums, sweet williams and Canterbury bells; ours was the only garden where knives and forks were planted among the flowers after accidental use – for meat as well as milk dishes, or milk after meat. Sometimes they were forgotten and rusted there. Sometimes the cat, or the gardener, would displace them. By the time I went to school, the custom had lapsed, like so many other remnants of the culture of my immigrant grandparents.

While I was still a small girl, my father ceased laying phylacteries. I used to peer round the dining-room door, watching him tie the little black boxes containing their tiny scrolls to his arm and forehead by their long, silky tapes. He was solemn in his white shirt and dark trousers, the spats already fastened on his glistening black shoes. The phylacteries, like the spats, disappeared after the war, discarded appendages.

When I graduated from nursery suppers to dinner with my parents, talk at the table centred on the refugees and the 'British'. This puzzled me. I knew who the refugees were: my nannies, with their starched aprons, chapped hands, a series of Ursels and Gretels rapidly replaced; later, the parents of my schoolfriends, those girls whose birthday parties always ended with pencil and paper games that were historical seminars, instead of crackers being pulled. German-Jewish parents seemed not to have heard of crackers. But who were 'the British'?

'Aren't we British?' I asked. Of course we were. Britain was the most civilized country in the world, said my mother categorically.

That was why my grandparents had chosen to live here, rather than to remain in Czarist Russia, or in Latvia. That was my good luck, because otherwise I might have been, like so many other Jewish children, a pile of ashes, or shut down in the hold of a ship making its way at night, past 'the British', to the coast of Palestine.

The ice-cream man's bell rang in the road outside. My mother's eyes were damp; my mouth watered. I could not interrupt her to ask for ice-cream, though the van was just outside, beyond the mountain-ash trees in the front garden. Why were the trees called 'mountain-ash'? There was no ash on them, but bright red berries, like drops of blood.

The identity of 'the British' only became clear later, when I was taken to Zionist meetings by my parents, and left in the cloakroom to finish my homework among the coats. While most of my schoolfriends collected autographs from Margot Fonteyn and Alec Guinness, I held up my album for Herbert Morrison and Harold Laski to sign. 'The British' were synonymous with 'the Foreign Office people', and Labour was going to do something about it. However, the Jews were accused by Bevin of trying to get to the head of the queue. Henceforth, I was careful to keep my place in all queues: bus queues, post-office queues, ballet queues. You didn't ask people to keep a place for you while you went off for a hot mug of tea; you stayed exactly where you were, even if the thermos leaked.

Palestine, the refugees' sanctuary, was an important part of my life in at least one sense: my parents had met at a Zionist conference in the late 1920s. That accounted for birth. But it was also a family graveyard. My paternal grandmother had drunk from a street-vendor's water-jug in Jaffa and within days died of typhoid. Her husband, a tyrannical white-bearded patriarch with a black-velvet skull-cap, had built a villa on Mount Carmel and died there, in traditional Jewish style, in his eighties. (His London house had a pair of stags' antlers over the fireplace – another early puzzle.) An uncle by marriage, sent out to Haifa to manage a branch of the family's glass business, a mild man with mutton-chop whiskers, had been dragged from his car and knifed to death in the Arab town during the revolt of 1936. His widow, who wrote novels, kept his study untouched in that villa, I was told, like Queen Victoria after Albert died.

My parents' Zionist sympathies were philanthropic, educational and sentimental. My mother said she would like to spend the winters there, but not the summers, because of the heat. I saw my father's early Zionism as parallel to his First World War pacifism, for which he was jailed and his health permanently damaged. He was a disciple of Bertrand Russell and the No Conscription Fellowship, and Russell's books, like those of Brailsford, Massingham, Romain Rolland and Shaw, with others who had influenced him as a boy, stood side by side on the bookshelves with the glass fronts that snapped down on unwary fingers, with the writings of Herzl, Hess and Weizmann. I thought this a natural partnership.

To help the refugees, I put pocket money in the blue money-box with the chain over the vent to stop you fishing it out again; but I noticed that when the man came to collect it, my mother would write a cheque. She had worked for the Zionist movement before her marriage, had met Weizmann, Sokolow, the Eders, legendary figures. She insisted on calling our suburban house 'Eglon' (an Amorite town) rather than Hillside, or The Beeches, as everyone else did, and kept a tin of Israeli sardines, first product of the Israeli canning industry and a souvenir of one of her many visits, in the same walnut-faced drawer as her jewellery. It was still there when she died.

We were never allowed a Christmas tree, though my mother would always give something to the carol singers, as she did to the man who switched the blue boxes with the chain. My father pointed out that we children had twice as many school holidays as our non-Jewish friends; two New Years, and chocolate Easter eggs kept until after Passover.

At the Jewish New Year, in synagogue, the old ladies wore fur coats, in warm Septembers already sprinkled with the snow of mothballs. On Yom Kippur, they all sniffed from little sea-green bottles of smelling-salts, began sobbing at the beginning of the Memorial Service, and dried their eyes neatly at its end. Were they weeping, I wondered, for the interminable list of the defunct rabbis of the United Synagogue, or for some private grief? I marvelled at the zeal with which businessmen, accountants and doctors tapped their chests and confessed to the lists of sins for which they deserved 'the four kinds of death inflicted by the Court of Law: stoning, burning, beheading and strangling'. Looking through the list of sins for one which applied to me, I found 'the sin wherein we have sinned before thee by despising parents and teachers', and beat my still-flat chest energetically. The priests (on ordinary days, plain Mr Cohens of the district) pulled their prayer-shawls over their heads and flapped them at us, amiable ghosts, during the final benedictions, sung raggedly, and never in unison. I pitied my Christian friends with their over-explicit prayers, and their absolute decorum, in their cold, odourless churches.

I lost my belief in God at puberty, for no memorable reason; it was not a subject for discussion but a private matter, like the family finances and the way my parents voted. My parents, tiring of the archaisms, eventually left the traditional synagogue of which my father had been a founding member, with his name in the stained-glass window, and opted for the Reform movement, plain wood. During the last years of his life, my father chose to spend the Day of Atonement in Paris, as it fitted in with his autumn business itinerary. He would leave the little synagogue in the rue Copernic at nightfall and stroll back down the Champs-Élysées, sublimely unaware of any incongruity, to break his fast not on herring, crackers and chicken soup as we had done at home, but on *sole meunière* and *fraises du bois*.

A series of teachers, most of them perpetual students, had been engaged from my early childhood to teach me Hebrew. By adolescence, I could read the books describing the struggles of the Palestinian Jewish pioneers, but they had no purchase on my imagination, unable to compete with the French Romantic poets. One of my teachers was an ex-Israeli who made a living by giving Hebrew lessons. He wore celluloid collars, which I had never seen before, and used one long grey fingernail as a pointer, like the ritual wands used in synagogue. His general air of physical neglect suggested contempt for the middle-class English homes where, as a supplement to the Hebrew textbooks, he taught the daughters of the fleshpots the ringing, obsessional verses of the prophets. I was at an age when even the word 'thigh' made me blush, and to read Jeremiah with this young man was torture, especially when I glanced at the English. 'For the greatness of thine iniquity are thy skirts discovered, and thy heels made bare.' Heels? Another euphemism, it emerged, of the faulty but superb King James Version. I was determined that we should never reach the neighings, whoredom and abominations which lay five verses further on, and fortunately the Israeli had a long roster of girls and a poor memory.

Before long I was the only Jewish girl in my class at school without an engagement ring, and with plans for further study and travel. I had been brought up to have an enquiring mind and I was as curious sexually as I was intellectually. That curiosity had no ethnic limits, and I was shocked when my mother informed me that if I were to marry a Gentile my parents would go into mourning. This did not square, in my view, with reading Tom Paine and Berdayev, and membership of the Left Book Club.

When I left home for Oxford, primeval sexual fears stirred in my mother. The dreaming spires suggested to her not only the studies she had missed (her father's repeated bankruptcies had interrupted her own university education) but an alien phallic threat. She wanted me to promise that I would not be alone in my room with a non-Jewish male. I countered by telling her that I would inform the college that I could not take up their offer because of parental prejudice. That worked, but I avoided further confrontations and kept my various adventures to myself, which was possible because from that time on I never lived at home. A discreet silence was maintained, and when I married a dozen years later, she destroyed the love-letters I had carelessly left in a cupboard at home and remarked that I had had 'a very good innings'.

Where Oxford was concerned, my mother need not have worried. There was no resemblance whatever between the Gentile seducers of my grandparents' nightmares and the inexperienced young men who visited my room at Somerville. My Picasso reproductions and my large photograph of Michelangelo's uncircumcised David (amputated at the loins by the framer at my mother's insistence) did nothing to make the room look less like the attic of a girls' boarding-school, the wallpaper mended with safety-pins. The young men came, unwound their college scarves; they toasted muffins, pink-knuckled, discussed Arnold and Freud, Catullus and Claudel, rewound their scarves and left. They looked no more like men to me than a row of parsnips; parsnips was my thought, as I sat opposite them at muffin-time, gazing at the only part of them revealed to me, half an inch of grainy shin between trouser-leg and sock.

One winter, when the snow had frozen in ridges along the Woodstock Road and we had crawled, hands mittened, part of the way to Merton, I was pulled into a cupboard and embraced vigorously by a handsome undergraduate, but when we started breaking crockery we were pulled out by the celebrated logician to whom the cupboard belonged. On the next day I received an apology on a card in Latin, and for some weeks afterwards I stood freezing on the sidelines of the rugger field holding the young man's sweater and watching his white legs tauten in the scrum, but when I showed more interest he shied away like a colt.

I was enjoying muffins with another young man when a postgraduate scholar I worked with on the university magazine, *Isis*, burst in and ordered me out, making it clear that he had prior claims.

Ironically, the only man in Oxford with the kind of designs on me which my mother feared was a New York Jewish painter with a noisy motor cycle, one of the crowd of university hangers-on we affected to despise, not much higher in the social scale than the American airmen from Brize Norton whom we passed, eyes averted, as they stood glued to the college scouts at the entrance to the college on Saturday nights. My demon lover was a buccaneering don, but he didn't exist. The real dons were bland or desiccated, like preserves left too long in an expensive grocer's.

So my dearest companion, in that first year, was a former rabbinical scholar, a rebel against Jewish orthodoxy, reading philosophy at Balliol, a chastely affectionate friend. 'Don't forget that Jews weren't admitted here until recently,' he warned me. 'The colleges were monastic foundations, and we're outsiders.'

I wanted to reject this, but had to admit the feeling of being different. It had been there from the first day, when the Mission people had canvassed my membership and, politely rebuffed, had tipped off the Socialist Club (which was in fact communist). No one else in the college, I found, was 'British', except perhaps for one Pakistani girl who became my friend. The London girls had memories of an old parish. I had none. I couldn't really claim Ystelyfera, my father's native village in Glamorgan, where the Bible-reading Welsh for miles around had come to press their noses against the windows at Passover 'to hear the old Jew sing'. My mother had been born within the sound of Bow Bells, but was not working-class. I resented, now, being taken up because I was Jewish and curly-haired – hence somehow flamboyant, exotic, oriental; I was none of these.

What made matters worse was my disappointment with the Oxford system. I craved intellectual rigour, but the teaching I experienced – philology apart – was undirected and superficial. I was reading the wrong subject – English literature rather than history, as I had quarrelled at school with my history teacher and walked out of her classes – and it was unheard of to ask for a change. My tutors were, I suspected, bored by undergraduates and would have preferred to be left to their own research. Mary Lascelles, my moral tutor, announced when she first convened us that, ideally, she would have taught no more than two students a year; there were ten of us.

Lascelles was a châtelaine in a medieval epic: beautiful, melancholy, immured in her rooms save for her excursions to the chapel, a building I never entered. Access to her rooms was a social ordeal. There was the challenge of judging the exact rhythm and volume of the tap on the 'oak', the social foreplay, the difficult balance between respect and familiarity, the atmosphere of fear and intimacy combined, which I was to recognize when I read Rubashov's encounters with Ivanov in *Darkness at Noon*. But, unlike Rubashov, I did not know what my inquisitress required of me. I bounded at her with quotes and ideas, like a puppy bringing pieces of bone and old slipper to an increasingly irritated mistress. It was after one of these tutorials that the thought occurred to me that it was somehow wrong, impertinent even, for me to be studying English literature.

My worries crystallized on the way back from the class on John Donne with Helen Gardner – the only intellectual experience of my Oxford years. Of the six young women who had been listening to Gardner's exposition of 'To His Mistris Going to Bed', five had been reduced to smirks and giggles. I had overcome the problem of reading erotic texts back with Jeremiah. But the absurdity of inexperienced nineteen-year-olds (in the English 1950s, inevitably so) reading texts about sexual passion was dwarfed by my sense of the incongruity of my studying the literature so clearly the product of a Christian civilization.

I wrote elegant little essays on *Piers Plowman, Religio Medici*; I knew Donne's sermons and devotions almost by heart. But what catechism had I ever recited? A three-personed God would never batter my heart, for the Lord of Israel was obstinately One. The New Testament, with the Christmas trees, had been outlawed from 'Eglon', and I wrote about Browne and Milton mentally omitting the name of Christ, as I had done in choir practice at school when, in flagrant violation of the concordat with the large Jewish contingent, the headmistress introduced explicitly Christian hymns into what was known as Universal Prayers.

The problem went deeper. My concept of history started with the Enlightenment and disappeared into the pit with Auschwitz.

8

My family thought Conservative but, I suspected, voted Labour. I could place them neither as Whigs nor Tories. Nor was I a High Sephardi. When Disraeli was buying shares in Suez for England, my forefathers had been dodging the cruel recruiting officers of the Czar. I admired Marvell and Wordsworth, but the countryside they described was almost unknown to me. My father had been raised in a village he never revisited, preferring to holiday abroad.

Here surely was a case for a moral tutor; but to consult Mary Lascelles was out of the question. I took my problem to a philosophy tutor whom I knew slightly.

'Typical of the way in which your subject is taught,' she responded. 'You gels are actually encouraged to make judgements on the basis of emotional response, which is rather, do you see, as if I were to attempt to construct a table from pink blancmange. In theory it is possible, but the table will not serve any practical purpose.'

Blancmange was served at college suppers, edible blotting-paper. Not a Jewish dish. Another area of ignorance yawned before me.

'When you say that you *ought* not to be studying English literature, I take it that, though you employ a moral term, you are not saying that in studying Chaucer, or Milton, you are offending against a religious code, a Jewish Index, as it were?'

I could not explain that she had the problem upside down. In any case, my rabbinical friend, not I, would have known the answer. Was a Jew permitted to read *Holy Dying*? My face burned.

'I'm not an orthodox Jew,' I said.

'Then what you *intended* to say', she went on, 'was that you are *ill equipped* to study the syllabus because of your ignorance of the Gospels and lack of familiarity with the more common plants and animals of the country. It seems to me that you could get yourself a copy of the New Testament, and join the University Ramblers – I think there is some such group – to solve the second problem.'

I read the Gospels, but didn't join the University Ramblers.

Instead, I went further afield after Oxford, to Paris and to Rome, and a remote Italian province. I earned my living in Paris as front girl in the British consulate, helping to repatriate Distressed British Subjects; and in Rome, teaching shopkeepers basic English. Like many young Jews with my background, I developed a passionate interest in another political struggle – in my case that of Italian socialism – and, like many young Englishwomen, fell in love with an Italian. I reappeared sporadically in London, where for a few months I worked for a well-known publisher of educational books. I gained little knowledge of publishing, save how to dispose of unsolicited manuscripts, which were temporarily stored in a metal cabinet in the corner of the office, and when that was full, tossed on top of it. One of these dog-eared notebooks dealt with the Israeli-Egyptian conflict; I gave it a bored and cursory look, and flipped it on to the top of the pile. A few weeks later the Suez crisis broke.

Suez and Hungary were both felt in our office, which was full of Labour people. We acquired two fugitives from the new Hungarian regime who were given work addressing Christmas cards three months early, as they had not a word of English between them. Having done its best for political asylum, the office turned its attention to the Middle East crisis and the vanished manuscript, which had slipped down the back of the cabinet. It was decided to march on Whitehall in protest against Eden's policies. Alan, the publisher, grasped his umbrella and prepared to lead our contingent. Everyone but the Hungarians fell into line behind him. Then he looked at me solicitously. 'I suppose it's difficult for you,' he said. 'Quite all right if you prefer to stay behind.'

I was odd woman out again, and stayed in the deserted office with the speechless Hungarians. Honour demanded no less.

'Where will you go now?' he asked.

We stood looking down from the roadside on to the Pope's summer residence at Castel Gandolfo. It was as good a place as any for a last meeting, a high place, and I felt as weightless as a kite. I let the last string binding me go and floated off towards another adventure.

'I think', I said, 'that I shall go to Israel.'

2

Terminus

I SRAEL WAS less than a decade old, and improvising. A worried official at the embassy in London asked my mother whether diplomats should lead the way when going up-stairs, or allow women to go first. I was a totally untrained gradu-ate, but the Hebrew University offered me a job teaching English. There was no description of the curriculum nor, despite enquir-ies, details of the salary. When I wrote for the third time request-ing information, the department head wrote back: 'No member of the English department has yet died of inanition.' This was true, but at least once during that first year I received a slip of paper explaining that my salary would be delayed because of adminis-trative problems. Probably a donor had forgotten to endorse his cheque.

Jerusalem, that autumn, was redolent of guavas and cordite. The stacks of guavas on the roadside stalls had an acrid, exciting new smell, but the taste was disappointing unless the fruit was eaten straight from the tree. The cordite hung in the air for seconds after the rock-blasting at the new campus in Givat Ram, to the west of the Jewish half of the city; the old campus was stranded in Arab territory. The building where I taught shook all day to the sound of bulldozers and compressors, gorging and grinding the earth and rock. Quiet intervals were followed by warning shouts of *'Barood!'* – Arabic, not because there were any Arab labourers but because the Jewish labourers were Yemenites and Kurds who still spoke little Hebrew. Then the charge would go off, and fragments of limestone hurtled into the air while I discoursed on Herrick's 'A sweet disorder in the dress', Joyce's story 'The Dead', or an essay on the role of cricket in the British Empire. When I suggested that the curriculum, left over from the Mandate period, was anachronistic, the students were indignant. 'There's a tradition in *this* university,' they told me.

Israel in 1957 was a country of veterans and refugees. The veterans ran the country dynastically, while the refugees did what they were told and went where they were sent. I was neither an immigrant nor a refugee, and bypassed all the bureaucratic ordeals of newcomers. I slipped into the rock-pool of expatriate Jerusalem where people of my kind – graduates of English and American universities trying out the country – swam round and round, creating their own little currents. We might all have gone on further east, had it been possible. But it wasn't.

Jerusalem, at this time, was literally a dead end, the furthest accessible point of a territorial corridor leading up through the Judean hills from the coastal plain. The frontier which bisected the city was the frontier between Israel and the entire Arab world, between Israel and Asia. The coastline of Israel was the end of the Mediterranean, and Jerusalem gave me the feeling of running up against a wall, of being at the end of the world. One could go no further.

An absurd little railway station, built towards the end of the Ottoman period, was the last on the line from Europe, with its single track ending in a lonely pair of buffers at a crossroads overlooking the Old City walls, not far from Mount Zion. The station-keeper's smalls fluttered from a wire clothes-line like a frontier marker. It was the terminus to end all termini. There were several points from which you could peer across the frontier; the best was the roof of the Notre-Dame Hospice where, cautiously parting the nuns' washing, you spied small figures, half a mile down the hill, entering and leaving the Damascus Gate. Across the fields it was a different world, through the looking-glass. There were parts of Jerusalem that were for ever England: sewer-covers, plumbing, pillar-boxes. Odd names adhered to odd places, such as 'Miss Carey's', a house to the south-west, according to some a stud farm for Polish soldiers during the war, now a mental home.

The border itself was marked by walls dotted with gunners' nests; houses with patched blind sides; barbed wire lagging rustily through overgrown fields, no-man's-land; church windows plugged with sandbags; sheets stretched between houses to discourage snipers. One of my colleagues lived in an Arab house on the frontier, by courtesy of the Custodian of Enemy Property. The Israeli frontier post was on the roof next door. When he played Wagner on his gramophone, the frontier guards on the Jordanian side, across the road, tuned in to Um Kultumm from Cairo. Sometimes they signalled to him. When Hussein's Bedouin were on duty, they would wave; Palestinians, however, made the obscene three-finger sign.

I had loved the light and warmth of Italy, but further east along the Mediterranean it was a different physical world. For months I was always dazzled, always thirsty. It was always too hot in the sun, too cold in the shade of the stone walls. The unfamiliar raw odours of carob sap and cement and the explosions on the campus were the least of the Middle East's assault on my senses. The brilliant light of Jerusalem drained colours from the landscape at the height of the day, shrank distances, changed perspectives. There was prolonged summer, then winter, then summer again: no autumn, no spring; and a twilight as rapid as a curtain being drawn. On my first return visit to England I felt that I was entering a long, green, damp cave, the light as gentle as a caress.

In Israel, the days of the old Norse and Roman gods were gone, displaced by the stark Day One, Day Two of Creation. The Jewish Sabbath pushed Sunday aside and made it Day One. I had been used to the idea of a weekend, but here the week lurched to a halt at midday on Friday and began again on Sunday morning. The Jewish Sabbath had been a private indoor matter in England, while the world outside went on as usual. In Jerusalem, a shroud of silence fell on the city from Friday afternoon. Jaffa Road, the main street through commercial West Jerusalem, emptied of traffic and looked like the empty street in a western before the bad men and the sheriff rode in.

Though the city was divided, the existence of three days of prayer was audible, though not visible: there were few Muslim Arabs left in West Jerusalem and their cemetery was neglected, a field of nettles and gravestones on the edge of a park. The muezzin's voice, recorded and amplified, would float across the valley dividing the Old City from the western town in the early hours of the morning, and the siren announcing the beginning of the Jewish Sabbath, as if it were an air-raid by God, could be heard all over town on Friday evening. On Sunday, church bells from the Old City competed with the slapping sound of Jewish housewives beating carpets from the balconies of the New.

People were curious, angry, competitive about the rival religions. Israelis crowded into the YMCA at Christmas to hear carols played on the carillon, and drove out to Abu Ghosh, an Arab village with two churches, to hear Jewish choirs sing the Bach Passions. When the event was moved back into a Jerusalem concert hall, orthodox Jews burst in shouting protests.

In this political cul-de-sac, it was easy to decode the presence of different national groups. The solid German Jewish bourgeoisie of Rehavia, behind neatly trimmed hedges, tended private libraries and window-boxes, while sonatas trickled out of well-aired rooms; old ladies with veils counted the grocer's change in German. In the former Arab areas, huge and dignified houses were broken up with partitions and extra stairways to accommodate immigrant families from North Africa and Eastern Europe. The ultra-religious quarters were designed like Polish and Hungarian ghettos; they looked to me like sets from Eisenstein's films about the Revolution, with galleried courtyards and fur-hatted men – all that was missing was the marauding cavalry.

There were no open boulevards and pavement cafés as in Tel Aviv, a real seaside town. Here each café had its own clique. The patrons of Finks Bar, where Dave Rothschild (no relation) served the cheapest goulash soup south of Budapest, were survivors of the crack Palmach fighting corps of the War of Independence, who dismembered the last of the legends of that war with scabrous wit, and foreign journalists. Visiting American Jewish scholars, treating a year in Israel as their contribution to Israel Bonds, gathered at the Alaska Café for waffles and toasted cheese. Weimar Germany lived on at the Grete Ascher Pension and other lunch-clubs where white-aproned matrons served vegetarian cutlets and fruit soup to philosophers and jurists. Middle Europe was the Atara Café, where the cash register was guarded by an old man with the face of an angry whippet, wearing an Alpine hat with a green feather, metal bracelets against rheumatism on his wrists and, at his feet, a Pekinese with a bow round its neck. Here they served *glühwein* in winter, and the walls were decorated with paintings donated in lieu of payment.

Life in Jerusalem was austere. Few people had cars; even fewer, telephones. Little pads with attached pencils hung by doors for messages. Concerts and recitals took place in cinemas after the evening showing. Chartered buses warmed their engines noisily towards the end; it was a Jerusalem habit to leave just before the coda lest the bus leave without you. The heating systems were hazardous (in the flat I eventually rented you lit a poker, then a kerosene-soaked rag, and plunged the whole thing into an oven where a frightful explosion followed as gas roared up a chimney), and people like me trudged from home to home begging hot baths in the winter. Kerosene vendors still plied the streets with donkey carts; and you could sell your cast-offs to old-clothes men to supplement your salary.

I finally found a flat to rent from an American entomologist and his Israeli wife on the ground floor of a house in the Street of the Abyssinians. My windows faced the Ethiopian monks' cells, and the rear of the house faced Mea Shearim, the orthodox Jewish quarter; I was sandwiched between the Copts and the Hasidim. Above me lived an Iraqi flautist and his wife, in a flat so small that he had to retreat behind the door if he wanted to open it; and above them were a couple of Polish biologists. Round the corner from my house, in an alley, lived Al Altman, who had served in the American army of occupation in Japan and was, at that time, one of two experts on Japan and its culture in Jerusalem. Al and his English wife often had Japanese guests, young scholars who made paper flowers while Al made the *wonton* soup. The other expert was the artist Jacob Pins, who had a private collection of sculpture and prints he would show, with his own work, to friends invited to his studio at weekends. I learned more about Japan during my first year in Israel than I did about Jewish culture.

Mea Shearim, just beyond the Altmans' alley, was a jumble of seminaries and synagogues, and hundreds of little shops: glaziers, carpenters, silversmiths, and grocers with olives in brine barrels, pretzels and bagels piled on dusty counters, every shop in confusion while the proprietors sat reading Talmudic tracts. I had never met Jews like these and it never occurred to me that I was in any way in contravention of their way of life until one summer morning, coming out of my gate in a sleeveless dress, I almost collided with a tall Hasid, in his fur-brimmed *shtreimel* and long frock-coat, leading a small boy with fair ear-locks and a velvet embroidered skull-cap. The Hasid cast an angry, furtive look at my bare arms, spat on the ground at my feet, and directed the child to do the same.

While I lived in Abyssinian Street, Otto Preminger began filming *Exodus*: the Israeli Army played the British, the Palmach veterans played bit parts, and the street was invaded night after night by technicians trailing miles of cable. I had to argue my way home past fake British officers trying to keep unwanted extras in the wrong clothes away from the camera's range. With the proceeds from renting out their church as a film location – for the scene in which a Jewish terrorist is run to ground by British soldiers – the Coptic priests repaired its leaking dome. For a while the monks' nightly prayers took place in their cells. Their one o'clock chanting rivalled the morning *davening* from the little synagogue behind the house. Sung in a tonal system I couldn't identify, it always woke me; I could turn in bed and see the immensely tall, black figures silhouetted against the light in their windows. They, too, rocked in prayer.

The Copts sang, the Hasidim sang, and I sang too. I had two guitars: a mellow-toned French eighteenth-century lady's guitar, decorated with mother-of-pearl, and a factory-made product bought in Rome that responded more easily to the strumming with which I accompanied my repertoire of Italian and French folk songs. Most of the people I sang with were Americans; Israelis sang in groups, to concertinas, at that time. But in those days almost every American in Jerusalem with a first degree could strum on a guitar, and anyone with half an ear collected folk songs, most of them interminable ballads taken from Appalachian miners and Abruzzi peasants who were probably glad to be rid of them. Once a week we gathered at a café in the German colony and listened to Lennie Shenson, an American social worker with a marvellous foul tongue, one of the great unrecorded blues singers of the fifties.

The company I kept, beyond the circle of my university colleagues, was similar to that I had kept in Paris and Rome. I had some formal introductions, but fled the deadly Friday evenings beloved of the Israeli middle class, where men sat on one side of the room, women on the other, and getting up and moving to the men's section was the equivalent of taking your clothes off and dancing on the table. Men were offered a thimbleful of Israeli 'medicinal' brandy, women sweet vermouth, and then the drink was taken away and mountains of cream cakes appeared. Switching the order of refreshments was like stamping on the national flag; I never understood it. But the aversion to hard liquor (apart from the matter of expense) was the first sign I had in Israel of its Diaspora roots. To ask for another drink was to be instantly labelled as a drunkard.

My flat attracted the same kind of expatriate hitch-hikers I had known since leaving Oxford. There was Tom, who had been ministering to the Sicilian peasantry with Danilo Dolci, and chose to have a near breakdown in Abyssinian Street; Dick, a writer who left a trail of bad debts through Israel and used my address as a collecting post; and Harry, an American philosopher who was homesick for his analyst and insisted on telling me repeatedly, usually at two in the morning, how – but not why – he had assaulted his father in Grand Central Station. Fortunately, my teaching work kept me in touch with Israel.

*

The first time I mounted a platform in a classroom on the campus I was greeted with applause, laughter and the suggestion that I get down quickly before the English instructor arrived. All the students were older than I was. Several generations of Israelis, preoccupied with military and political duties during the first decade of the state, were now going back to school. There were army officers, from generals down, civil servants, kibbutz pensioners, political functionaries, and a sprinkling of young people a couple of years after their military service. I thought I recognized, with nostalgia, middle-class girls looking for husbands (one pretty girl actually wore skirts and white cotton gloves) and young men with rumpled hair and eyes still sticky with sleep. The fatigue, I soon learned, was from having spent the night walking the baby and most of the day in an office. Any memory of gowns, Oxford rituals, hangovers, lazy afternoons in the Meadow vanished. What was far more relevant was the year I had spent teaching basic English to the shopkeepers after they had rolled the shutters down in the Via Sistina.

I taught in the Basic Studies section of the English department and then, for a few terms, took a class in Shakespeare. By that time Israel was growing respectable and I was told that to teach a proper literature class I would need to acquire a doctorate. Snobbishly, I declined.

Basic Studies was a circus. The students came in order to acquire the reading skills necessary to decipher their political science, economics, medical and legal textbooks and agricultural manuals. What they learned were nautical terms from Billy Budd and archaic bawdiness from Shakespeare. I realized that I had never actually learned any English grammar, and improvised. I invented a few rules to please the civil servants, and explained things away, as I had done in Rome, as 'exceptions'. I demonstrated the difference between Hebrew and English use of tenses with the sentence I had picked up from my friend Philip Thody, a British student of existentialism, in Paris: 'Without that tree that he is hanging at, he will be fallen down a long time before.'

My colleagues improvised no less. Arieh Sachs, who had

recently returned from studying philosophy in Baltimore, was told to teach eighteenth-century literature. All he had read, at that stage, was *Gulliver's Travels* in an abridged school version. Pnina Eliash, formerly one of Mary Lascelles' pupils, took her duties too seriously and failed an entire class at the end of her first teaching year. The department head discreetly upped the grades. Arab students, we were given to understand, were not to be failed under any circumstances.

Adults though they were, my students loved disrupting a young woman's classes. One psychology student, dissatisfied with my paraphrases of professional terms, sat shaking his head and groaning in the front row. Another argued that Elizabethan metaphors were unnecessarily complicated, and quoted a line of Czhernikovsky: 'Put out the candle; the light needs to rest.' There was *real* poetry for you. In one class, the students chatted and threw paper pellets; in another, they slumped with their heads on the desks. I picked up my books and left. There were aggrieved deputations. Didn't I realize that they were paying for these lessons with hard-earned cash, not grants? I said that I did, and if they shut up I would get on with it. A male colleague, veteran of New York's notorious public schools, cracked under the strain and left in mid year.

We English instructors were the lascars in the boiler-room of the university; above, on the deck, were illustrious figures, survivors of the glorious Middle European years on Mount Scopus, the campus now visited once fortnightly by policemen and librarians who travelled via the Mandelbaum Gate in armoured trucks. There was Martin Buber, cheered and chaired by philosophy students on his eightieth birthday. Gershom Scholem still lectured. I knew the historian Jacob Talmon, an endearing man (I did not know his ferocious reputation in the classroom), always ready for a talk on politics, so intensely organized that once, in a ride between the university and the town, he described to me the exact limits of his productivity and hence the date of his early death. The scientist and philosopher Yeshayahu Leibowitz was then engaged in a titanic argument with Ben Gurion over the place of religion in Israeli society. Ben Gurion, he told me, by his accommodation with the religious politicians, had made Judaism the whore of Zionist politics.

Adam Mendilow, the head of the English department, encouraged personal tutorials on the 'British' model. The advantage of this system was that I came to know many of my students personally; I visited several in kibbutzim and Arab villages.

In one kibbutz, I insisted on working in the fields, something women no longer did. It was less rewarding than I had expected. The rows of marrows looked inviting at dawn, but their leaves were sharp as scythes, and it was only after my hands bled freely that I noticed that all the men in my row were wearing thick gloves, which no one had offered me. Setting my teeth, dragging my heavy sack, I filled it with the largest and most impressive specimens I could find. Someone upended my sack and laughed. The big marrows, he explained, were for the cows. It was the small ones which tasted good and sold well.

After that, I put in time in the laundry which, in the late 1950s, still served in this kibbutz as a common pool for clothes; men and women took their rough sizes at random from a heap. The food was mush, reduced to geriatrically acceptable pabulum, and living conditions were tough. Even very pregnant women shared the communal showers, appearing not to mind. It was the women, I thought, who had the rough end of kibbutz life. The men organized and ran the show while the girls, once paired off, became no more than communal housewives.

The kibbutz ethic was still the Israeli gold standard. Half the Government consisted of men and women who commuted to Jerusalem from the kibbutzim; Cabinet ministers could be seen doing their stint of kitchen duty during weekends. Austerity, the contempt for city life and material goods, was marked. The converse of this, though, was that the rare luxuries – radios, electric kettles, even the number of bulbs used in a couple's 'room' (a term used even when it became a bungalow) – were the subject of intense debate and inspection, to ensure that the benefits were shared and used equally. Among some of the older women the private domestic instinct was already reappearing; once a woman had a gas-ring in her room, she used it to bake cakes.

I liked visiting kibbutzim but thought them rather anachronistic. Elderly men and women referred to their life partners as 'comrades'. Ideological battles were fought out over the question of whether small children should be allowed to sleep in the parents' house rather than in the communal nursery. Some aspects of kibbutz morality looked dubious to me; during a lesson I attended at one kibbutz school, a woman teacher tried to discover which children were failing to make their beds, or turn off the taps firmly, or who was stuffing wet underpants into the laundry bag; the system she used was to encourage the children to inform on one another.

Perpetual intimacy made many young kibbutzniks look elsewhere for husbands and wives. As one boy told me: 'It's difficult to get excited about a girl when you grow up sitting next to her in the row of potties.' In a country which virtually ostracized bachelors and spinsters, to be single on a kibbutz was difficult, to be homosexual impossible. The Jewish family was nowhere stronger than in the once revolutionary nucleus of the kibbutz.

Even when they were on their way to becoming landed gentry, the kibbutzniks clung to the idea that they were the real 'workers' of the country. Once I was at a kibbutz during the visit of a couple of European puppeteers who were touring the Galilee giving shows for the children. The 'culture committee' of the kibbutz vetted the programme very carefully. There was a puppet policeman, a French can-can dancer, a Dutch milkmaid, a bullfighter and a fairy-queen in a red cloak. The kibbutz teacher who compèred the performance translated and invented Israeli parallels. The policeman was a British soldier from the Mandate, he explained; the Dutch milkmaid, like Rivka, from the cowshed; the can-can dancer was left without comment; and the fairy-queen was a British princess who had come to visit the children of the kibbutz. One of the little girls who watched the show, the granddaughter of a founding family, was rapt with admiration, and the woman puppeteer made her a parting present of the fairy-queen's red cloak. For days after the puppeteers left, the little girl treasured the cloak, lending it to friends (everything was shared) but keeping it under her pillow at night. When she was taken to visit her grandmother in the veterans' corner of the kibbutz, she danced around with the cloak on her head, explaining that she was a beautiful princess. The strong-faced old woman with a Russian accent cut this short. 'Give me that thing, *bubele*,' she said firmly. 'You're not a princess, you're a member of the working class.'

That was the generation of the pioneers, the rebels against their Diaspora parents, the intellectual peasantry unparalleled elsewhere. Those who survived malaria and Israel's wars lived on into their eighties and nineties, sustained by their pride in the past, the prestige they enjoyed by continuing to work, and the total absence of financial worries. The romanticism of the early enterprise was reflected in the epitaphs carved on gravestones in the little cemetery of Kinneret, on the shores of Lake Galilee – inscriptions which have no match elsewhere in Israel: 'Died of disappointed love'; 'Died from a kick by the mule'.

Disused mosques with empty minarets; stockades of prickly pear marking the boundaries of vanished villages; a prayer-niche or dry fountain on a side road; the base of walls now indistinguishable from the terraces in the Jerusalem hills; names of crossroads fast slipping out of use; renamed squares in Jerusalem; redecorated houses whose main room, windowless, was a kind of entrance hall – all these I learned to recognize as signs of what was once Arab Palestine. But visiting Arab villages, in the Little Triangle between the coastal plain and the Jordanian frontier, or in the Galilee, meant going into a different world, one of formal hospitality and barely concealed bitterness. Israel's Arabs were still living under military rule, which did not mean the presence of soldiers but that they needed permits to move around. At that stage only the mukhtars, or clan leaders, could afford to send their sons to university, and they welcomed me like a memsahib, as they did the Labour party officials for whom they collected votes and distributed favours.

The homes I visited were elaborate villas with huge colour photographs as decorations and spangled wallpaper covered with bluebirds. They faced on to streets where untreated sewage flowed. Some of the villages still had no electricity and most of the schools I saw had crowded, ill-equipped schoolrooms where the children sat bundled up against the cold in winter. The mukhtars suavely deflected my questions, but the students were less discreet, bitter against both Israel and their elders. When I questioned Jewish Israelis, they told me that this was the way the Arabs lived and preferred to live, that things had been worse before and their children now lived instead of dying, and that the country had other priorities. Much later, as a journalist, I learned of the unwritten pact: taxes were not strictly enforced, services were not regularly provided. Ten years later, the children in those classrooms had come of age and Labour was losing their vote to the radical left.

Three times I renewed my contract with the Hebrew University, not for love of Melville's whaling stories, or Hornby's patterns of grammar, but because of the challenge of my rude, opinionated but likeable sabra (Israeli-born) students. They were Israelis my own age or slightly older, in their mid-twenties, mostly of European parentage, and they disagreed with everything I said, not only about the curriculum but also during the 'debates' which I made the pretext for getting to know them. I stayed on in Israel through perversity, because what I learned in those four years was that there was an unbridgeable gulf between myself and the world of the sabras. I hadn't been in a youth movement, I hadn't been in the army, I had missed all the formative experiences and it was too late to join the club, though for some time I wanted to. I envied the sabras their certainties and arrogance and single-mindedness.

24

I had expected them to hate everything English, but that was a simplification. They had grown up with parents in the British Army, listening to British bands playing in the parks, and picked up their first phrases in English from colonial readers. As colonial rulers, they said, the British were better than the French. As for my being 'British', the very suggestion would have been comical. I was often questioned about where my family 'really' came from; the answer satisfied them that I was just a Polish Jew like anyone else, with a few airs picked up *en route* through London. My Diaspora background made me a stranger. They were on first-name terms with Jewish antiquity but totally estranged from the world of their grandparents.

The post-war period had embittered people against 'the British'. My students remembered British soldiers disarming Jews and shooting on sight at people out during curfews (not every family had its own radio to alert it). The most famous case, still raw in the memory when I arrived, was of the death of a young girl, Bracha Fuld, who stood guard on the balcony of a Tel Aviv house and was shot dead in a gun battle. So though English was necessary, many of the young people were out to show that this meant no love for the British; English teachers had a notoriously bad time in the schools.

The sabras' attitude to Diaspora Jews was one of unveiled contempt. Jewish life anywhere but in Israel, they had been led to believe, was one long humiliation. A young woman psychologist, newly returned from studying with Piaget in Geneva, asked how, in England, I could stand to have my race and religion marked in my identity card. She clearly didn't believe my denials.

Galuti, the adjective describing Diaspora Jews, meant subservient, cringing, psychologically maimed. One of my students, later a professor of sociology, told me that he could spot any Diaspora Jew, by his 'servile manner', from a distance of thirty feet. As Israelis began to travel more and became superficially more worldly, the contempt was concealed, but it never disappeared altogether. Thirty years later, the novelist A. B. Yehoshua, writing in a newspaper supplement about relations between Israel and the Jews abroad, argued that the Diaspora was 'a cancerous phenomenon', 'a people which clings like a fungus to the body of other nations who do not want them'. He went on to blame Diaspora Jewry for most of Israel's troubles, and recommended that primary-school teachers should take a critical view, in Bible lessons, of Jacob and Moses, for 'having preferred to die in foreign lands' rather than in the Land of Israel.

It took me some time to understand that all this started in school. The long roster of pogroms and persecutions which scarred Jewish history revolted the young sabras, and the Eichmann trial, held during my second year in Israel, intensified their revulsion, and increased the sense of shame that, in that shabby phrase, 'the Jews had gone like sheep to the slaughter'. Sabras couldn't understand the psychology of minorities, or the defenceless loyalties of so many Jewish communities in the Diaspora. There were at that time very few books about the Holocaust. I had been brought up to understand that only chance and luck had enabled me to survive the Nazi period; it didn't make me feel any the less at home in England – problems with the Gospels apart. If Zionism meant thinking that Jews could not live anywhere but in Israel, then I was not a Zionist. I found myself locked in impossible arguments. Many of my students thought the Jews could have 'fought back'; some of those who wore skull-caps saw the fate of the Jews of Europe as an obscure punishment. Both arguments were to me so patently preposterous that I was left speechless.

'I've had an idea all my life,' a student told me, 'that with one good machine-gun, the Jews would have been able to prevent the fall of the Second Temple.' Not only could I not imagine defending the Temple in the year AD 70 with machine-guns; I was entirely unable to visualize the people of ancient Israel in the way my students did every day. Many of them had never been inside a synagogue and used the Bible as a kind of archaeological handbook. I was as amazed at their casual familiarity with the Jews of biblical times as at their inability to identify with young Jews of their own age in the Diaspora. I could identify with the

Jews of Europe rounded up by the Nazis, felt one of them, as my students did not, but I was unable to feel any empathy with the warriors and sages of the first century. No doubt this was the fault of my education. It was as if British history had ended with Boadicea. I had met classicists whose mastery of their subject was such that any personality or incident they described came to life, but this was something different: a collective archaism which made me subtly uneasy.

When I took refresher courses in Hebrew during my first year in Jerusalem, the young woman who taught me was shocked that I had never heard of Masada, the Herodian rock-fortress overlooking the Dead Sea, whose Jewish defenders allegedly committed mass suicide rather than fall into the hands of the Romans. The Masada cult was created by Israel. The Talmud makes no mention of Masada, and it was only with Jewish nationalism that the legend was revived. In torchlight ceremonies on the summit, Israeli paratroopers now took their oath and swore that Masada would not fall again. At the same time as the zealots fled to Masada, another group of Jews, rabbis, fled to Yavne on the coast, with the agreement of the Roman authorities. There they set up one of the most famous Talmudic centres of the ancient world. But that was not very heroic, and didn't lend itself to military celebrations.

The story of Masada, which my students took very seriously indeed, failed to thrill me. I brooded and thought and read about it for some time, and then told an archaeologist friend my conclusions. The mass suicide repelled me and I found arguments to rationalize my aversion. The story is known to us only through Josephus, the Jewish historian, with an echo in Pliny. Josephus was a survivor of the wars against Rome, and also a defector who both admired his Roman patrons and wished to rehabilitate his fellow Jews after their defeat and humiliation. Suicide rather than surrender was a Roman virtue, particularly suicide by the sword. The philosophical arguments that Josephus put into the mouths of Eleazar, the defender of Masada, did not in the least resemble the arguments for suicide elaborated by the

Tannaitic sages of Yavne under the terrible pressure of events. It seemed to me just as likely, I said cautiously, that the defenders of Masada had been killed (a score or more of skeletons were found, later to be buried with full military honours by Israel) as that they had killed themselves.

My friend, no mean iconoclast himself, looked at me sceptically.

'All right,' I said, prepared to back down. 'Where did I go wrong?'

'It's not that you went wrong,' he said. 'I'd just hate to see you strung up in Zion Square.'

I stuck to my heresy despite the warning. From time to time I advanced it in private, always meeting with furious protest. We were back with the old problem: I was an incorrigible Diaspora Jew, in favour of ignominious survival.

The clank of the gate on Abyssinian Street, late at night, signalled the beginning and the end of a number of affairs, most of them evanescent. I thought sexual life in Israel very Jewish in its combination of licence and puritanism. Sabras of my age (always excepting the religious) were supposed to relate to one another *dugri* – an untranslatable term meaning in a frank and straightforward manner, without any hypocritical nonsense. This carried over into sexual relations. In Israel courtship, if there was any, followed bed rather than the other way round. It was a waste of time to take trouble over a man or girl who was difficult. This was hard on the sensitive and hesitant. Just as 'manners' were considered hypocritical, eroticism was suspect and decadent; these *dugri* relationships were notably short on the arts of pleasure.

As I learned, this was a new era in Israel. The sabras of an earlier period, though they had set no great store by marriage, had been even more inhibited. Politics came first and sex second, and Netiva Ben Yehuda, one of the survivors of the Palmach generation, insisted that many of the young fighters had gone to their early deaths still virgins. But my own observations suggested that the drink-of-water theory – that sex was no more complicated than thirst – had survived in Jewish Palestine, like other outdated Marxist slogans, long after it was condemned by Lenin. *Dugri* sex didn't mean that contraception was available to women, either, unless they were prepared to pay for it – there were no birth-control clinics at all – and abortionists had a field day. There were some hair-raising theories about how to prevent conception, and a very beautiful young Yemenite girl I knew insisted that an extra wriggle at the right moment always worked for her.

By the late 1950s I saw that sex was taken very casually indeed. By chance one spring, I joined a tour of the Galilee organized for office workers. We were to spend the night at a hostel, near the southern end of Lake Galilee, where the men and women occupied separate dormitories. During the night one of the men stole into our dormitory and, guided by encouraging coos from his mate, found his way to her bed. Springs creaked, stifled pants and groans followed, and everyone else pretended to be asleep. 'Good night all,' said the man cheerily before he left.

This incident was no doubt rare. But even among the young Israelis I now knew, most love-affairs were public knowledge as soon as they began. My own preference for privacy, even secrecy, belonged to an alien world. The Hebrew phrase about the Israeli 'who finishes fast and runs to tell his friends' was self-mocking, but had a basis in truth. Obsessive passions were deplorable and mad. Romanticism, like unrequited love, was absurd.

In the Israel of that time, when the children of the founders went to school and the generals went into business, there were still a few genuine solitaries: living in huts on still-unspoiled beaches, pioneering desert farming, or in abandoned houses forgotten by the Custodian of Enemy Property, piloting peace missions, or simply camping out on a stretch of border by courtesy of the security services which, like nature, abhorred a vacuum.

A decade later, and many of these loners had become restaurant-owners, Diners Card bohemians, directors of safari tours, agents for inns with tethered camels and Bedouin playing two-string violins. Like the celebrated raconteurs of Finks Bar in Jerusalem and Kassit in Tel Aviv, they were soon to succumb to the vulgarity of a wider fame, to be signed up for their memoirs, or emerge as candidates for expensive alimony suits. There was already a strong whiff of the public relations industry about them.

But there was also a smaller handful of people who needed to escape the predatory intimacy of the *chevra* – in other words the kids in your class, the friends in your army unit, the people you had always known and whom you met every Friday night to talk gossip and politics. Some of these people preferred to be alone because their memories were too painful to be shared, others because they were disillusioned with the way Israel had developed, some because they hated all forms of institutionalized living. Bezalel lived alone for all three of these reasons.

Beyond the banana plantations of Kibbutz Ginossar, on the north shore of Lake Galilee, beneath the Mount of the Beatitudes and less than three miles from the border with Syria, was the deserted German Catholic hospice of Tabgha where Bezalel Rabani lived. His neighbours to the east were members of a sedentary Bedouin tribe in their black goat-hair tents. This corner of the lake, before 1967, was one of the loneliest places in Israel. At night there was no sound but the shouts of fishermen calling across the water, and the thud which meant that, against the law, they were dropping dynamite to drive dead or stunned fish into their nets.

The Syrian artillery positions on the Golan Heights commanded this part of the lake and the Huleh valley further north, but untilled land between Tabgha and the border, fields studded with the sinister outcrops of black basalt rock from which the older cottages of the region were built, was dangerous for a different reason: bored Syrian recruits from the frontier positions sometimes crossed into Israel and ambushed unwary travellers. A British diplomat's wife staying at the Beatitudes hostel went out one morning, just before my first visit, to pick wild flowers and was found shot dead some hours later. A young Israeli hiker, exploring the region on his own, was killed in the same way. Against such dangers, Bezalel had an old rifle and an affectionate half-Labrador mutt called Kushi.

It was typical of Bezalel that when we arrived one evening at Tabgha in the fast-fading twilight, he immediately proposed a tour of all his territory, Kushi going ahead first to ward off snakes or scorpions.

Bezalel looked fifteen or twenty years older than his age – he was thirty-nine – when he came out to meet us in a singlet and ragged trousers; he had a high, Shakespearian forehead, slightly protuberant eyes that gave him the look of an enquiring child, and the abrupt manner of a man more used to thinking aloud in solitude than talking to others. His young wife, Tirza, had gone to study in Paris for a year, and that autumn he was alone.

Tabgha was then, and for a few years to come, a magical place, with hidden springs and ruined water-mills. The hospice was in great disrepair. Stone steps, wreathed with cascades of bougainvillea, led down from the crumbling terrace straight into the lake. The water that lapped against the slippery rocks was deep and cold, save where jets of sulphurous hot-springs created their own pools of warmth. A path, which had to be cleared each spring of the undergrowth that grew up during the rainy season, led to a small, pebbled beach between the hospice grounds and the fields of Kibbutz Ginossar, and a family of peacocks pecked and strutted in the yard.

Bezalel and Tirza lived in two rooms on the upper floor of the hospice, bare save for beds and improvised bookshelves made with planks and bricks, and a table for dining and study. Now that Tirza was away, the bathtub served to contain the overflow of Bezalel's library: archaeological works, histories of nineteenth-century travellers in the Levant, and English detective stories. For bathing, and to do his laundry, Bezalel walked into the lake.

Bezalel was from the Baltic port of Riga, like my mother's family; it was a frail first link in our friendship, for I knew nothing of Latvia and Bezalel did not talk about his European past. All his family had died in the camps, but he had managed to escape to the Soviet Union and join the Red Army. After the war, he made his way to Palestine, where for a couple of years he had lived on bread and radishes as an itinerant labourer. For a short time he worked as beekeeper on a kibbutz. He was badly stung, but it was not the bees that drove him from the kibbutz; like so many Jews who had lived in the Soviet Union, he couldn't stand the mandatory intimacy of a commune. He joined the anti-British underground and concealed a stack of arms with friends in an Arab village. He was caught and put on trial, where, to the surprise of the British district judge, he insisted on conducting his own defence, displaying a mastery of British legal procedure and Roman law. When he told this story, it was in tones of wonderment, not boastfully. He had found an unexpected opportunity to make use of knowledge which, like all the other subjects he had mastered by himself, had been acquired almost accidentally. Of course, the knowledge did not help him. He was imprisoned in Acre fortress, and released only when the British left.

Bezalel had begun studying archaeology on his own during the first years of the state's existence, helped by a British archaeologist, Philip Guy, who pioneered a technique of filming digs from an aerial balloon. His first work on a site was as volunteer policeman – an important job, as amateurs made off with whatever they unearthed. The Tiberias police force was, in Bezalel's stories, a Dogberry and Verges setup with an oriental cast; having once signed with them, he was pursued ever after by the Night Watch looking for recruits.

He said that Tiberias, the low-lying, humid, lazy lake-town of the Romans, had always been backward and corrupt, and now that it was run by Levantine Jews it had changed not at all. He went into Tiberias only for work and provisions, and to check that the local contractors laying sewers didn't disturb the sarcophagi which lay everywhere. He and Tirza had taken over an abandoned lakeside mosque and made it into a tiny museum, housing finds he had salvaged from the immediate vicinity – glass jugs and oil lamps, and glazed pottery from a medieval Arab site, Hirbet Minye, near Tabgha. Almost unaided, he and Tirza had uncovered the beautiful mosaic floor of a Roman bathhouse, but no budget was found to protect it adequately, and the local people soon vandalized the site; eventually it was reburied. The Mayor of Tiberias saw no reason to prevent people taking pieces of ancient masonry to decorate their homes or graves, and only occasionally consulted the Rabanis as to whether they wanted them for the museum, or to have them sent to Jerusalem. On one occasion, reproved for having removed a Roman pillar from the little municipal park, he argued that a friend of his had wanted it for his wife's grave, and since it had been 'rolling round the streets for ages', he couldn't see any objection.

Bezalel also tried to forestall the ruin of antiquities by developers digging quarries, farmers levelling ground, or kibbutzniks seeking finds for their own little museums. Farmers who knew the rules planted eucalyptus trees whose deep roots became entangled in Roman remains; kibbutzniks used bulldozers for excavations, smashing the retaining walls of Byzantine houses; the orthodox, expanding the old Tiberias cemetery, ploughed into anything they were assured was not a Jewish grave.

Bezalel lived in Tabgha like a lord, but his tenure was tragically insecure. The army had allowed him to occupy the hospice because it was convenient to have an ex-soldier near the frontier. His refuge was invaded first in 1953, when the Israeli and American governments decided that the hilly ground to the north, useless for farming, would be ideal as a cattle ranch. Tabgha (the Arab name) was renamed Karei Deshe (Green Pastures), and Bezalel found himself quartered with trainee cowboys. The Sinai Campaign won him a respite, but as more families appeared in the area, the Rabanis attracted the attention of Israel's bureaucracy. Local farmers did not enjoy the exemption allowed to people in other border areas. The taxmen came down on the Rabanis, who owned no more than the clothes they stood up in, but what distressed Bezalel most was the suggestion that he had gone to live in Tabgha in order to avoid taxation. This was like telling Dante that he had loved Beatrice in order to get a family allowance. He wrote to the Income Tax that he was 'offended and hurt by their insinuations'.

Trudging and hitch-hiking from site to site (he had to refuse the offer of a motor cycle because of a chronic liver inflammation which made the jolting painful), waiting for hours by a roadside to conduct government officials on surveys, Bezalel had all too little time for his own research. But for his few friends he would spare the time to scour the markets for odd finds – a discarded Bedouin cooking-pot, a rare stone. He took us to see a Moroccan immigrant woman who was an expert on the evil eye, along with Geoffrey Hartman, a visiting scholar who wanted to write a monograph on the subject.

Together we climbed the steep hills to the Arbel caves, the retreat of the Maccabeans, and visited the Horns of Hittin, where the Crusaders made their last stand against Saladin: the Arabs had taken up their position between the Crusaders and the nearest stream; the Christians were trapped in the blazing heat in their heavy armour. It was clear why they had lost.

In the late summer of 1959, with Tirza back from Paris, Bezalel was pleased to be invited to join a dig organized by the French archaeological mission under Jean Perrot and the University of Michigan. The site was Hirbet Minye, the remains of a winter palace of an Ummayad Caliph, which had been partly excavated in the 1930s. Bezalel hoped, during this dig, to be able to learn from an earlier layer, dating back to the twelfth and thirteenth centuries, how to date medieval Islamic pottery in Palestine, which had become his special interest. Carefully, year by year, travelling to Jerusalem to consult the books he could not afford to buy, teaching himself yet more languages (he was learning his sixth, Italian, with a Benedictine priest), he was building up his knowledge of a subject which then interested few people in Israel.

But he only managed to make notes for three days of the excavation. On the fourth, a wasps' nest was accidentally disturbed and the infuriated insects stung him repeatedly on the head. He knew, having been warned from his time on the kibbutz, that this could be fatal. In the car taking him to hospital, he lapsed into a coma from which he did not emerge. On his last evening in hospital, the old Arab in the next bed, who had offered comforting words each day to Tirza, turned away his head when we arrived. That night Kushi, who had sat whining under Bezalel's bed in Tabgha, suddenly gave a howl and dashed off towards the hills.

Tirza slashed her wrists, and the scars were still raw when I invited her to live with me for a while in Abyssinian Street. She was a Romanian immigrant, as withdrawn and shy a person as her husband, and I wondered how she could survive without him. My invitation was one of those gestures, made impulsively, which fails. She went back alone to Tabgha, and later, in a second attempt, managed to kill herself.

Soon after her death, I was commissioned to write a film script about the National Water Carrier. As part of the co-ordination of all its available resources, Israel was to begin pumping water from Lake Galilee, replenished every year by rains and by the northern tributaries of the Jordan. On a trip round the lake, I was guided down into the vast underwater chambers where the great pumps were being installed. I suddenly realized that the surface installations, guarded by double fences and lit by powerful projectors at night, were situated near Hirbet Minye, by that little pebbled beach where we had chatted and bathed only a few years earlier, while Kushi retrieved sticks from the shallow water. The dig had been reburied.

When I last visited Tabgha it was unrecognizable. At the gate was a kiosk where parking tickets were issued. Green, purple and yellow tents were scattered everywhere. The path to the beach had been blocked by a giant fall of rock. The peacocks had disappeared. The lake had filled with pleasure steamers, paddle canoes and motor boats tugging water-skiers. In Tiberias, hotels with black-glass façades and flashing neon signs dwarfed the little old houses with their square-cut basalt walls. Smoke puffed from dozens of barbecues on the shore. Attempts to revive the little museum, cared for over some years by a friend of the Rabanis, had failed.

At Kibbutz Ginossar, a multi-media museum displayed to busloads of visitors the history and zoology of the region, which – had they time and interest – they could have discovered by themselves. Enlarged photographs of the lake, seen through reeds, spared them the trouble of walking out and looking at it for themselves.

There are probably some places which should never be revisited.

'It is very dangerous', said the Russian consul, frowning. I must have looked worried, because he smiled suddenly and added, 'to speak English with a teacher' – and stamped my visa.

We all received our visas only after personal interviews at the Russian Embassy, then in Tel Aviv. I was the joker in the pack of seventeen Israelis who set out via Cyprus, Athens, Salonika, Belgrade, Katowice and Warsaw to visit the Soviet Union in the summer of 1960. It was only four years after the 20th Party Congress, in the early years of de-Stalinization. Not all the statues of the Soviet tyrant had been toppled from their plinths, and wherever, on plaques, Stalin's face had been partly superimposed on that of Lenin, as at Brest Litovsk, where we crossed the frontier, it still remained in place. I thought of the Via Salaria, a route through the Apennines I had often travelled, where in the mid-fifties the saplings planted after the war had not yet effaced the word DUCE, visible from twenty miles away, carved out of the living forest.

Ours was the first organized group, apart from official diplomatic delegations, to visit the Soviet Union. Nineteen-sixty was the year of the Soviet spaceship Sputnik and the downing of the American U2 spy-plane, but also of exceptional relaxation in relations between the Soviet Union and Israel. We were hosted by the Russian students' travel organization (naturally called Sputnik) and were defined as students, though none of us actually were. Our group included a leading authority on Herzen, professional people and journalists, as well as a number of kibbutzniks affiliated to the Marxist Mapam party. I was the only one not fluent in Russian.

When we arrived in Athens, some of the young kibbutzniks, who had never been out of Israel, sighed enthusiastically over the Doric façades of the banks in Omonia Square. One tried to barter a packet of Israeli cigarettes for a pear, unaware that this system had gone out in the post-war period. We crowded into two third-class carriages of a train on which child beggars worked the corridor right up to the Yugoslav frontier, and travelled non-stop right through to Poland. In Katowice, the young Israelis who had never been abroad were fascinated by the sight of ivied gables, autumn leaves in August (it was a cold wet summer in Poland), and our Polish guide, Magda, who wore plastic sandals on her tiny blue feet. We stayed in a bug-infested Polish hotel (when I tried constructing a Maginot line of Israeli soap-powder they simply ate their way through it) in a town at whose centre was the giant planetarium with a replica of Sputnik. The Poles we met kissed hands and warned us of spies and surviving Stalinists, and the food we were served reminded me that what is known elsewhere as Jewish cuisine (*cholent, kishkes* and the stuffed sausages from which you unwind yards of twine) was actually Polish.

Cracow was for us a way-station to Auschwitz. We travelled there on a little local train, rather like those in Switzerland on branch routes where the journeys are so short that they provide few seats. It was not like visiting a cemetery or a memorial. I had read a great deal about the camps and the visit itself made a less powerful impact on me than what I had read. I found that my mind stalled. Auschwitz was just a disused camp with a deserted barracks. The extinct ovens, the smokeless chimneys, even the glass cases stacked with exhibits of the crime – hair like grey straw, battered suitcases or discarded shoes – failed to evoke the horror. On one wall of the display hall was a greatly enlarged, blurred photograph of naked women fleeing into a forest. The shadows of leaves dappled their backs and legs. My mind refused to interpret what I saw. I was reminded of an impressionist painting, even while knowing that the association was obscene. None of our party said a word either on the way to Auschwitz or returning. Afterwards, one or two protested that the inscription on the memorial to the Nazis' victims did not mention the Jews.

In Warsaw, in a park in the pouring rain, young Thomas, who had taken over from Magda, lectured us on Polish history, emphasizing (well out of range of any possible listeners but ourselves) Polish victories over the Russians. He said nothing about the Jews. The old city of Warsaw had been reconstructed; the ghetto was represented by a blank wall. The Herzen expert, Michel Confino, and I went to visit one of the handful of Polish Jews left in Warsaw, who was an authority on Rostand. It took some time to track him down, and he proposed that we meet in the lounge of a vast, seedy hotel, surrounded by smart whores and their clients. I noticed old scars across the insides of his wrists.

Elsewhere we were given a cardboard box which we were instructed not to open until we were on the train for Russia, at night. Inside were Hebrew prayer-books, little candelabras for Chanuka, postcards with views of Israel, Stars of David on necklets, Israeli cigarettes, and chocolate wrapped in several layers of paper closely printed with Zionist propaganda. Someone had clearly relied on its being a cold summer during which the chocolate would not melt. All this was distributed among our various shabby suitcases.

On our last night in Warsaw, Confino had called us together and informed us solemnly of the significance of our entry into the Soviet Union. We were going into a country which only recently had relaxed some of the harsher measures of the police state. The leaders might have changed, but the apparatus was still in place. We would have to be careful to whom we spoke, and remember that we might endanger Soviet Jews, perhaps even ourselves. We were not to involve local Jews in any way with the authorities, or discuss politics; nor should we forget that we were official guests of the Soviet Union.

I am afraid that we did not all obey these instructions. Once inside the Soviet Union, we behaved like no other group of visiting tourists that we met, still less like the official communist student delegations we occasionally came across from Germany, England and other places. Several of our group had relations in Russia. One young man had been smuggled out of Eastern Europe as a baby, during the war; his mother met him on the station platform in Moscow and accompanied us on our travels. Another went off to meet uncles and aunts, who also travelled with us. He financed their trip by selling off the shirts, sweaters and trousers he had brought with him, so that when he returned to Athens a month later he owned one shirt, and one pair of trousers, underpants and socks. And, of course, his shoes. We were all easily identified as foreigners by our shoes, and I became used to the people we met immediately looking at our feet.

The other student delegations housed in the same hostels marched en bloc behind their guides, filed into tourist buses, and turned up obediently at official receptions and student jamborees. We split up into groups of two or three, escaping the supervision of official guides, who were unable to control these Russian speakers who could find their way alone. To report this situation to their superiors was to risk punishment. So they came to an unofficial agreement with our deputation. Each day, we elected one or more victims to be 'group leaders' who were duly accompanied, while the rest of us went free.

But we did attend a mammoth student reception at a vast Palace of Sport and Culture, where we were asked to perform our national dance. I had only the vaguest idea of how to do the *hora* (actually a Romanian folk-dance) and the others were sheepish and self-conscious, not having danced it for years. Toes were trodden on, and the well-drilled communists were amused.

We were not harassed by the police. The Russians' lackadaisical attitude to our unruly group was probably due to the fact that the KGB were as snobbish as anyone else and couldn't believe that, travelling as we did, sleeping in train compartments and dossing down in the cheapest hotels and hostels, we posed any threat to internal security. If they were aware of our agitprop activity (Russian Jews did not yet dare apply for emigration), they made no attempt to stop it. We distributed all our prayer-books and postcards, cigarettes and chocolate, both in synagogues and to individual Jews we met, some of whom literally scented us out, or heard us speaking Hebrew. Sarah Malkin, wife of the director of the Israeli Labour party college, a very emotional woman, was moved to tears by every Jew she encountered; she found herself followed down a street in Leningrad by a poorly dressed woman walking unsteadily and muttering to herself. She was an ordinary drunken beggar, but Sarah concluded that she must be a Jewess in trouble and thrust a Star of David into her outstretched hand.

While the Soviet authorities took no discernible interest in our presence, our own left-wing kibbutz members were deeply shocked and disturbed by the discovery that what they had assumed to be capitalist propaganda about the low standard of living, poor housing conditions, food shortages and backward technology was actually true. Even the recent doctors' trials of the late 1950s, when many Jews were falsely accused, condemned and executed, had been debated and excused at Israeli left-wing seminars. So our kibbutzniks were distressed to see women labourers operating pneumatic drills in the Moscow streets and shopkeepers calculating sales on an abacus.

The only victim of our visit was a Soviet non-Jewish engineer who was, like ourselves, a visitor to Moscow. Two of us picked up Sverdlovsk, as we nicknamed him, one sunny afternoon at a bar in Gorky Park. He was an ordinary Russian tourist from that far northern city, lonely and naive – too naive to be afraid of foreigners, let alone Jews from Israel. We met him several times and on our last evening in Moscow went dancing in the park with a couple of African students. I partnered Sverdlovsk, who danced like a steam engine reversing down a station platform, and then we settled down to chat in one of the trellised arbours surrounding the dance floor. The conversation in Russian, translated into French for me by one of the Africans, was about party politics. Because I could take no active part in it, I had the time to look around me. I noticed a man in a nearby alcove listening rather too

attentively to the conversation – during which Sverdlovsk
faithfully toed the party line – and remembered Confino's advice.
But my worries were dismissed as panic. When I looked round
again, the man had gone.

Just before eleven the lights began flickering on and off as a
sign to leave the park. We strolled away in couples, but when we
joined up outside the gates Sverdlovsk was missing. We asked the
Africans if they had noticed where he went. 'He went off with
friends,' said one. We were alarmed; he knew no one else in
Moscow. 'Two friends, one on each arm,' said one of the
Africans. There was nothing to be done.

Six months later, we received a letter from Sverdlovsk which
appeared to have passed through half a dozen communist
countries. It had obviously been dictated by the police and was
clumsily devised. It asked us to send him the names and addresses
of Jewish friends of ours in the Soviet Union so that he could look
them up. None of our party's relations was ever harassed, so
clearly we had done no great harm, save to the unfortunate young
engineer.

Three of us dropped out of the organized group on our way
back, to visit Budapest. In the main tourist office we asked for
advice about a hostel. The Hungarians looked us up and down.
We hadn't washed for days, we were filthy from the Kiev–
Budapest train journey, and our remaining luggage was rudimen-
tary. They ordered us to entrain forthwith, as we had only transit
visas; otherwise we risked arrest. We protested that to leave
Hungary without seeing the jewel of the Austro-Hungarian
empire was impossible. One of the officials suddenly grinned,
conferred with his colleagues, and handed us a slip of paper with
an address.

We walked miles, drawn by the shop windows of Budapest
which, after Russia, looked like Paris; it took twenty-four hours to
realize that most of what we saw was kitsch. The address we had
been given, to our surprise, turned out to be that of a huge
mansion in a quiet residential street. It had glass doors which
yielded to a push and led into a splendid lobby. As we stood there,

wondering whether we were soiling the carpet, a pinafored manservant appeared, read the note, and showed us wordlessly to our magnificent rooms.

There was no reception desk and no sign of other guests. Finally, we discovered a pile of magazines on a table and made a few discreet enquiries. The Hungarians, justly famous for their sense of humour, had put three filthy Israeli scarecrows into a guesthouse for visiting Soviet chiefs.

3

On the Road

A FTER MY first four years in Israel, I turned in my job at the Hebrew University and took to the road. I had had enough of the rock-pool and wanted to see more of the country. In those days, everyone hitch-hiked. Most of the cars on the roads were official, or army vehicles, and even Cabinet ministers would tell their drivers to stop for a hitch-hiker. Minister and driver always sat side by side, dressed alike, and ate *hummus* and *falafel* together at pull-ups. Parties of schoolchildren were crammed into lorries and trucks, swaying and singing in the back, their heads wound in Arab headcloths against the dust, khaki water-bottles on their belts. They were deposited in canyons or wadis, and marched off on gruelling treks, with water sometimes rationed as a matter of discipline.

I went wherever the drivers were going and never worried about where I was going to sleep. Once or twice my ignorance of the country led me into awkward situations. A trade union official offered to drive me one night from Tel Aviv to the Dead Sea, where he said that the national theatre, Habima, was putting on a performance of *The Caine Mutiny*. When we reached Beersheba, he dismissed his driver, doused himself with cologne and lunged at me. I spent the night in a nearby soldiers' hostel, where I met a South African physiotherapist who had had the same experience a week earlier. We disconcerted him by appearing the next morning together in his office and asking how he had slept.

Hiking around Israel was exhilarating because, although the country was so small (from one end to the other was a mere seven hours or so on the road), the sea and the desert, the mountains and the plains were so close together that as you drove, the landscape changed almost minute by minute. So did the people. Israel, when I arrived in 1957, was quite literally not the Israel of 1961. In the early 1960s, immigrants arrived in a new batch from North Africa and Eastern Europe; Algeria was going through its pre-independence struggle with the French and – though the editors of the daily papers agreed not to print the news – boatloads were arriving from Romania.

When Bezalel had arrived in Israel immediately after the war, immigrants (most of them illegal, as he was) were spirited away from the beaches at night by volunteers. In the early years of the state, they had been housed, temporarily, in the transit camps or *ma'abarot* of which there were still traces in Jerusalem, Tiberias and elsewhere – shacks and Nissen huts, with improvised grocer's shops in upturned crates. Now there were what were called 'development towns', mostly dormitory settlements, in permanent buildings, whose locations were strategically rather than economically planned – any space on the map that seemed open to Arab infiltration – and the work of looking after them was done by officials and not by volunteers. There was much talk about the 'wilderness generation' and their children, who were to be turned into socialist pioneers by the influence of school and army. It didn't quite work out like that.

My new job was working freelance, writing pamphlets and documentary film scripts for the Jewish Agency, one of the institutions left over from the pre-State period, which now handled, among other things, immigrant settlement and information (or propaganda) for export. I had bought a Morris Minor, which boiled over every time it made the ascent to Jerusalem but whose carburettor I could adjust myself with a now obsolete wavy-edged coin worthless for any other purpose. At this time there were very few women drivers in Israel. Gangs of children in remote villages would dart in front of the car, fall on the road, and

scream 'Compensation!' Brawny-armed taxi drivers, if I overtook them, would shout 'Women to the kitchen!' But the Minor
helped me explore parts of Israel very few people visited unless
they were sent there as social workers, doctors, or officials
representing Diaspora investors.

The chance to write film scripts came through my friend Helga
Cranston (later Keller). I had met Helga, who left Germany as a
girl, in London, while she was working as chief film editor for
Olivier on his Shakespeare films. I'd thought her well adjusted to
English life, and was surprised when she suddenly confessed to
me, in a shared taxi-ride, that she missed her *yiddische neshome*,
Jewish soul, and wanted to go to Israel.

Despite her background, she was warned to get work before
leaving England, as Western immigrants were coveted but looked
down on once they actually arrived. Helga met what she called the
Genesis complex. Israelis, she said, never believed that anyone
had ever before done what they were now doing. No one had
founded a university, no one had drained a swamp (save
Mussolini, perish the thought) and no one, certainly, had made a
film. In Israel, she was treated as a novice, and I was her novice. I
had never written a film script. Helga told me to divide the pages
of a school notebook into two columns with a ruler, head them
'Sound' and 'Vision' and write down my ideas. We worked
together on several documentaries.

Our boss was an Agency official whose favourite expression
was 'Give me time to think'. I went out to do research, brought
back reports to Jerusalem and then, once the project was
approved, wrote the script. My first assignment was in Kiryat
Shmoneh, a 'development town' founded a few years earlier.

Beyond Bezalel's territory was the Huleh valley, formerly
swamp land, rich in plant and animal life, and humming with the
malaria-carrying Anopheles mosquito. The draining of the
Huleh, which was in its final stages when I arrived in Israel, was
one of Israel's more ambitious projects. Much later, ecologists
were to question its scale, but in the early 1960s no one doubted
the value of reclaiming the land for farmers. The swamp had

shrunk to a small nature reserve, and all around, in the upper Galilee, was the rich farmland allotted to the kibbutzim further north. Towards the centre of the beautiful valley, in the area of the kibbutzim, was Kiryat Shmoneh, first a transit camp, then a town of uniform concrete blocks that looked as if they had been planted there by helicopters.

In 1961, Kiryat Shmoneh was a town of fifteen thousand people, most of them from Persia, Iraq and North Africa. Visiting the place was my first experience of what was called immigrant 'absorption' – which meant taking people from widely different backgrounds, none of whom spoke Hebrew, and putting them in the middle of nowhere. What was to be done with thousands of dispossessed shopkeepers, craftsmen or pedlars in a brand-new town with no capital, industry or agriculture? The answer was simple: early every morning, the able-bodied male population of Kiryat Shmoneh was bussed out to work in the fields and factories of the kibbutzim, leaving behind a ghost town of old men, women and small children – some at school, others in the little shopping centre, and the rest playing *shesh besh* (backgammon). Half the population was living on relief. There was one social worker and an indignant woman teacher called Alisa Levenberg, who was doing the work of tens of veteran Israelis who preferred to be somewhere else.

The older part of the town, formerly an Arab village, had weathered stone houses, with gardens or yards where goats and sheep wandered, and every few yards another little synagogue. Each community, and sometimes each clan, observed its own rites. The shacks of the transit camp, now almost empty, were dotted on the hillside. The concrete-block permanent housing had become instant slums, with graffiti-covered walls and filthy staircases (people kept their own yard in order, I saw, but public property, as throughout the East, was no one's business – a lesson Israel's town-planners gradually learned). The two-and-a-half-room standard 'housing unit' split at the seams where families had eight or more children, and when school was out the children were in the streets.

I visited the town in late autumn, when the fields between the buildings and the transit camp became stubble easily ignited by a discarded cigarette-butt. In the Mayor's office, one of his children, wearing a baseball-player's cap, kept watch from the window, continually interrupting our conversation – a list of the Mayor's grudges against the Government – with fire alarms.

'Dad, the football field's on fire!'

'Never mind, it'll get rid of the snakes.'

'Dad, the fire's getting near the huts.'

'Never mind, it's time they took them down.'

Towards evening, the buses returned with the kibbutz labourers, the tribal elders held their council meetings sitting on the ground in the shopping centre, and the unemployed threw dice to the music of Radio Cairo. The Kiryat Shmoneh wind, which rose in the late afternoon and didn't drop till near midnight, was like a Galilean banshee; trapped between the Golan Heights to the east and the ridge of hills to the west, it howled until exhausted.

All the men I talked to were bitterly jealous of the kibbutzim where they were employed, where they were fed in segregation, and where their children were not wanted in the schools. The kibbutzniks, for their part, argued that the immigrants 'didn't share their values', had 'petit-bourgeois' habits and needed separate treatment. No contrast could have been greater than that between the manicured lawns, spotless dining-halls and whirring factory dynamos of the kibbutzim, and the cheerless façade of Kiryat Shmoneh, its centre with *falafel* stands and haberdasher's shops that sold embroidery-kits featuring French shepherdesses and medieval castles. Even the poultry behaved differently. The kibbutz hens were lined up in batteries, dropping eggs relentlessly in their *lux perpetua*, while the immigrants' hens strolled around in the yards in the *laissez-faire* tedium of the day.

The hostility towards the kibbutzim was to have political repercussions less than two decades later. Previously, the ruling Labour party was the boss and the employer, and the Agency the favour dealer. Later, in conversation with me in the seventies, Moshe Katsav, one of the first right-wing Cabinet ministers, once the child of an immigrant family from Iran in a transit camp, said with great bitterness, 'What did the kibbutzim ever do for this country?' The question was outrageous, but I stayed silent.

The drive back to Tel Aviv took me through Wadi Ara, a narrow valley with Arab villages on either side which leads from the Galilee to the coastal plain. I had driven alone in the Galilee many times, but I had noticed that my Arab hosts were far more nervous than I if the Morris developed an engine fault which threatened to delay me until after nightfall; they would have been in trouble if anything had happened to me. So I tried to set out early enough not to drive through Wadi Ara in the dark. But talking to people kept me longer than expected, and Alisa Levenberg, with whom I had stayed, asked me to give a lift to a woman with a small girl, who decided half-way through the wadi that she needed to pee. It was getting dark and the car whose sidelights I had been following disappeared. I opened the car door and kept the engine running. Ahead of me were two lorries heading in opposite directions; both suddenly drew up, side by side, and the Arabs sitting in the back of each climbed out and gathered in the road. I suddenly remembered my murdered uncle. It was irrational, but my fear was strong; he had been in this situation and suspected nothing. I got the child back into the car and drove on slowly, my hand on the horn. The men looked round and parted to let me through; of course they were just groups of village friends meeting on the road.

I was angry at myself for my racist, paranoid suspicions. But when I told the story to my archaeologist friend, he shook his head. 'Yadin never takes that road without a gun,' he said. 'If they hadn't made way you'd have had to put your foot down on the accelerator and driven straight at them – over them if necessary.'

I was sure that he was wrong. I'd learned to drive at the Speedwell School of Motoring and been taught to jam my foot on the brake, not on the accelerator, if anyone moved out in front of the car; that reflex would have been the strongest.

Back in Jerusalem, I summarized my findings on Kiryat Shmoneh, prefacing the report with the words 'The film should present the town as a challenge and not an achievement' –

diplomatic enough, I thought. Our boss was furious, and told Helga: 'I was in Kiryat Shmoneh a couple of months ago and it's a success story. You Anglo-Saxons!' But the project was cancelled. Instead, he sent me to Ashdod.

Ashdod, later to become Israel's third port, situated some twenty miles south of Tel Aviv, appeared on the map then only as an archaeological site. I decided to drive as the crow flies and ended by piloting the Morris through orange orchards, through gaps in fences, and under sprinklers in fields; then, in first gear, urging the reluctant little car up an embankment on to the coastal road. Eventually I found the town by following a line of electric pylons to a power station on the horizon. The town was so new that when the wadi separating the town from the road flooded, it was cut off, because the access road had been laid too low. There were platforms for factories as yet unconstructed, scaffolding for others, and the first houses, elephantine blocks with garlands of washing hanging across their flanks. From a distance, it had looked substantial; on approach, it disintegrated into half a dozen streets separated by sandy hillsides. But from the outset it was alive in a way that Kiryat Shmoneh was not.

All kinds of excrescences had already appeared on the face of the town, interfering with the planners' model. The little igloos humped here and there in the yards of the first cottages were ovens for baking pitta bread, because the square greyish loaves bussed in from Tel Aviv were not to the immigrants' taste. The shacks slapped up against the walls of the housing estates were shops made out of the crates in which their goods had been brought to Israel. The municipality building had formerly been the local water tower; its lower levels were filled in with offices. Outside, an Egyptian who claimed to have owned a chain of shops in Cairo and Alexandria laid out plastic goods on the sand, under a tattered umbrella covered with Arabic lettering – a floating spar from his past.

What Helga and I were supposed to be documenting was

'immigrant absorption'. No one had to wander the country as Bezalel had done, living on bread and radishes. There was now an enormous bureaucracy to run the immigrants' lives. The officials had a peculiar language of their own: people were 'human material'; places to live were 'housing solutions'; and immediately on arrival the immigrants were handed a booklet called *A thousand words*, containing all the vocabulary necessary for their existence. The 'In-gathering of the Exiles' meant standing on a hot evening in the middle of an empty space called the town centre, waiting to see who would climb down out of the next lorry. There were Poles and Romanians running away from communism, shopkeepers from Algiers and Tunis who thought of themselves as French, and village Jews from remote mountain areas almost all of whose customs were Arab but who knew quite well that they were not Muslims. Some of the European Jews who arrived at this time were the survivors of the last gutted ghettos and many of them were broken people. Mickey Kidron, a friend of mine who was one of the first psychiatric social workers in Beersheba, was summoned to Haifa to meet a boat from a Baltic port loaded with immigrants among whom the Romanians had included the entire population of a Bucharest asylum. Many were probably not Jews, but they were sent off to be 'absorbed' with the rest.

We watched them arrive. When the buses or lorries came to a halt, the immigrants peered out doubtfully at the sandy space, the handful of buildings, and the three 'absorbers': a Moroccan woman with high blood-pressure, swollen ankles and a bruise on her arm left by a dissatisfied client the week before; a Hungarian with a briefcase stuffed with hundreds of documents and forms to be filled in to keep track of the new arrivals; and a very lazy young Romanian whose main activity was patting people on the back.

It was easy to tell Europeans from North Africans. The first wore sober, threadbare suits, trilby hats and mufflers; their knickerbockered children wore wilted paper hats someone had given them at the port, and carried tin trumpets they had tired of blowing. The North Africans wore rainbow-coloured cottons and leopardskin-patterned nylon scarves knotted round bare necks. The young men were in jeans so tight you could see the shape of their genitals, and their legs moved like scissors. Bearded elders, almost all with rheumy diseased eyes, nursed the smaller children.

Decanted from the lorries with their cardboard suitcases and bundles, the 'human material' was led to the shacks and huts which housed the newest arrivals and introduced to the 'equipment' they had to sign – or leave a thumbprint – for. There was the standard-issue iron bedstead, the famous Jewish Agency mattress, which came in two sections (one for your body, the other for your legs) and which had a habit of parting and leaving you like a suspension bridge, primus stoves, lamps and petrol, two blankets, and a complimentary bottle of synthetic orange juice. The next day they were introduced to the 'institutions': the labour exchange, the school, and the adult and baby health clinics.

'Dead professions, that's what I call them,' said the manager of the labour exchange. 'Dead professions.'

The labour exchange was built like a fortress, with steel doors, no outside windows and grilles on the inner windows at which the immigrants queued up with their documents and references the day after arrival. It was built like this not because vast sums of money were kept there but because in the development towns the labour exchange was so often besieged by discontented or resentful immigrants. The manager was a burly young sabra with an expression of continually outraged patience.

'There's full employment in this town,' he explained, 'but they can't expect to come to a new country and carry on in the same jobs. What can I do with so many cobblers, tailors, furriers? Even carpenters. How many carpenters do you need in a town this size? The factory-owners want mechanics, fitters, men with technical training – they give me an order and I have to fill it. It's hard for the older men, but if they can't stand the pace, they'll just have to go on relief.'

The queue pushed its way forward. At its head was a plumber, an elderly Moroccan who had brought not documents but all his portable equipment, wrapped in old newspaper, and plans of the distant buildings in Marrakesh where he had installed the plumbing years ago. Behind him, pressing close, was a Tunisian wearing a checked cloth cap that gave him the air of a mad golfer. He smiled vaguely at the request for documents, and offered everyone a handful of nuts from the paper bags that filled his pockets – he was a peanut-vendor. Then came a bespectacled Turkish shopkeeper, protesting that he couldn't go to work the next day on a building site in the only suit he possessed and that no one was offering him work-clothes.

The manager shrugged. 'If he wants to fix himself up somewhere else, it's up to him. There's no official traffic between development towns – too complicated. At least he's got a roof over his head.'

The first problem was to round up the 'primitives'. These were the ones who didn't send their children to register at school or appear at the baby clinic as instructed, who hung their washing on the fence, or laid it out on the ground, rather than use the clothes line provided, who couldn't be trusted to take medicine home. All these families had their old patriarchs who were given work as casual labourers, picking up dry leaves from the street one by one or planting bushes in erratic lines. If they were totally unemployable, they sat at street corners praying.

I went to the baby clinic to see how the nurses dealt with the 'primitive' mothers. The social worker noticed that one woman on the list was absent and we went to look for her. She was a tiny woman from a village in the Atlas Mountains, with so many visible bones that she looked as if she had the skeleton of a fish. Her fin-like feet were clad in sequined sandals bought *en route*. She spoke a dialect no one understood, and had produced four children in six years of marriage, most breast-fed into their third year, which did away with at least one current old-wives' tale.

Three of her children had been removed that morning for kindergarten or injections. None of the bundles on the floor had been opened, and various relations sat around eating freshly baked pitta. There was no sign of the youngest baby until the nurse noticed a hump, with a little tuft of black hair, under the shawl on the woman's back.

'Take her off at once!' ordered the nurse angrily, and hissed at me, 'Two years old!' 'How's she going to walk? Get her dressed warmly and bring her to the clinic. And clean the floor!' The little mother had obviously not understood the words, but the gestures and tone were clear, so, anxious to obey orders in whatever sequence, she bent down, the baby still on her back, and began brushing the dirt away with her hands.

The other mothers in the clinic were amused to receive instructions from a nurse who, by her own admission, had only one child herself. The social worker was annoyed that the nurse spoke to the women only in Arabic. 'Talk Hebrew to them! Never mind if they don't understand, get them used to the sound of the language.'

A pregnant woman stared horrified as the nurse massaged a newborn baby's chest; the little chest and belly were so swollen with milk that the end of the umbilical cord stood up straight like a tiny trumpet. The child had been born on the mother's arrival, in a local hospital. The pregnant woman touched the nurse's elbow timidly: 'Madame, don't they bind the babies here? To make the navel go in? Surely they don't let them stand out like that for good?'

The nurse was too busy to reply, and it was left to someone else to reassure her that Israel was not going to change her children's anatomy.

There were children everywhere: bare-footed, bare-bottomed, in the huge sandpit that was Ashdod, clinging to the lintels over the doors, playing in the most dangerous corners of building sites, gathering wood to burn, exploring and conspiring.

'Children are wealth,' said one Moroccan woman in the clinic.

'Wealth!' snorted another. 'It's just because the men are selfish; they won't stop half-way.'

'They told me there was something called a ring,' said another, 'but I don't know how you use it.' She looked at the nurse, who pretended not to hear. They were offering prizes to women who bore ten children or more.

Every night carry-cots stood in the aisles of the new cinema; children under three could be brought in free of charge, and were cuddled and suckled throughout the screening. The Mayor called a special meeting to review the situation, with the cinema proprietor, the nurses and a community worker.

This young man, earnest, rather breathless, with a windcheater saying 'Chamonix' on the sleeve, summed up the problem: the stuffy crowded cinema was unhealthy for babies, and the suckling annoyed older members of the audience. Leaflets, posters and announcements over loudspeakers were to tell nursing mothers that they would be turned away from screenings.

'And what if they've got tickets? I can't turn away anyone with a ticket,' objected the proprietor, who looked like the doomed hero of a French police film; narrow-shouldered, fidgety, with dark glasses and a cigarette flapping on his lower lip. 'Don't I suffer too? A beautiful new cinema like mine with damages every week. If a kid tells his mother he wants to piss, she tells him to take his trousers down and not bother her. And I have to pay people to clean up every day.'

No solution was found. The cinema was the only recreation in town. The Jewish Agency provided organized entertainment in the Red Shield of David (Red Cross) building, where the only person usually around to sample it was the red-haired Romanian bachelor who was both ambulance driver and unofficial midwife, since the nearest hospital was half an hour away and the multiparas left things late and gave birth fast. But lectures by Foreign Ministry spokesmen on the Arab refugee problem, or Israeli folk-song recitals, didn't draw the crowds. I went to one lecture which attracted twenty people, leaving 7,908, according to an official count, who spent the evening some other way, if not at the cinema, then at a wedding or a circumcision party with arak and *falafel*, the women trilling ululations and the men doing parodies of belly dances to a violin and drum; where the tables creaked under the weight of chicken and rice, salads dripped oil, pastries scattered sugar, and no one bothered to rinse the glasses.

The line of pylons that had guided me into Ashdod was the town's lifeline. The power station and the port – still only a few piers reaching out to sea – were going to ensure the town's future. The experts and technicians of the Israel Electricity Company lived in bungalows near the seashore.

Motti, one of the sabra technicians, commuted from home to the power station daily, rarely passing through what his wife called 'the Kasbah'.

'Always trying to pick quarrels,' he said about the North African employees at the station. 'You can't have a peaceful word with them. The only way I manage to keep my temper is that I say to myself, "You're superior," and then I feel all right. I *know* I'm superior.'

The bungalow was modestly furnished. Outside stood a motor cycle and side-car, bought with his parents' reparation money from the West German Government. The bookcases, which he had made himself, held the usual sabra library: a Bible concordance, the book of the Palmach, and beside the Hebrew fiction a few paperbacks in English, including *The Fountainhead* and *The Naked and the Dead* – both favourites at that time.

'They're lazy, too. Never get them to do a job properly. Head cleaner's worse than anyone. I won't say you don't sometimes come across a hard-working one, like one of our best electricians, been here since 'fifty-one, but he's the exception. I'm not sorry they're here, of course; I wouldn't say, keep them out; they've a right to be here. But they don't like us, either. The only time the tune changes is when one of them gets his sister married to an Ashkenazi.'

A Moroccan employee at the station saw things differently. 'The easy jobs go to the Ashkenazim because they've got the pull. There's a pile of papers on the desk at the labour exchange and some high-up comes along and says to the fellow behind the desk, "*Vus hertzach*" – Yiddish is the password – and then he says, "So-and-so's my cousin, get hold of his papers, there's a good fellow, and put them on top of the pile." We North Africans all know it, so we shout and make a fuss. Lots of us had good jobs in the old countries – tailors and hairdressers and jewellers, and look at us here. Building, sweeping streets, packing. It's a hard life for us blacks, I can tell you.'

At that time there were very few intermarriages between Ashkenazim and Sephardim. Miriam, a Moroccan, was an 'absorber'. She was also a skilled mechanic; she could fix any car in town, was as notable as the Polish immigrant woman who was a building labourer, clambering nimbly over the scaffolding with the men. Shmuel, Miriam's electrician husband, was a Polish concentration camp survivor. I spent many evenings in their flat. It was perfectly organized despite Miriam's eighteen-hour working day. But their ten-year-old son refused to go to bed on time, and when they did manage to get him to bed, he was soon awake, running in with screaming nightmares. The child seemed responsive and friendly enough and I couldn't understand the trouble until one evening I heard Shmuel telling him the usual bedtime story.

'We got them all together and pushed them into one of the wooden huts they used as a latrine. They were shaking, I can tell you, the bastards, they knew what was coming. I don't know where we got the strength from. We were shaking too. We got them in there and they started begging us to let them out. We had to be quick, before the soldiers arrived, so we found some petrol they'd hoarded for their getaway and we poured it all round the hut and set fire to it. How they screamed, I can tell you, and how we laughed. We all joined hands and danced round the hut . . . '

Helga and I followed the immigrants from the labour exchange to their first day at work – on the building sites, in the power station, or in the new factories. Private investors were represented by a young man who went round the town expostulating at all the pitta ovens and makeshift shops. 'You've got to plan every detail of a town like this or it'll become a slum straight away!' He pointed at the government housing estate on the main street. Shutters and blinds had not been provided, so anything was strung across the windows against the sun – an old skirt, oilcloth, brown paper. 'We've got experts here who've worked out exactly how many shops we need. We can't just sell shops to anyone who asks, and we can't lower our standards. If these people can't make good, they can go on relief.'

Maurice ran a furniture shop in the main street, but not in the new shopping centre backed by investors – he couldn't afford it. He was from Casablanca; he'd been a fire-fighter at an American air-base, and a taxi driver, and in Israel he had tried out one immigrant centre after another. During five years in Israel, he had been at Afula in the Galilee (all the decent jobs had gone), in Kiryat Shmoneh ('They put it there just to keep the Syrians away; I wasn't going to work for the kibbutzim'), Nes Ziona, a veterans' village in the plain, where he ran a café ('No chance of doing business there – those old Russians just come in for a glass of lemon tea, and when the Moroccans found out I was one of them they ran up bills for beer and *arak* and never paid'), and finally opted for Ashdod. He was no agrarian socialist and he didn't ask for hand-outs.

Furniture was good business in Ashdod, and so too (*pace* the man in the labour exchange) was carpentry, which Maurice had taught himself. Families who had brought ten children and a big mahogany wardrobe had either to get rid of the children or the wardrobe; Maurice would chop the wardrobe in two and sell the halves to smaller families. He bought second-hand furniture in Tel Aviv, treated and varnished it himself and sold it on hire-purchase. His shop opened and closed at odd hours of the day ('Back Soon'), and stayed open late at night in defiance of licensing laws. Maurice bought and sold other things as well: pianos, barbers' equipment, stoves, anything that would work. He had come to Israel, he said, because of his children, three girls and a plump cosseted son whom he slapped when the boy got his Sabbath clothes dirty. A robust, handsome man, he said that he had been a good athlete in Morocco but never dared touch Arab boys who insulted him in the street. 'Here, Jewish kids will jump off a roof and you're sure they'll break every bone in their bodies, but they don't. When kids like that grow up you can put machine-guns in their hands and they'll use them if they need to. I like that. They're brave as . . . as Japanese suicide-pilots! In Morocco we were scared from the word go.'

We filmed in two schools, the state and the state religious, which were at opposite ends of the town. The Bible was taught exhaustively in both. In the state school, which Maurice's son attended, I recognized the constant hum of conversation which went on in most Israeli classrooms (and had gone on in mine), but the teacher, very pregnant but very mobile, had her own system of keeping order, snatching away a box of pencils here, confiscating a book there, removing a handful of nuts from a desk and throwing them unerringly into a box in the corner ('Goal!' – applause), and occasionally wielding a ruler, in the style of a more amiable Dotheboys Hall, to emphasize a point.

The passage in Proverbs about sparing the rod and spoiling the child was under discussion.

'When the father doesn't hit the kid, then the kid's happy?'

'The stick's got to be small.'

Prompt cue from the teacher: 'What happens if you hit your little sister and your father doesn't punish you?'

One boy saw the light. 'He shouldn't use a rod, he should use a plank.'

In the class for the newest immigrants, a nature lesson: origins and uses of water. Blue rain fell on brown earth in the teacher's blackboard drawing; water sank through to rock and was drawn up through wells. Only two children out of twenty had coloured pencils and the blue pencil circulated feverishly.

'What's the blue, teacher?'

'Rain, of course. The rain's blue.'

The child glanced surreptitiously out of the window. Grey rain was falling into grey sand. She shrugged, made the rain blue and passed the pencil on.

One little boy was expelled regularly from the class because he wouldn't sit next to a little Indian girl. Each time the teacher asked him if he would share her desk he shook his head; he said he was afraid of black people.

'Homeland' lesson: the children were learning the shape of their new country. The teacher explained that there was a 'historical frontier' and a 'political frontier'. She had been talking for ten minutes before she realized that the children didn't understand the word 'frontier' in Hebrew. When this had been translated into French and Romanian, there was more trouble. If the Land of Israel lay on both sides of the Jordan, the red frontier line looked less important. One little boy said fearfully, 'Then the Arabs are everywhere, the Arabs are in our country!' Panic in class.

In the eighth grade, the final class of primary school, they were learning European Jewish history. The subject was Hassidism, Jewish mysticism, about as comprehensible to Moroccan, Indian and Egyptian children as the Diet of Worms. They obediently wrote down, under columns headed 'Advantages' and 'Disadvantages', the ideas of *Hasidim* and *Mitnagdim* (participants in the greatest eighteenth-century theological quarrel in European Jewry). Guessing which arguments belonged where was like a game of roulette.

None of this got into our film, because we hadn't the budget to record scenes live. There was just a commentary I wrote, and background music. No one stopped Helga filming, save when a fight broke out in the street outside the labour exchange, and the police intervened and confiscated the film. But the real problems started when the film was complete. The message, we thought, was reasonable: Ashdod was a town with a future, but getting used to life in a new strange country wasn't easy.

Five separate government institutions had to endorse the film, and they all hated it. If it was shown abroad, we were told, fund-raisers wouldn't like it. The message wasn't positive enough. It showed Israel in a poor light. It would have to be scrapped.

Fortunately Helga had two allies: one was Haim Hefer, a celebrated Israeli poet and songwriter and Palmach veteran, who was writing the Hebrew commentary. He threatened to hold a press conference condemning the way the Government was withholding information. At the crucial moment, Heizi Zinder, whose background was similar to ours, was appointed the new head of Information Services, and he liked the film. It won a prize at a town-planning congress.

I stayed on in Ashdod for a couple of months, in a room rented from an old Romanian couple so poor that if they had put margarine on a piece of bread they didn't eat, it went back into the icebox for the next day. He was a cobbler, and travelled an hour each day to Yavne, the dismal nearby development town; he had found a gap between two buildings where he set up a stall.

The officials and the sociologists and the political analysts I knew in Jerusalem all told me that in a few generations all the differences between 'ethnic groups' would be ironed out. In other words all the little Sephardi Jews would become Ashkenazi Jews.

Maurice wanted his son to be an engineer, or a pilot, or a doctor. Half the children in the boy's class said they wanted to be archaeologists. There had been an expedition to the Ashdod excavations and the children had seen that archaeology was a 'status value' profession, with boys and girls called Shai and Tami (not Armand and Arlette), in shirts and shorts (not patterned nylon and synthetic velvet), volunteering for work during their summer holidays.

I sat in on a visit by an Education Ministry official who had analysed the psycho-technical tests that were going to decide the immigrant children's future. He tried to explain to a Moroccan mother that her fourth son had no talent for abstract thinking. She looked blank. The headmaster tried to explain abstract thinking to her in halting Arabic peppered with French. Nothing helped. She wanted her son to be a pharmacist.

The man from the ministry told her he was better at manual skills. He advised vocational training as a mechanic.

'All his brothers are mechanics. I want something better for him.'

The official was embarrassed. The headmaster intervened. 'Let's see what the boy wants for himself,' he suggested. Under 'Choice of Profession', the boy had written, 'Private detective'.

Maurice's wife didn't want her daughters to go into the army; she had heard too much about what went on there between boys and girls. The daughters thought otherwise. They had heard that girls had fun in the army and on the kibbutzim. But they wouldn't rebel.

Post-school, though, was the angry age – between leaving school and the army. A trade union official was invited to give a lecture on opportunities for temporary work. The thirty boys present had already seen the film at the town cinema twice. They paid little attention to the lecturer, shouting, jeering, scraping their chairs and competing for the attention of a little group of girls clinging together at the centre of the hall like sirens on a rock. Raising his voice, the speaker explained that Ashdod employers wouldn't pay the boys more than a token wage at their age. 'Boys can spoil machines. Boys go from one job to another. Boys leave to go into the army. Boys aren't responsible.'

For the first time the boys exchanged looks of something like pride.

The speaker told them Israel was one of the most advanced countries in the world for teenage employment. The boys were hysterical with laughter, and the little Yemenite who was the local trade union man shot to his feet in a rage.

'You don't know what it was like ten years ago,' he shouted, trembling visibly. 'When I came out of the army I walked the streets looking for crusts. There wasn't anyone to look after me the way I look after you.'

'Lies, all lies!' shouted one of the boys. 'Why can't we study? We want to study. Abroad we could have studied as much as we liked.'

'Yes, study, study,' they all yelled, and scrambled to their feet. They knocked over all the chairs on their way out. A serious little girl who had been sitting alone at the back came up to the discomfited lecturer. 'What about work for women like me?' she asked. 'I've got a family to support.' She was fourteen.

'In Casa there was much more than the cinema,' said Maurice. 'We had cafés and dance halls and all sorts of attractions, you didn't have to spend much money. Here, if I go to Tel Aviv for Independence Day, there's nothing much to see. A big football match is too expensive. Now in Casa, there were plenty of *entraîneuses* in the cafés, Spanish women who danced with the customers. All very *distingué*. On the fourteenth of July we had fireworks, and dancing in the streets. The sea was full of little boats and the air was full of balloons.' His hand rested thoughtfully on the table-top he was polishing. 'Ashdod's just a village. Now the Gardens of the Sultan in Marrakesh,' he murmured, 'that was something.'

Fifteen years after I first visited Ashdod, I toured Israel to interview the new Sephardi leadership, most of whom were now supporters of the Israeli right wing. Almost all of them said that they wanted a different kind of socialism, anything but the old Labour leaders who had been their patrons, their organizers and their educators. In Yavne, a byword for immigrant misery in the 1960s, its clever young Mayor, Meir Shitrit, a biochemist and a captain in the army, was now an ardent supporter of Menachem Begin. He had removed the names of various Labour founders of the state of Israel from the streets of his town, and replaced them with the names of birds.

In Ashdod, in the sixties, there were still rabbis with two wives, one for the living-room and one in the kitchen. No one forced such couples to undergo divorce, and the custom died out. Among the 'primitives' there were families who immolated their daughters if they got pregnant outside marriage. Cases like this disappeared too; the customs of the country triumphed, the Sephardi birth-rate fell. But the celebrations lived on, like the spring pilgrimage to Meron in the Galilee.

This had very ancient origins. It commemorated the life and death of Simeon Bar Yochai, a second-century rabbi who had defied the Romans after the conquest of Jerusalem and was said to be buried in Meron. The pilgrimage to his tomb had long been celebrated by Hasidic Jews, who made it an occasion to collect charity; it was also when the hair of three-year-old boys was cut for the first time (leaving only their side-locks). For the North African Jews, it became a huge jamboree, like the Maimouna or spring festival of the Moroccans, a gathering of the clans.

I drove up to Meron in 1962, after I heard about the celebration from people in Ashdod, and by the time I reached the winding road leading up to the shrine I was part of the vast convoy of lorries, vans and cars making their way through the hills. Meron is a tiny village almost hidden in a knot of forests, but the route was clear from a distance, marked by hundreds of tail-lights climbing up out of the valleys. Seventy thousand people attended the pilgrimage that year – the number later reached hundreds of thousands – and police were posted at intervals along the roads. The fields all around were dotted with tents and the narrow path to the tomb was fringed by family groups with barrels, boxes, lamps, rugs and straw mattresses. This path was bordered on the one hand by a solid mountain-face, and on the other by a steep drop to dry scrubby fields, a drop only partly fenced off by coils of barbed wire.

The crowds moved slowly up the path, each family propelled by those behind. Sometimes the flow was blocked by a sudden meeting, as families sent to different parts of Israel by immigration officials met and embraced, or when a group of Hasidim, having gone down the hill to meet a respected rabbi, escorted him up again with dancing and singing. At one point they caused chaos, and several women, screaming hysterically, were hauled back from the edge of the drop, or clambered down into the fields.

The tomb was concealed in an inner room of a stone building with a flat roof and inner courtyards and staircases. In the courtyards, under the eye of Simeon, whose portrait was pasted up everywhere, families lay sprawled on the flagstones, leaving little room for the crowds to pass. Many of those prostrated there were old, ill or pregnant, for a visit to the tomb was believed to cure the sick and prevent miscarriage. As far as I could see, it was more likely to have the opposite effect.

As we pressed through the last door into the room of the tomb itself, the effect was hallucinatory. The heat was intense but for a moment I thought it was snowing, until I realized that the snow was hundreds of candles and their fragments falling from the upper balconies. The pilgrims up above were hurling candle after candle on to the tomb, a slab of stone surrounded by a high iron railing. As the candles, most of which were lit, fell into the tomb area, they piled up high in curlicues of tallow, while bogged down in the white grease were scraps of paper, prayers tossed hopefully through the railing. Men keeled backwards and forwards in prayer against the railing, their eyes fixed on the tomb, while the women kept up the ululations. The noise echoed from the low dome, the air was thick with the smell of candles, garlic and sweat, and the policemen at the door drove the crowds in and out with half-coherent shouts, like goatherds. When we finally got through to the open air again, a sudden burst of song and flame made us look up to the roof. A bonfire flickered wildly in a huge copper bowl; pilgrims burrowed through the crowd and up the steps to the roof with their arms full of old clothes and cheap jewellery, which they began hurling energetically on to the flames.

Below in the fields, soldiers with skull-caps were dancing, and an old Moroccan couple jigged placidly to the tunes of a fiddle and tambourine. Rabbis were selling copies of the Zohar, the mystics' key text. I recognized a young orthodox soldier from Jerusalem, who was looking on indignantly. 'That's not the Jewish religion, that's Arab. Those people don't even know what they're doing. I asked one woman why she was throwing candles and she just stared at me.' The Hasidim, however, were more encouraging. At this time they began courting the Sephardi immigrants, and within a few years, in Safed and in Jerusalem, you could see the pilgrims' children studying in Ashkenazi seminaries, wearing the long black frock-coats and fur-brimmed hats of the Polish Jews.

The immigrants who were sent to Ashdod were the lucky ones. There were other towns, particularly to the south, where the site seemed to have been picked out by a blindfolded official with a pin, towns which from the outset had no chance of success and from which the Europeans, or anyone with savings or gumption instantly fled. One such town was Yeruham in the Negev.

The Negev was the scene of many peculiar experiments. Ben Gurion went there to live in an isolated kibbutz, Sde Boker, hoping to draw the children of the cities after him like the Pied Piper; but they didn't follow. Michael Evenari experimented with water conservation on the Nabatean ruins of Avdat, growing tomatoes with dew. A sculpture garden was erected on the edge of the Great Crater, the most desolate spot in Israel. But the people of Yeruham were not tomatoes or modern sculptures. The town had been plagued by feuding between the Moroccan clans who had been running it, after a fashion, for the previous decade. Things were not improved by the arrival of the Bene Israel, Indian Jews who were not welcomed by the hidebound rabbinate. As no recognized rabbi had supervised the community since the eighteenth century, the rabbinate declared that their 'purity' was questionable, and it took years for them to be formally accepted. They did not get on much better than the Moroccans, and I was told that a number of them had taken to the bottle.

I arrived in Yeruham, to write a report, in the middle of a crisis. The week before, two of the Moroccan clan chiefs had quarrelled, the town council had fallen apart, and the Ministry of the Interior had sent a couple of officials to run the town until peace was made. The Mayor I was going to meet was therefore probably an Ashkenazi, but just as in Arab villages you had to make for the mukhtar's house, in a small Jewish town there was no bypassing the municipality. It was about midday when I arrived to find the town hall almost totally deserted, though I had made an appointment by phone. A solitary clerk looked up when I came in. Yes, she seemed to remember talking to me on the phone. No, the Mayor wasn't in; he had gone to a cricket match.

I looked out of the window at the usual dreary blocks of public housing and the tawny pebbled desert behind them. A cricket match?

Yes, she said. An American donor had contributed a football stadium to the town, but at the moment it was being used for a cricket match. Did I know anything about cricket? Not much, I said warily. But did I at least know the rules, more or less? I said, I thought so. Well, in that case, she was sure that the Mayor would be delighted to see me and hear how the game was played. I might even get my interview.

I followed her directions to the football ground and found, in the huge but empty stadium, a puzzled group of Jerusalem Ashkenazis who had been sent to Yeruham to cope with the Moroccan clan-war and the alcoholic Indians and were now sitting glumly, chins in hands, trying to make sense of cricket. On the field was a smartly turned-out group of Indians, the home team, batting, and in the field, a group of tall, pink-kneed, red-faced Englishmen from Harrow. How and why Harrow had made contact with the Yeruham first eleven I never found out. I was too busy explaining a maiden over to the ersatz Mayor.

By the end of the day, the Indians, exhilarated by their memories of a half-forgotten skill, were on their way to victory. The municipal officials, and the few Moroccans present, were impressed. For the first time since their arrival, batting for Yeruham, the Bene Israel had risen in status. The Harrovians, floored by the savage heat, had by losing done a great service to the In-gathering of the Exiles.

4

Matters of Life and Death

I MET my future husband, as befitted two convinced social-
ists, in a private swimming-pool – at other times a reservoir.
The guests swam round holding glasses of white wine, ser-
enaded by the tree frogs in the eucalyptus trees separating the
house from acres of orange orchards. I had hardly been in the
pool for a few minutes when a burly, sandy-haired, snub-nosed
young man who looked like a British major, save for his slanting
Slav eyes, tossed his glass into the bushes and made for me. I had
seen him once before and we both knew something of one
another. He was the aide to the current Minister of Labour, had
been drama critic on a left-wing monthly, and belonged to a Tel
Aviv set I knew only slightly. We swam round and round, between
and under the other guests, in a wordless aquatic mating-dance. I
was annoyed and teased; the Slav major seemed confident that no
words at all were necessary.

Later, when most of the guests had left, and those who
remained had paired off and disappeared into the various
bedrooms, my host, a teaching colleague from the previous years,
asked me discreetly if I wanted the Slav major to remain.
Certainly not, I said primly. I thought the whole thing too public –
as usual. The major, now fully dressed if still damp, took his
rebuff with perfect good humour, and handed me an engraved
card with his address and telephone number. This was rare in
Israel at that time, and since he had neither a home of his own nor
capital, rather like putting a Rolls-Royce emblem on a motor
cycle. Then he drove off grandly in a wealthy friend's large car.

I spent the summer that followed, as always, in Europe, partly in Denmark, and from Copenhagen I brought back a dozen cigars in metal jackets to distribute among various men-friends. The Slav major, whose name was Yehuda, received more than his fair share because he was the first sabra I had met who wooed me with gourmet dinners and classical records. Unlike all the other men of my acquaintance, he knew the chefs in restaurants, liked Yiddish jokes, regularly got drunk with artist friends in Tel Aviv, and liked to pamper women. His strait-laced, principled, German-born Minister, Giora Josephtal, might reprove him for 'rolling around from bed to bed', but I detected the family man in Yehuda and was not surprised when he told me that he wanted a crowd of children who would line up to salute him when he came home at night. He proved as direct and single-minded about me as on that first night in the pool, and had no reservations about my Diaspora background. Unlike most of my friends, he had never read a textbook of psychology and refused to analyse himself. He was young, and unsoured by experience.

Like other sabras, he had changed his surname – from Lichtblum (his father's family had been candle-makers; on his mother's side were generations of rabbis) to Layish, meaning lion-cub (it went with his leonine appearance). He was one of the first batch of Israelis to be delivered in the Tel Aviv hospital in the mid thirties. His father had been a teacher in Warsaw, but in Israel worked as a labourer, breaking stones on the roads – the classic progression; later he became a clerk in the vast Israeli bureaucracy. His mother belonged to a famous rabbinical family, of the Bratslav Hasidim, and though Yehuda never went near a synagogue after his bar mitzvah (his father was staunchly anti-clerical), he had an affectionate familiarity with Jewish customs – that agnostic *Yiddishkeit* which must be scarcely comprehensible to a non-Jew. To hear the gusto with which Yehuda led a Passover Seder was to realize that orthodox Jewry had lost a great cantor. His very Gentile appearance was, in my view, partly explained by a Freudian interpretation of a family legend about a Cossack raid on the little village where his great-grandparents had lived. His great-grandmother, so the story went, had just baked a Sabbath loaf and put it on a windowsill to cool; but she had no time to close the wooden shutters before the cavalry swept through the village. In the story, one of the Cossacks, spurring his horse through the village, had reached out with his sabre and speared the still-steaming *chala*, carrying it off on the tip of the steel.

An only child in a family that led a very austere life (there was no nonsense about foreign travel, birthday parties or even eating out), Yehuda, like my own father, had gone out to work at fourteen, doing clerical and even manual work, and received his secondary education at the Working Youth night-school of the trades unions. This, I found, explained some of the lavishness with which he always entertained others once he had a regular salary; he had a very endearing gesture, a wave of his arm, which said the hell with the expense, whenever anyone queried the price. As I had spent my early independence starving in garrets as a matter of principle (there was nothing I didn't know about fleas and dysentery by the age of twenty-two), to impress my father – but always knowing there was security back home – we proved to be extremely bad housekeepers, never budgeting, never counting the cost. I teased Yehuda that, though a socialist, he always had a ministry limousine and driver at his disposal and never travelled by public transport. He himself had never learned to drive, never having had a car, and always kept one hand prudently on the door-handle when I drove him, in case, he explained, he had to make a quick exit by rolling out on to the roadside as he had been taught in the army.

Yehuda and I had absolutely nothing in common: neither background, upbringing, experience, professional training nor even a common language of which both had mastery; his English remained as poverty-stricken as my Hebrew. What this meant was that we had to make strenuous efforts to understand each other, which was constructive. My schoolfriends had all dreaded leaving school without an engagement ring – the Jewish girls in particular were terrified of the fate of a spinster. My friends at Oxford had solemnly told me that they couldn't imagine marrying anyone who didn't have the same upbringing and education as themselves.

I had found both absurd, but the language barrier, nonetheless, was considerable. Speaking a language less than instinctively means that you say what you can, not always what you mean. On the other hand, it makes for honesty; the effort to disguise and to pretend is easily decoded. The problems and the rewards even out, with time.

After nearly two years, we married. This meant my first encounters with Israeli bureaucracy. I acquired an Israeli passport and identity card, and became, after six years as a temporary resident, a citizen of the Jewish State. When I went to the Ministry of the Interior office in Jaffa Road to register myself, a little self-conscious about the importance of the act, I was faced with a bearded, skull-capped clerk, a brass tray with lemon tea and a half-chewed bagel in front of him, and thousands of dusty files behind him. He looked over my documents, eyed me critically and, rubbing his nose said, 'Something smells here.' With those historic words, my status was altered.

My parents arrived and we all went to the rabbinate to register our request to be united in a religious ceremony; there is no civil marriage in Israel. The new clerk, more rigorous than the first if no less brusque, looked hard at my parents. My father, with his white hair, formidable expression, and the cane he carried from choice, like his father (an American friend called him the Judge) was unapproachable. In any case, it is the mother's religion which determines that of the child in Jewry. So the clerk turned to my mother and asked, 'How do you know you're Jewish?'

This left the former first secretary of the Women's Zionist Federation speechless with anger. 'Oh, all right,' muttered the intimidated clerk, and put us on the register.

Yehuda was asked how much money he wanted entered on the *ketuba*, or marriage contract. This is the sum the husband is obliged to provide for his wife in case of divorce – to deter him from too easily abandoning her. 'Ten pounds,' said my prospective husband. The poor clerk was forced to note this down too.

I was ushered into a little office for a confidential talk with a woman clerk, who from her wig, hat and dress, designed to deter any sexual interest, was clearly a married woman, probably a rabbi's wife. It was her job to fix a date for my wedding according to the date of my last menstruation, a procedure designed to prevent couples fornicating during the wife's period. Though furious, I wasn't going to make an issue of this, so I told her a date I had calculated and watched her work out the marriage day we had in mind. She handed me a slip of paper to give the clerk at the ritual bath-house, I deposited it in the gutter outside, and we found a friendly rabbi (unbearded), employed by the Ministry of Tourism, who gave us the kind of talk we would have heard in a registry office. The only thing that wasn't clear to me was whether I had to suffer the various customary indignities (which to my mind included wearing a veil over an ordinary suit) in the cause of upholding Jewish tradition, or merely to prop up the latest coalition government between Labour and the religious parties.

There was one propitiatory rite, however, that later I was sorry I did not observe. Tova Touashi, the Syrian Jewish cleaning woman who had been coming to me once a week since I had moved into a flat of my own, suggested that I should cut a chicken's throat and sprinkle its blood in the four corners of our new living-room, as this would bring good luck to the marriage. 'But,' she added tactfully, 'perhaps you have other customs?'

We hadn't; except that my mother spent the night before the wedding with me, insisting that Yehuda and I must approach the synagogue from different directions. Just as we were about to leave for the ceremony, a water-hydrant burst in the road outside, and since I had written a script on Israel's water-carrier I was very sensitive to the sight of wasted water. I used my brand-new phone to try to alert the municipal officials, though my mother was nervous that I would miss my wedding. The clerk on the other end was suspicious of hoaxes and, like the clerk at the rabbinate, wanted more information about my identity and origins. In the end I told him that I was getting married in ten minutes and couldn't be more precise – which only served to confirm his suspicions.

Wedding presents arrived from my parents' friends in England, who had been cheated of a wedding: damask table-napkins, Swedish glass, Spode – all too elegant, too formal to be used. They were treated like someone else's possessions, laid by and dusted once a year. My piano, the one thing I had wanted from that other life, now that I was anchored in Israel, should never have been transported.

It was a Vogel, a Viennese instrument, a native of temperate zones, too delicate to stand the change of climate. The wood contracted and expanded with the first *chamsin* (desert wind), sighing and cracking. At night, when other sounds were stilled, I heard its agony; sometimes the strains were so great that a string would break loose and whiplash against the lid with a twang like that last stage direction in *The Cherry Orchard*. I was told to stand a bucket of water beneath it, to alleviate the dryness, but nothing helped. The pedals creaked, keys stuck and had to be shaken loose in mid-arpeggio.

Suddenly the night-sounds stopped. No more complaints. But when I sat down next to play I realized that the piano's voice had changed; it had the hoarseness and quaver of age.

I called in the blind tuner whose fingers, passing over the soundboard with its gilt decorations, detected a hairline crack I hadn't noticed. Nothing more, he said, would happen now. It was not a reassurance.

The ordeal at the rabbinate was, to me, the first indication of the gap that existed between my perception of Judaism (the heritage of my English upbringing) and Judaism in Israel, embodying Eastern European orthodoxy. Before this, only one thing had stirred memories of stories I had been told about my grandparents: the Mahane Yehuda street-market in Jerusalem on the eve of Yom Kippur, during the ceremony of *kappara*, by which sins are transferred to a rooster which is waved above the sinner's head and then ritually slaughtered.

When I saw that, I remembered my grandmother, who had

arrived in London from Riga at the turn of the century. My grandparents considered themselves to be observant Jews but by orthodox standards they were pagans. My grandfather loved Wagner and my grandmother loved Shakespeare. They had lost track of the Jewish calendar during the voyage from the Baltic. Under the impression that the day after her arrival was the eve of Yom Kippur, my grandmother had spent all day buying food and cooking for the large meals that precede and follow the fast, only to find that she had spent the fast-day wholly preoccupied with food. She rushed to the nearest rabbi, who happened to be an orthodox member of one of the sects that dominate religion in Israel, expecting him to prescribe a specific prayer to be read in penance. Instead, he instructed her to buy a live cockerel, wave it around her head (my grandmother never went out without gloves), and slit its throat at once. She backed away nervously, convinced that she was dealing with a dangerous lunatic, and was never seen in his synagogue again.

After the indelicate enquiries of the rabbi's wife, I began to feel rather like my grandmother. I also started seeing things I hadn't noticed before, such as religious Jews kissing the *mezuzot*, amulets, nailed to the doorposts of every building where Jews lived, both when they went in and when they came out; and I was surprised by all kinds of customs in Yehuda's family I had never heard of, like eating apples dipped in honey at the New Year. On the other hand, I knew far more about what went on inside a synagogue than Yehuda's friends, many of whom would not have known how to behave if 'called up' to read from the Law in a foreign country.

In Israel, boys had to be circumcised, most teenagers had bar mitzvot, and everyone was buried according to Jewish rituals (there was no cremation), but it was possible for a Jew to get to the end of his or her life without ever having entered a synagogue or observing a single precept of the Jewish religion apart from the interrogations and formulae of the wedding ceremony. All the vast edifice of law and dialectic built up over the centuries had shrunk to the dimensions of the skull-cap kept in the glove

73

compartment of Israeli cars, to be hastily put on at funerals (in Jewish law, and because of the climate, held within hours of death).

Israelis were *hiloni'im*, secular, or *dati'im*, religious, a division unknown elsewhere, and people tried to persuade me that in Israel you didn't have to know anything about Judaism; it pervaded you by a kind of osmosis, simply through your living in the Jewish State. I thought this nonsense. I started to read books about Judaism, like Foot Moore's classic on the early Christian era, good for apostates like myself, and a religious magazine which explained how a modern state could be run in the spirit of ancient Judaism. When Israel was still running a merchant and passenger fleet of its own, there was serious discussion as to whether its ships should not shut off their engines and drift at anchor through the Jewish Sabbath. The scholars, with advice from engineers and sailors, worked their way through an argument which went like this: what happens when engines are switched off? The ship may drift aground. If the drift is corrected, what happens when the Israeli cargo arrives a day later than that of its competitors? The Government loses money. Welfare services are cut back, people (i.e. Jews) suffer. And so on, until famine and despair looming, a solution was reached. For reasons of *pikuah nefesh* (the saving of lives) the entire argument went into reverse, and the ships' engines, theoretically stopped, were theoretically set in motion again.

I did not become devout, but reading about how the problems of levirate marriage complicated the lives of seven hypothetical deaf and dumb brothers, I did understand why Jews produced some good mathematicians.

Such debates were not academic in Israel at all. The rabbinical synods, poring over volumes of precedent, reported to the ultra-orthodox political parties. These leaned on the Labour party. Labour hegemony formally came to an end in November 1976, when a contingent of F16 fighter-planes inadvertently landed at Ben Gurion Airport a short time after the start of the Sabbath (calculated by rabbinical fiat as the time at which, allowing for cloud conditions, three stars were deemed to have appeared in the sky). The religious departed the coalition and the Government fell.

But I also observed that there were a number of quiet accommodations. The sanctions of the rabbis extended so far and no further. When the Knesset still met in a converted biscuit-factory in King George Avenue, the amiable Moshe Kransdorf sold pork chops, ham and bacon at a side entrance to the building. Even when the new anti-pig-breeding law was passed, years later, the kibbutzim, who did a roaring trade in pork sausage, camouflaged their pig-pens and troughs, army fashion, while inspectors from the rabbinate hired helicopters and telescopic lenses to try and locate offenders. When the whole country was supposed to be cleansed of leavened bread before Passover, the agreed fiction was that select Israeli Arabs would 'buy' what remained, just as during the Sabbatical year, when fields were supposed to lie fallow, they were 'sold' to Muslims. It is intriguing to think what might have happened had the Arabs taken this seriously.

So my own partial collusion with the woman at the rabbinate – who, I am sure, knew exactly how seriously I took the whole business – was perfectly in the spirit of what was going on in the country as a whole. It was of no interest to her whether I was chaste or intended to observe the laws of ritual purity. The main thing for Jews like myself was to observe the form. I might think that monotheism, the Ten Commandments and the strictures of the Prophets were the essence of the Jewish faith. The rabbinate knew these did not constitute Judaism. My personal objections to the rituals, the hypocrisy involved and the humiliation of having to conform to a procedure I found objectionable did not concern her.

Curious to know more about undiluted Jewish life, I got to know a post-office employee in his fifties, Solomon Hirsch, and his son Jacob, a sabra. Solomon was the son of a wandering Jewish tailor who had travelled from Galicia to England, to Palestine, and back to Belgium in the thirties, from where the family was deported by the Nazis. Solomon, who was British by birth, managed to get a certificate to enter Palestine and worked as a postal clerk throughout the Mandate. His whole life was organized around the three main prayers of the day – the first in the synagogue; the second in the post office, where Solomon and his colleagues gathered in a corner among the mailbags, facing east; and the third, in the evening, back in the synagogue near his home. His life was mapped out into four geographical areas: home, a place of observance and study; the synagogue; the post office; and 'the street', the outside world with its temptations and distractions. What looked to me like dingy little shops in Jaffa Road were to Solomon dens of trickery and vice; for him, the cafés and restaurants were either not sufficiently kosher, or places where the 'dust of slander' was spread. Cinemas were boring, for the only films advertised as permissible in the religious newspapers were war films, 'the same ships and cannons and soldiers over and over again'. Window-shopping was out, unless you were rich, because it was a sin to go into a shop and ask the price of an article you had no intention of buying.

Solomon had studied in the ultra-orthodox Mea Shearim district, but despised these people for living on charity and letting their wives work while they studied. Like most orthodox Jews in Israel, Solomon worked by day and studied a page of Talmud every evening. Some of the other post-office workers were so devout that they would turn their heads away from a woman when handing her a parcel, but Solomon was mildly tolerant even of a female free-thinker like myself. He knew that the Law was infringed in all kinds of Jewish institutions, such as banks (taking interest from Jews was forbidden), but he insisted that the sheer busyness of the orthodox kept them out of 'street' mischief ('like orgies, that French thing'). Pain had to be borne stoically, the sick had to accept their fate, he said, and took me to a religious hospital.

These hospitals, originally founded to outwit the missionaries, kept Jewish law in detail. No bread was served during Passover and medicines were tested for starch. No lights were lit on the

Sabbath (they came on automatically) and the nurses could not even use cotton-wool, as 'squeezing' counted as labour. If essential machines broke down, the *Shabbes goy* (Gentile worker) would mend them; or an orthodox electrician who would then receive a retroactive sanction from a rabbi.

Orthodox Jews had their own form of alternative medicine; praying disciples would visit the rabbis; boiled flax-juice would be used to relieve bronchial congestion; and it was not unusual to see a jaundice patient's visitors placing a pigeon on his belly. Post-mortems, incidentally, were out of the question, for the body must be intact to be reassembled at the last trump. I would not have wanted a really orthodox doctor – one who did not work in hospitals at all – to treat me, for these worked on plastic models for their anatomy studies.

Solomon kept up with contemporary rabbinical rulings rather as a doctor might read *The Lancet*. The problems of debts that fell due on the Sabbath (promissory notes or cheques did not count as money), of cooking without lighting fires, or of whether false teeth counted as crockery to be changed at Passover were just as important as the potentially drifting ocean liners of the merchant fleet. But the ordinances which concerned all of us, religious orthodox or not, were family disputes and cases relating to divorce; for the rabbinical courts were the only ones competent to deal with marriages or separations. I learned, somewhat to my horror, that Yehuda could divorce me but I could not divorce him; that if he were to get the next plane to South America and fail to return, I would become an *aguna*, an 'anchored' woman who cannot marry again if her first husband's whereabouts are unknown. But if he failed in his conjugal duties the courts could force him to release me. In theory. A visit to the rabbinical court with Solomon indicated that things were not so simple.

The couple before the judges came from one of the poorest districts of Tel Aviv, inaptly named the Quarter of Hope, where they had moved from an immigrants' transit camp. These were the people who were totally dependent on the rabbis' rulings. People like Yehuda and myself could, if the worst came to the worst, marry in civil ceremonies in Cyprus, or further west, and ignore the problems (until children came), or find other less stringent rabbis abroad. Others, like the couple in court, could not.

They had been separated for six years after a marriage of only two months, and the wife had appealed to the Rabbinical High Court for more alimony, having stubbornly refused to accept a bill of divorce from her husband. They were obviously not observant Jews; the wife wore no head-covering and her blouse was transparent; the man was dressed in his best suit, clearly in an attempt to influence the court with his respectability. As soon as they entered the court the wife made a beeline for the husband, but the lawyers insisted that they sit apart. The wife's lawyer spoke first; he was in his shirt-sleeves and spoke confidentially, man to man.

'Listen, rabbis! He left his wife and she had to go back to her parents. Imagine the shame! But anything rather than live alone, rabbis! What he gives her isn't fair, it was before the last devaluation. What's it worth now? My client's not a strong woman; the separation has made her ill, she has doctor's bills to pay.' He handed up a dog-eared collection of receipts; the woman stared wistfully at her husband's profile.

'All she wants is to go back to her husband, rabbis. All she wants is to be a faithful wife.'

The argument was torn to shreds by the husband's lawyer, a dapper young man whose approach was more formal.

'Your Honours of the High Court, my client maintains that this demand for extra money is only a pretence, an excuse, an attempt to force him to return to live with a woman he doesn't love. Why does she need more money? She lives with her parents, she has no one to support. For the last six years, your honours, this man has had to support a woman who refuses to accept his divorce. How much longer can this continue?'

At this point, the husband, who had sat with his head down, raised it and muttered, 'This hell, it can't continue.' His lawyer reproved him. A slight, almost imperceptible smile crossed the woman's face.

One of the rabbis had been leafing back and forth in the file. The eldest rabbi, after a consultation, leaned forward to ask a question. Immensely dignified, rubbing at a spot on his robes, he asked why the husband originally left his wife.

The husband's lawyer hesitated a moment. 'Well, you see, he said she wanted three and even four times a night, your honours; she wanted relations all the time, and he's a hard-working man, your honours.' The rabbis all nodded together, understandingly. The case was adjourned. I never found out how it ended.

I attended the marriage of Solomon's son, Jacob, to a Tunisian girl. It wasn't at all like our wedding. Men and women were kept apart at all stages of the ceremony, and Solomon had to apologize for not shaking my hand.

Jacob was a teacher of new immigrants – this was how he had met his bride. He was far more militant than his father, seeing himself in constant combat with evil: ignorance (especially that of the Sephardim), anti-religious forces, and unpatriotic Israelis. 'The religious soldiers take off their skull-caps when they go dancing. The oriental boys had never even heard of the Holocaust, and they knew hardly anything about Jewish history. They asked me why the Germans did that to the Jews. So I told them that the Germans were afraid of the special power the Jews have. I told them that the Torah teaches that anti-Semitism will never end, and assimilation with other nations is impossible. Every nation belongs to a group, and only the Jews are unique; we have to keep ourselves unique through our religion. That's our only claim to this country, being religious. Otherwise, why did we take it away from the Arabs?'

Solomon took me to visit one of the religious associations administering charity, which granted free loans without interest to the orthodox, and even built houses leased at low rents to the poor.

There were sacks full of the worn and precious belongings of the borrowers piled high in the strong-room behind the counter of what looked like a banking-hall (men on one side, women on the other). It was like a giant pawnshop. There were also ritual

79

objects for loan – from candlesticks to wedding-rings and prayer-shawls. Most of those who applied for charity were well known to the lenders, but if not, they could offer jewellery or household goods as security.

'Well run and very reliable,' said Solomon. 'Much better than a bank that charges interest, or social workers, may the Name forbid. They come prying into your house, asking all kinds of questions, and we orthodox don't like dealing with them. Here, they're very discreet, and you know you're among friends. Most of the money comes from abroad, and you don't know who the donor is. That's real charity, in the right spirit, as the Talmud prescribes.'

But Jacob was against the whole notion of charity; he did not even like the State of Israel borrowing from the United States, though he had no suggestions as to how this could be avoided. His opinions about Diaspora Jews were as negative as any I had heard from my students. 'The only real life for Jews is in Israel. It's a great sin to live in the Diaspora as a religious Jew. Each time the Lord refers to himself, he doesn't say, "I am the Lord who created the world," but, "I am the Lord who brought you out of Egypt." The Jews who died in the Holocaust were punished for not coming to Israel.'

Solomon was much milder. 'You can be a Jew anywhere. It may be more difficult to be observant abroad, but you can still be a good Jew. Jacob has more education than I have, and more status, but I don't think, for all his ideas, that he has enough religion to know what a Jew should do. We haven't the authority to say such things.' He told me that he wanted to go on learning, if possible in the country, with his books and a few hens.

Jacob was among the first to join the religious settlers in the West Bank, some years later.

During the two and a half years preceding the birth of our first child, our small flat was overrun by friends who, like most single people, took marriage more seriously than the married. They

assumed that the ceremony had automatically conferred maturity, that all passion was spent (or could be deferred until they had
left), and that we could offer unlimited hospitality, sympathy and
time to those in emotional trouble, without a home, or short of
cash. In a flat of some sixty-five square feet, this was difficult. We
were at first flattered, then tolerant, and finally desperate. Unlike
my friends and colleagues, Yehuda actually worked as hard as a
dock labourer; like most people in important civil service jobs, he
was at his desk at seven-thirty, if not touring the country. I had
several jobs writing and translating (mostly reports of Israel's
hopeless trial soundings for oil). We tried to ignore the couples at
daggers drawn or in tears in the kitchen, and the people sleeping
on the carpet in the living-room, whom we had to step over in
order to get to the front door. I even pinned up a notice in two
languages asking for contributions towards food, and saying that
'Emotions should be deposited with the management for safe-
keeping; guests should be in possession of a valid date of
departure on arrival.' No one was impressed. Eventually we took
to going to bed at eight, turning off the lights, and refusing to
answer the doorbell.

Shortly before I married, I began writing for the *New
Statesman*, which in those days was an influential weekly, though I
regarded it chiefly as a bridge to my English life and the crowd of
friends with whom I never lost touch. I had already written a
couple of sketches for John Freeman, then editor; the first from
Paris and the second from Rome. Now, I simply walked into
Great Turnstile and asked whether they wanted someone to write
regularly from Jerusalem.

I had about as many qualifications to be a political correspondent as William Boot, but I knew the country well from my tours
in the Morris Minor. When I wrote my first article, in January
1963, about tensions on the Israel-Syrian border, I didn't need to
make a special journey there. I knew that the kibbutz farms that
had drawn the shelling were sowing lentils that season, that the
farmers had built a wall between the children's house and the
kindergarten to deflect blast, and that the shelling of fishing-

boats near Tabgha could be seen from the terraces of Tiberias. From my four years of teaching, I could call on a long roster of Hebrew University political scientists, sociologists and Arabists for informed comment. I never went to a press conference, and the stencilled hand-outs left in my box in the Government Press Office were useful later as children's scribble-paper.

Israeli politicians each had a favourite journalist, and the trick was not to sum up the views in the Hebrew press but to work out who had leaked what, to whom, and why. But most important, I had at hand an adviser who had grown up in the Labour movement, rubbed shoulders every day with Cabinet ministers in the Knesset, and knew the details and history of every political *cause célèbre*. After a few months' apprenticeship, I was able to make my own informed guesses as to what was behind the news.

Unfortunately, the mark of the Lascelles tutorial was imprinted on everything I wrote. I tended to over-research and to read hundreds of pages of transcripts, or documents, or social studies, in order to write a piece of five hundred words, which went through as many drafts as the midnight essays I wrote as an undergraduate. I translated Israeli politics into the language of an Oxford common room. Just as I had leapfrogged my way into university teaching without qualifications, and into script-writing without any training, I became a pundit without ever having been a reporter. As I only wrote for prestigious papers, I was paid scarcely anything for my pains. When I stopped writing for the *Statesman* and other weeklies, after the right wing took over in Israel fourteen years later, I was still earning, from journalism, about forty pounds for a thousand words, which in terms of woman-hours resembled the pay of the patriarchs for rearranging the sand in Ashdod.

Writing for foreign papers posed the problem of assessing which aspects of Israeli politics would interest friends in England and America. In England, in the sixties, my friends were concerned with nuclear disarmament, world credit facilities, the Vietnam War, the admission of immigrants from the Commonwealth, comprehensive schools and 'streaming'. In Israel, no one was interested in nuclear warfare, money from abroad was spent with virtually no accounting, Moshe Dayan was touring Vietnam to see whether he could learn from the Americans how to deal with irregular warfare, and no one could buy their children out of the comprehensive state-school system.

In England, children were growing up who knew nothing of the Second World War and confused it with the First, and even historians were beginning to run them together. Everyone hated 'militarism' and soon even National Service ended. Israel was rapidly becoming an anachronism both in its preoccupation with war and security, and – after 1967 – as a colonial power. The slow decline of Labour in both countries might have provided some common ground had it not been for the fact that although, when I began writing political commentary, British Labour was a traditional friend of Israel, with Labour ministers touring Israeli factories and kibbutzim and mouthing 'Hatikva' (the national anthem) at Zionist dinners, it was eventually the Tories who were to sympathize with Israel's security and colonial dilemmas, while the left fiercely condemned its attitude to Palestinian nationalism and its political reliance on the United States.

On my frequent visits to England, I found that both those who admired Israel and those who condemned it had a lopsided view of the country, largely because of the early successes of Zionist propaganda. Sympathizers thought Israel was the kibbutz and that the Jews had gone back to the land, whereas in fact the kibbutzim were a mere three-plus per cent of the population (despite their lead in experimental agriculture and their prominence in the officer corps of the army), and eighty-five per cent lived, like Diaspora Jewry, in towns. Those who attacked Israel saw its people as white settlers oppressing a native population, when actually the majority of the settlers came from a very similar background to that of the natives – often disliking them the more for that very reason. Critics suffering from colonial guilt argued that Israel should 'merge' into the surrounding area, which was ruled either by military regimes or run by a semi-Westernized elite. Diaspora Jews didn't understand the polarization of 'secular' and 'religious' Jews.

What happened eventually was that I explained Israel rather as I had explained English grammar to Israelis; I made clear what I could, invented rules where none existed, and labelled the rest as exceptions.

I never wrote in Hebrew. When I was about to be married, I had been called to the army's Jerusalem recruiting office. In the early sixties, women were still regularly called up for reserve duty, even when married, for as long as they were childless, and I had romantic ideas about my ability to contribute to the country's defence, if only as a driver. I filled in a number of forms describing my education and – as I thought – useful experience. The young woman soldier scanned them, and then asked me to write down a number of sentences in Hebrew as she dictated. As she read them, she stifled a laugh and told me to go home. Misspelling a word can totally alter its meaning. I once addressed a letter to a friend as Lecher of the Antiquities, and informed a child's teacher that I was coming to school the next day to shoot her. Hebrew speakers will work these out for themselves. My erratic spelling had ended my chances of soldiering.

It was too late to acquire a different culture, and perhaps I did not wish to. Others had tried and succeeded; there were Europeans who wrote faultlessly in Hebrew. But I never wished to change my name to a Hebrew equivalent. I was, and would remain, odd woman out.

In the spring of 1965 Jerusalem enjoyed a field-day when the Israel Museum was finally opened. The kings of whisky and real-estate and show-business and textiles descended on Jerusalem, bearing every man his endowment, his Rembrandt or his Maillol, and the governors of forty museums sent every Moses, Tower of Babel or Golden Calf they could spare for the opening exhibition. There were fake Israeli shepherd-dances to flutes and cymbals, Giulini conducted 'Pictures from an Exhibition', and Billy Rose, the New York showman, rasped over the microphone, 'And if there's a war here, you can melt down my sculptures and make bullets of 'em!'

This event was organized by the great impresario of Jerusalem, Teddy Kollek, in the face of what only the Israelis knew were serious obstacles. The budgets wouldn't stretch, and the curators and labourers lived on Benzedrine and arak. Two days before the official opening, they were still dynamiting rocks in the gardens (*'Barood!'*) and pinning up donors' names (in lower case – in those days everything was in lower case), and in Billy Rose's sculpture garden the Japanese-American architect Isamu Noguchi sat astride the fountain with a pneumatic-drill, and much of the sculpture was still stuck in the ports because of dockers' strikes. In the Shrine of the Book, the monument housing the Dead Sea Scrolls, people had been throwing coins into the basin around the dome, and orange-peel floated like water-lilies above them.

The religious faction in the municipality announced that it would refuse to contribute to the upkeep of the museum because of the graven images in the sculpture garden. One of the museum officials suggested that under each sculpture should be written PLEASE DO NOT BOW DOWN. Noguchi and Billy Rose were not on speaking terms. Israeli artists were furious at their under-representation and staged an alternative exhibition at a nearby hall. 'What a pity you have no Queen Mother to help with this,' said John Russell, who attended the opening with our friend Bryan Robertson, then director of the Whitechapel Gallery.

But the real show began when the celebrities had left. It was the first free Saturday. People came in their thousands, with babies in arms and *in utero*, carrying picnic-baskets, water-bottles, bags of sesame seeds, and kittens. The Persians and the Yemenites gazed at glass cases full of their old clothes, hurried past the Klee and the Rembrandt drawings (the finest loan exhibits, but much too small and sketchy for the crowds) and were interrogated by a roving curator who wanted to know the origins and purpose of a sickle-shaped, honeycomb object in the archaeological wing. To this day it is still unidentified. The attendants, some late of the town's cinemas, were as unused to the crowds as the crowds to a museum. 'You've been in front of that picture for five minutes,' said one of them reprovingly to an old man in a burnous. 'Move along now.'

Noguchi, alone of the famous figures, had wanted to see the crowds gather on what he called the new Acropolis. 'It will be exciting,' he had said, 'but very ambiguous.'

Our flat was on the fifth floor of a block overlooking the Vale of Gehenna, exactly on a level with, and in sight of, the southern-most position of Jordanian soldiers on the Old City walls. One morning I was having breakfast when I heard rifle-fire. This was not unusual, but it seemed heavier than usual. I rang Yehuda, already at work in Tel Aviv, and asked him which was the safest place in the flat. He told me to sit with my back to the bookcase, as books are good bullet-stoppers. When the shooting was over, I went to pick up what I thought was a heap of cellophane lying on the carpet a couple of feet away, and found that it was the shattered glass of the french window leading to our balcony. I hadn't heard the report. I looked all over the room for the bullet, and finally noticed that the entire front of our Pye record-player had disintegrated. Next to the turntable was something the size and shape of a chewed date-pit (leaving such things in such places was typical of our guests): this was the bullet.

Later that day I went down to Tel Aviv for a lunch given by the Foreign Press Association, of whose committee I was a member. The guest was Levi Eshkol, then both Prime Minister and Minister of Defence, and as I was sitting next to him I produced the bullet at what I thought a good moment and said, 'I've just come from a border settlement and I don't think much of the security. This missed me this morning by inches.'

'Which settlement?' he asked.

'Jerusalem.'

Eshkol laughed. 'Make it into a brooch,' he said, handing me back the bullet.

The more I learned of Labour politics, then run by Eshkol – Ben Gurion was still in his kibbutz in the Negev – the more it reminded me of the Jewish patriarchal family, which is dominated by its strongest member, but eventually turns and rends him. The founding generation clung to power and emasculated the 'youngsters' – in their fifties. I thought of the family house in Haifa, which my paternal grandfather had left to six of his ten children, ensuring permanent feuds. It was a charming pink-stucco villa in a garden on the French Carmel, with a balcony that overlooked the whole of Haifa Bay. Three daughters and their husbands had originally shared the house, but when they quarrelled the beautiful villa, with its elegantly designed staircase running from the living-room to the upper floor, was chopped in half. The staircase, which could not be removed, was duplicated; the original ran straight into the ceiling.

The Labour party veterans had held power for too long, and their resentments and jealousies exploded that year during the Lavon Affair. In retrospect, the terrible psychodrama played out on the stage of a concert-hall in Tel Aviv that spring, which I witnessed, marked the beginning of the decline of Israel's Labour movement.

I never wrote about the Lavon Affair. It seemed at the time both too parochial and too complicated to be understood abroad; many details were still unclear, or, if known, were sure to be suppressed by the censor, to whom I had to submit every article.

The drama of 1965 centred on something that had happened eleven years earlier. Like my warring, deadlocked relations, Labour could not put its quarrels behind it and was doomed to relive them. The Lavon Affair originated in 1954. Someone in the Defence Ministry had had the bad idea of blowing up the USIS Library in Cairo to implicate the Egyptians and turn the United States against Nasser's regime. The plan was amateurish, and the young local agents, Egyptian Jews, were caught; one was hanged and the rest jailed for long terms. Israel denied involvement. But the Fiasco, as it was called, refused to lie down, chiefly because of the tensions between the Labour leadership and the movement's father-figure, Ben Gurion.

The question was: who had authorized the Fiasco? At the time, the Defence Minister, Pinhas Lavon, resigned. But in 1960, when fresh information came to light, Lavon asked Ben Gurion to clear his name. Ben Gurion refused to help, insisting that this was not a political but a legal matter, and that only a judicial 'committee of enquiry' could decide. The party thought otherwise, and a political Committee of Seven cleared Lavon. The stage was set for a battle royal between Labour, and Israel's intellectuals, on the one hand, and the old leader, with a rump following, on the other. Ben Gurion's opponents saw him as an ageing dictator, and his principled stand as a personal vendetta against Lavon.

By 1965, and the 10th Labour Party Congress, Ben Gurion was back in self-imposed exile in the Negev, but his giant shadow still fell on the new Prime Minister, the pliable easy-going Eshkol.

Two days before the Congress, when these tensions were to surface, the foreign press held another of its monthly lunches, with Ben Gurion as guest of honour. With his pink complexion and brilliant white hair, he looked newly laundered and ready for a fight. He was still the Russian revolutionary Jew. In his article that day in the Labour party newspaper, *Davar*, he referred to the need to educate the oriental immigrants who were 'entirely without a culture', and to the 'wilderness generation' of their parents as 'human dust' (*avak adam*).

I didn't fare much better. I realized from his questions about my background that he could not accept that Jews had ties to any other country than Israel. When I asked him whether he didn't think Church and State should be separate in a democracy (it was he who had legitimized religious politics), he answered me mischievously, 'No. Look at England. The Queen is head of Church and State.'

Finally he was asked about Lavon and the 'Fiasco'. Was he really going to bring the matter up at the Party Congress and possibly split the Labour party? 'The State comes before the party,' said the old man.

The 10th Congress opened at a time of crisis for Israel. Bonn, with which Israel still had no diplomatic relations, had suspended arms shipments to Israel under pressure from Nasser; a united Arab front between Syria, Jordan and Egypt was in the making – a union which bred the Six Day War, two years later; Syria was threatening to divert the Jordan waters, a *casus belli* by Ben Gurion's definition; and Ahmed Shukeiry was proposing the formation of a Palestinian Army. But the hottest issue at the Congress was 'who had given the order' for the Fiasco and whether 'the third man' (a then anonymous intelligence officer) or Lavon was the guilty party.

When I got to the Mann Auditorium, the concert hall where the Congress was held, on the second afternoon, I had to burrow my way through huge crowds, waving my press card in order to reach the wide glass doors. Later, those doors splintered under pressure from party delegates who were entitled to be present, but had been elbowed out by curious members of the public. The hall should have accommodated all the party members, but when I reached the press seats, on the stage behind the party leadership, the sight was alarming. Every seat in the hall and balcony was occupied, the aisles were jammed solid, and yet more and more people were streaming into the building. As the time approached for Ben Gurion to appear, there were people sitting on the parapet of the balcony. The Mayor of Tel Aviv took the microphone to announce that the engineers who had built the hall were warning him that the balcony might collapse under the strain, and requested all those without seats to leave. Not a soul moved – either on the balcony, or, more surprisingly, under it.

Ben Gurion was forty-five minutes late, and it was not clear till the last moment whether or not he would take the rostrum. Eventually he appeared, made a plea for 'truth and justice' and defended the principle of a judicial enquiry. However, he was upstaged by Moshe Sharett, Prime Minister during the Fiasco and for years Ben Gurion's faithful Foreign Minister. Everyone knew that Sharett was dying of cancer; he had broken a leg and was brought on in a wheelchair, which shook visibly when he gestured. All his bitterness and suppressed envy broke through when he spoke, his voice trembling, of his own 'modest, inferior' contribution to the State. Soon he launched a bitter, scarcely coherent, personal attack on Ben Gurion, who, he said, was destroying not only Labour's leadership but the prestige of the State itself. Sharett was continuously heckled by Ben Gurion's supporters in the hall, but as far as I could see from his profile, the old man, his head resting on his hand, was not moved by the attack. The really telling blow was yet to come.

It was nearly midnight (we had been there since four, and no one had moved) when Golda Meir rose to deliver the *coup de grâce*. Sharett had never actually mentioned Ben Gurion by name. Golda Meir, turning to the old man, addressed him rhetorically.

'Ben Gurion! Why did you not resign when the Committee of Seven was appointed? Ben Gurion! Why did you appoint Lavon, against our advice, as Minister of Defence!' The old man flushed deeply and threw Meir reproachful glances. Every party member knew of the affection and near-dependence that had existed between the two. The attack was a personal betrayal. When Meir had finished, Ben Gurion scribbled her a note ('*Et tu*, Golda?' suggested someone near me) and left the hall without a word.

That summer, Ben Gurion resigned from the Labour party and founded his own splinter party with his lieutenants Peres and Dayan; it was to vote itself out of existence three years later. My last sight of Ben Gurion was when, at the next elections, I went to see him campaign for his little party on a windy winter night, at a street corner in Jerusalem. Only a handful of people had gathered to hear him rehearse 'the Affair' for the last time and to call, in his reedy, Russian-accented Hebrew for 'truth, justice' and a judicial committee of enquiry.

While my parents were alive, with doctors in the family in England, I gave birth in a very privileged medical environment: the Lindo Wing of St Mary's, Paddington, where each door carried the name of the patient and her obstetrician. After my parents' death, my children were born in the delivery room of Hadassah Hospital in Jerusalem, where I lay in the maternity ward among women of every possible background, from Europe to North Africa, from Arab villages and sometimes even from Bedu tents.

In London, I attended the natural childbirth classes of the famous Betty Parsons in Seymour Street; in Jerusalem, most of the women screamed vigorously, not only from pain but to avert the evil eye. In London, no one whispered to me that if I went to the zoo I would have a baby like a giraffe, but on the other hand I had never handled a baby in my life and Spock was a poor substitute for the extended family. The ladies in the Lindo Wing, segregated in their little cells, gave birth discreetly. In all the time I was there, I never heard a shriek or groan, or anything more than a faint ladylike sigh of 'Oh dear!' In Israel, Moroccan women called on their mothers and cursed their husbands' penises. Hadassah was a teaching hospital, and giving birth was public, in one case witnessed by some visiting Japanese, whose eyes, peering at me over their masks, made me wonder if I was delirious. In the ante-room, nurses called out to one another as in an auction room: 'Two fingers!' 'I've got three fingers here!'

What I saw in the maternity wards of Israel convinced me that the idea that peasant women, or those who know little about their internal anatomy, give birth more easily, was a myth.

When once I had to spend some weeks in the pre-natal ward, I noticed a North African girl who was at an advanced state of pregnancy but, to the doctors' alternate anger and despair, refused to eat. With her generally anorexic appearance and huge belly, she looked like a parody of pregnancy, as if she really was carrying an incubus. Nothing the doctors gave her stayed down, and eventually she survived on intravenous drips. They could find nothing organically wrong with her, but they feared for the baby's health. This girl only had two visitors, her husband and her father. After a while, I saw that whereas when her husband, a lacklustre young man, visited her, she remained listless and dull, her father's arrival made her bright and nervous; she never failed to make up her face before he came, and chattered and blushed and flirted. I decided that for one reason or another she was trying to vomit up her baby, and suggested bringing in a psychiatrist. Of course, they didn't.

The idea of automatic bonding between mother and baby was contradicted in different ways in the different hospitals. Some of the more privileged English mothers appeared to have little more contact with their babies, in transit to Nanny, than a bonded warehouse has with its contents. I was in the nursery, learning how to bathe my son from the redoubtable Matron, Nurse Henly, when Lady Someone, elegant in a Fortnum négligée, swept in uninvited. Assuming that I was an assistant minion, she gazed absent-mindedly at my son and said, 'Harry's looking rather yellow today, isn't he?'

'This isn't Harry, this is Joshua,' said Nurse Henly (Doesn't recognize her own child).

'Ah,' said Lady Someone. 'Tell me, Matron, what are you giving Harry at the moment? I must know so that I can tell Nanny about the formula.'

Nurse flipped Joshua deftly on to his stomach and sloshed water over his behind. 'Steak,' she said with a glance at me (They never breastfeed).

In Hadassah, many women in the oriental communities, if they gave birth to girls, had fewer presents and fewer visitors – sometimes none at all. One middle-aged woman with long hennaed plaits, in the next bed to mine, refused even to look at her daughter, the last of thirteen children. She said her husband would beat her if she brought home another girl, and asked the hospital to keep her; better luck next time. Another woman, of European background, was so delighted with her new son that she ignored the wistful little girl brought to see her, and complained after she left that during her absence from home the child had broken pieces of her best tea-service.

Both hospitals were famous for their medical expertise, but the way they treated babies was dissimilar. In the Lindo Wing, mothers were allowed in the nursery only by invitation (although Lady Someone made her own rules), and babies were so tightly wrapped that I had to free my little son's hands so that he could grasp me while I suckled him. In Hadassah, it was open season in the nursery, and mothers who allowed their babies to scream with hunger were urged to get out there and remove the baby, as it was waking the others. A pacifier was as likely to appear in the Lindo

Wing as a hand-grenade; in Hadassah, harassed nurses plugged bottle-teats with cotton-wool and shoved them into screaming babies' mouths. The circumcision, in the Lindo Wing, was private (only near, male relatives were allowed in), but the ritual circumciser involved had not been adequately trained and might have compromised my elder son's future; some months later he managed to castrate an unlucky baby and was henceforth banned from every London hospital. In Hadassah, in the circumcision-room in the basement, huge crowds ate and drank while the baby howled in the corner. An English-educated Israeli friend, father of two sons, shook my hand on that occasion and commiserated. 'I don't think a fertility rite should be the occasion for a cocktail party.' I agreed, but by this time round I no longer cared.

If birth was different in England and Israel, so were the ceremonies of death. In Israel, the body is wound in a shroud and carried to the grave on a stretcher – sometimes the head may sway sadly from side to side, as if shaking its head at death – and the gases which distend and deform the corpse are clearly visible. The religious rationale against the coffin is the ruling that the body, to be reconstructed at the last trump, must be in contact with the soil of the Holy Land. The exception is the case of soldiers, who are buried in coffins, often because their bodies are no longer intact – the pieces are carefully collected by army chaplains. In this way the obvious mutilation of the body is concealed from the mourners' eyes.

While my elder son had been growing inside me, cancer had been growing inside my mother. When I left to return to Israel, with a six-week-old baby, I didn't realize that I would not see her again. An operation revealed that she had only a short time to live, but my father and relations in the medical profession were adamant that I should not return immediately, insisting that she feared death, did not want to know the truth, and that my return so soon after leaving would confirm that she was going to die. When death was imminent, they reassured me, I should be alerted so that I could see her. But they had reckoned without the rule of orthodoxy in Israel. My mother's condition suddenly deteriorated on the eve of Passover, when no planes took off from Ben Gurion Airport. By the time I left, with the baby, although I did not know it, she had already been dead for hours.

As I was still nursing, I was not expected to attend her funeral, but the proceedings in London confused and maddened me. An orthodox burial-society was called in, and the mirrors in my parents' flat were covered with cloths – something 'secular' Israelis do not do but which I thought fitting, eliminating even a hint of narcissism in grief. But when the women who officiated at the body's washing came up to me with scissors to effect the ritual rending of garments, they only reached inside my dress and made the smallest possible nick in a shoulder-strap. In Israel, where the secular conform to orthodox practice at the cemetery, no one would have dared approach the mourners in their homes. Of course, I could have refused the rite; but I thought that if celebrated, it should be done properly or not at all.

By 1967, I had been living in Israel for a decade and, despite the bullet in the living-room, the shellfire I had heard in the Galilee, and the knowledge that civilians were sometimes killed in 'border incidents', I had no sense of the menace of war. By the time I had reached Israel, the Czech arms deal had been completed, Britain was supplying Israel with Centurion tanks, and every year, on Independence Day, there were military parades – later discontinued.

Details of the parade were duly communicated to the Jordanians through the Mixed Armistice Commission, and when tanks rumbled through the streets, the Jordanian soldiers could be clearly seen on the Old City walls, watching the procession through binoculars.

I knew of the horrors of war from a distance. There was scarcely a family I knew which hadn't lost relations either in the Holocaust or in the War of Independence, that most costly of

Israel's wars. Most of Yehuda's friends, who were rather older than himself, had fought in that war, the women running between Israeli positions carrying messages under fire. My friend Mickey Kidron, a South African volunteer, had, as a 'cultural officer' for the Jerusalem fighters, lugged an old-fashioned wind-up gramophone from post to post during the battle; an Israeli position had literally collapsed on her head, but her skull-fracture, thought to be no more than concussion, was never diagnosed or treated.

Yehuda's army experience to date was not impressive. The Slav major wasn't even an officer in the reserves, but a mere corporal. He was Education Officer in a tank regiment, and in the army photographs he showed me of himself, some in the paramilitary farming settlement of Nahal Oz, he was either pulling a cow's tail, inspecting a rifle with the barrel firmly in the pit of his stomach, cuddling girls, or fooling around with the actor Haim Topol. In the Sinai campaign he had seen no action. So he was, as yet, neither as bitter nor as battle-scarred as the other sabras I had known.

His army boots were kept greased; periodically we checked on his identity disc and the state of his uniform. Once a year he went off to do reserve service and came back tanned, thinner and healthier, praising the cooking of the Hungarian chef in his unit. Like almost all Israelis of army age, he automatically turned on the radio on the hour, every hour, for the news. This was standard practice on most Israeli buses. Occasionally, there were alerts during which his unit's code-name was announced and he would report to the Schneller military compound for orders.

The frontiers were clearly signposted, the enemy was on the other side, and if Jerusalem was sometimes claustrophobic, the green hills of Galilee, the Negev and the sea were only hours away. My own childhood memories of war – of air-raid sirens and bombing and hot shrapnel lying in the drive in the morning; of men who went away to war and returned not weeks but years later; of rationing and of black-outs; of the arrested whine of flying bombs; and of squeezing into the Morrison or the school shelters, usually after the explosion of the V2s – were still vivid enough to

95

make Israel's dangers look pale by comparison. By early May 1967, I had written often of war threats, or of border incidents which might escalate. But it still wasn't real to me.

Only one incident, in early April, seemed more serious. When Israeli villages in the Galilee were shelled more heavily than usual by the Syrian artillery, Israeli planes were used to silence the guns. In the succeeding dogfights, Israel shot down six Syrian planes, a piece of news I heard in a communal taxi, or *sherut*, driving from Tel Aviv to Jerusalem. Syria had recently concluded a military pact with Egypt, but Nasser, who had repeatedly said that the time was not yet ripe for a 'final round' with Israel, did not react to Syrian predictions of an impending Israeli attack. April passed uneventfully. Nasser was bogged down in his Yemen war, and his relations with Hussein of Jordan were acrimonious.

In early May, Syria again maintained that Israeli forces were massing on her border; but diplomats and journalists, for whom the whole area was a couple of hours' drive from their offices, knew that this was not true. In mid May, Syria sent a delegation to Cairo. The jousting looked routine, but I was worried because I was about to leave on a visit to my father, who had been deeply depressed since my mother's death. Though I didn't know it then, he had only a few more months to live.

In Jaffa Road, on my way to the travel agency, I met Aharon Kidan, a friend of ours who was then the Prime Minister's economic adviser. I repeated the question I had already asked several times: was it all right to leave? If there was a crisis, I didn't want to be cut off from Yehuda and the country. Of course it was all right, there was absolutely no chance of war, said Kidan, smiling reassuringly. This was presumably the view in Eshkol's office.

I had only been in London for a few days when Nasser demanded the withdrawal of the UN emergency force in Sinai, all that stood between the Egyptian and Israeli armies. The UN Secretary-General, U Thant, agreed without demur. Encouraged, Nasser sent thousands of troops into Sinai and then, on 20 May, closed the Straits of Tiran to Israeli shipping. This, an economic blockade, was a *casus belli*. Israel called up its reserves. When I rang Yehuda at the flat that night, there was no answer. His secretary, next day, told me that he had been mobilized. There was no question of my returning to Israel and an empty flat. I had an eighteen-month child with me, was in advanced pregnancy and had no relations in Jerusalem to whom I could turn for help. So I covered the Six Day War for the *New Statesman* from Hampstead.

Two further agonizing weeks passed, during which time Israel realized that it could count on little diplomatic support from its supposed friends in the West. It could not indefinitely hold a reserves army at the ready without destroying the economy, and Nasser was threatening Israel's annihilation. I could only imagine the feeling of vulnerability in Israel. Friends of mine who shared a house with an Arab family – one of the few which had remained in Jewish Jerusalem – were told by their neighbours that the Arab radio stations were promising rapid victory over the 'Zionist entity'. I knew how unprepared the civilians were for war. The shelters and blast-walls, which looked ineffective compared even with those of my childhood memories, were left-overs from 1948. In our six-storey building, we had never had shelter-drill, and our emergency stairs (rare in an Israeli block of flats) were for some reason constructed *facing* the Jordanian emplacements.

Given my condition, and the fact that I seldom wrote straight reportage, I was able to write political commentary on the prelude to the war, and the conduct of it, much more efficiently in London than if I had been in Jerusalem. Censorship there was tight. In London, I had contacts with the Israeli Embassy and – what was more important – daily conversations with a close friend of Yehuda's, Haggai Eshed. Eshed was then *Davar* correspondent in London. He had close ties with the Labour leadership and defence sources, and was the author of the book on the Lavon Affair which Ben Gurion had tossed into the political ring two years earlier. My talks with Haggai enabled me to write confidently, ten days before the outbreak of war, that although Israel's diplomatic situation was bad, and though challenged by the Arab states, Israel's military situation was in fact more favourable at that moment than it might have been at the future period Nasser had set aside for the definitive battle. A week later, when war was obviously in the offing, I pointed out that while the Government was still dithering, Israel was now prepared for the fight. Three days later, Israel launched its pre-emptive air-strike and destroyed the entire Egyptian air force on the ground.

I heard the news minutes after it happened, but ironically enough, as writer for a weekly which appeared four days later, could make no use of it. Mike Elkins, the BBC's correspondent in Israel, who scooped the world and defied the censor by a clever reference to areas known from the Sinai Campaign, had his report downplayed, for his pains, by a sceptical commentator in the London studio. But before that, I had attended the *States-man*'s editorial staff meeting at which my news, delivered in as nonchalant a tone as I could manage, was not accepted. Paul Johnson, the editor, and the others obviously did not believe what I was telling them. Israel had been portrayed for weeks as on the verge of destruction. My announcement that it had wiped out Egypt's main offensive force was received with embarrassment. Poor girl, said the faces of the men sitting around; husband in the fighting, stranded here in her condition, obviously wants to believe some cock-and-bull story leaked to boost morale. Paul demurred gallantly, and after a short pause the conversation changed to other world affairs. Later in the day I was allowed to write my piece.

By the time it appeared, Jordan had begun shelling Jewish Jerusalem and I was watching, on television, the Dormition Abbey, which stood in full view of our balcony, burning, and shells landing in our street. My piece on Israel's war aims was published on 9 June, the day on which Yehuda was wounded, thrown out of a jeep with three other soldiers, either as the result of a Jordanian shell which landed nearby or, as Yehuda, not wanting to play the hero, claimed later, because of the driver's lack of skill. The others were badly wounded. Yehuda landed on all fours, and his wounds were superficial. I knew nothing of this until I spotted his white bandages, under a black corduroy jacket, when he visited me in hospital just over a fortnight later. War, death, victory, were all over in less than a week.

'What do we do with all this?' was said to be Eshkol's reaction when apprised of the full extent of Israel's territorial gains. That was a very good question. Because I hadn't been in Israel during the two weeks before the war, I felt more apprehension than relief. Yehuda, too, preoccupied with his unit's dead, did not take part in the celebrations. After leaving me in hospital, he sat over a solitary supper in a London restaurant and overheard a couple talking about Israel's new 'imperialism'. He turned round and said to them, 'I was there. It was a war of survival.'

Many London cars bore stickers declaring, 'We Stand Beside Israel', and in some circles there was a high tide of approval for Israel. I wasn't happy with either of the extremes, thinking that those who cheered Israel on now were those who were pleased to see someone else take revenge on Nasser for Suez. Above all, the reaction abroad trivialized the conflict. I saw a girl in the Underground wearing jeans and a T-shirt with Moshe Dayan's face printed on the back. As she walked just in front of me down a long corridor on the Central Line, Dayan's eye-patch wobbled on her backside. I was glad to go back to Jerusalem.

5

─────◆◆◆─────

Intermezzo

T OWARDS THE END of 1967, someone organized a
performance of the Verdi Requiem in Bethlehem's
Manger Square, with Zubin Mehta conducting the Israel
Philharmonic Orchestra. The idea was to emphasize that all was
well under Israeli rule, that Christians, Muslims and Jews were
living in harmony. The Philharmonic was a messenger of culture
and peace.

Wooden chairs had been lined up in front of the basilica and a
platform erected for the orchestra. The players looked resigned:
they were used to playing at unlikely sites where sand got into the
strings and sheet music was ruffled by the wind, like that blowing
on this night out of the Judean desert. The soloists filed in, and
Mehta raised his baton. But in the split second before the chorus
began the *Requiem Aeternam*, another, unscored voice responded
to the conductor's gesture. *'Allahu Akhbar,'* it chanted from the
minaret of the nearby mosque. Mehta lowered his baton and
crossed his hands in front of him, the classic gesture of
conductors waiting for coughing to subside. By craning my neck,
I could see a small group of soldiers hurry into the side-street
leading to the mosque. After a few minutes the muezzin's call to
prayer (which was not customary at this time of the evening)
ceased and only the obstreperous desert wind interfered with the
performance.

The signs of war in Jerusalem, now one city and under Israeli
rule, had been as quickly removed as the chanted protest in
Bethlehem. (The muezzin's call relayed from the Al Aqsa
mosque on the Temple Mount, moreover, no longer woke us at

100

three in the morning. The volume had been reduced and the sermons were monitored.) By the time I returned to Jerusalem in August the familiar blast-walls and tank-traps had gone, and there was little to show that the city had ever been divided. But my first sight of the Wailing Wall was a disappointment. I had been expecting a great, towering bulwark of stone familiar from nineteenth-century paintings. But the artists had all set up their easels in the narrow alley between the Moghrabi (Moors) quarter and the Wall itself. In that alley, Jews had been tolerated, or harassed, or stared at, for centuries. The Mayor, Teddy Kollek, had seen to it that within hours of Israel's victory the Moghrabi quarter was torn down. Entering the enormous open space now facing what in Hebrew is called the Western Wall, I lost my bearings. For a few seconds I wondered which, of the enclosing walls of stone, was *the* wall. The perspective I'd expected had gone, and with it the awe, which I never experienced.

I went with Adam Mendilow and others who remembered Jerusalem under the Mandate to revisit the landmarks of the Old City, the churches, bazaars and tombs long lost behind the frontier. Their excitement was moving, and so were the meetings between Arabs and Jews who had worked together during that time – a few doctors, lawyers and civil servants. For a very short time, the Israeli occupation was believed by the Palestinians to be temporary, while Israel believed that a peace settlement was in the offing. Both were wrong.

The most popular song in West Jerusalem, in those early months, was 'Jerusalem of Gold', a *schlager*, or hit, composed before the war and sung by a young English immigrant, Shuly Nathan, in a high pure voice. It was nostalgic, sentimental and misleading, for it spoke of yearning for a return to the 'empty' Old City bazaar – empty of Jews, its composer meant. The bazaar had not, of course, been empty, nor was it now. It amazed me that the war was followed so rapidly by a buying and selling spree. The bazaar teemed with curious Israelis buying up everything in sight: spices and *fistouk halabi* (pistachio nuts), rush-weave baskets, Bedouin saddle-bags, untreated-sheepskin coats, blue and turquoise Armenian pottery, hubble-bubble pipes, Red Chinese ballpoint pens, alarm clocks from Taiwan, wreaths of orange dates, plastic ivy and English tea-biscuits. All were equally exotic for Israelis and equally in demand.

But at the same time as every Israeli was humming 'Jerusalem of Gold', the most popular tune in East Jerusalem was 'The Flower of Cities' sung by a Lebanese woman, Farouz, given me within weeks by a Palestinian I met. Its opening, too, was nostalgic and sentimental, but the second part of the song was neither; there were drum-rolls and cries of 'We shall return'.

The key word on both sides was 'return', and it had a number of meanings. 'We have returned to our holiest of shrines,' Dayan had said, 'never to be parted from it again.' Palestinians from the West Bank returned in lorry-loads to the sea, which they hadn't seen for nineteen years. Old women rolled up their skirts and plunged gnarled feet into the surf. Israelis returned to Jericho and Hebron, where legend (if not archaeologists) insisted that the patriarchs common to Jewish and Muslim tradition are buried in the Machpelah Cave. For the first time Jews were able to pass beyond the seventh step, and a synagogue was partitioned off in a corner of the shrine. It rapidly became a place of confrontations. Palestinians returned to revisit their former homes in West Jerusalem. In one case, a family politely asked to look over their old house in the Baka'a quarter. This granted, they returned monthly, then weekly, and finally, when the tenants refused to open the door, squatted opposite, staring defiantly at the building. Eventually the owners called the police. The Jews returned to the Jewish quarter of the Old City and evicted those who had taken over their homes. Long white underpants hung over balconies from the old Yeshivat Hakotel seminary and recordings of cantorial music were switched on when parties of tourists arrived. The original owners of Arieh Sachs' house on the frontier were shown over it; they thanked him and his wife for looking after it so well, and requested that he go on doing so. They clearly assumed they were soon going to reclaim their property.

Arieh and a group of other Jerusalem poets met with the writer

Jorge Luis Borges, the first recipient of the new Jerusalem Prize. He told them, 'You are fortunate, you are living in an epic,' and then reconsidered. 'No. You are living in a western.' The author of those esoteric, kabbalist stories, who, it emerged, had always wanted to write the script for a genuine Texan western, saw the Arab-Israel conflict in terms of cowboys and Indians.

At this stage we all thought the situation was temporary. When it became clear that it wasn't, even personal relations with the Arabs in what were called 'the Territories' became un-authentic, forced, and finally corrupted.

Our first journey round the West Bank, in September, was hedged with menace. Our driver, Benny, a Turkish Jew who remembered the roads from before 1948, had a loaded gun propped at his side and a glittering cartridge-belt strapped round his waist. I thought all this over-dramatic until, walking through a bazaar in Nablus, we were hustled out by soldiers making arrests and heard for the first time the take-cover sound in Palestinian towns – the rattle of iron shutters hastily pulled down over shop-fronts and stalls. I was taken through the refugee camps in Gaza in a taxi driving at top speed and with an army escort, guns at the ready, for the camps were reputed to be arsenals, and the hatred of the refugees for Israel was uncon-cealed. The merchants and municipal officials I talked to in Gaza were all hoping for an early end to the occupation.

For a period of about six months we had social contacts with a handful of Jerusalem Palestinians; we visited their homes, they visited ours. Among them was Suleiman Dajani, a wealthy businessman who owned the Imperial Hotel just inside the Jaffa Gate. We met through my friend Mervyn Jones of the *New Statesman*, who stayed at the Imperial briefly when he visited Israel just after the war. Suleiman had a daughter who taught at the refugee camp near the Kalandia Airport, and a son who clearly hated his father's fraternizing with the enemy. One day, driving in Salah ed Din Street with his father and myself, the boy turned and said bitterly, 'We are in hell.' Suleiman shot back, 'No, you aren't, you are sitting in my very comfortable Mercedes with nothing to complain about.'

That was true of very few Palestinians – mostly wealthy businessmen who had been pro-Hashemite and were keen to make contacts with influential Israelis and the 'authorities'. The war was referred to as 'the catastrophe', but the illusion that Jerusalem would be reorganized politically at a peace conference lasted only a short while. Soon the Dajanis disappeared from our orbit and the Imperial Hotel, with its starved-looking waiters, was leased to the Jewish Agency as a hostel for new Jewish immigrants.

The person who really objected to my Arab visitors was my cleaning woman, Tova. If she was there when they arrived, she would start dusting (something she never usually did), shaking the dust out vigorously under their noses and glaring alternately at them, and at me.

'Why do you want to ask Arabs to your home?' she would ask me afterwards.

'But Tova, you always said that you got on well with them in Damascus,' I said. She gave a contemptuous sniff and patted my arm. After all, we were friends.

Cleaning women, in Hebrew, are called 'helpers' because of outdated socialist prudery about calling them anything else. But Tova really was a helper. As I had no mother at hand, she had helped me in pregnancy, tying raw onions to my leg when I sprained an ankle, and was the first to visit me after I gave birth, bringing Turkish delight and malt beer, which she said was good for the milk. She had looked after Joshua when I had to go to England after my father's death; every time he opened his mouth to cry, she put food in it, and when I returned he was as round as a barrel. She came to the sea with us every year; no one in her family, she told me, had ever thought of taking her. She couldn't read, and when on those boring seaside evenings we sat in our dentist's borrowed bungalow with our books, she sat with her hands folded in her lap and just rested. Looking at her, I realized for the first time what it meant to be illiterate. She said it was too late to learn, but her family might have tried; she was highly intelligent.

Tova had come to Israel on a bus from Damascus in 1947, too early to qualify for all the various hand-outs the Government gave to those who came later. Her husband, who had been a shopkeeper, appeared to do no work and looked a broken man, one of the many who found themselves redundant in the new country. Tova hauled water to neighbours in the siege of Jerusalem in 1948 to earn her first wages; thereafter she was the family breadwinner until the first of her seven children went to work. They all finished school, and the family never went on relief. Her boys, and all but one of her girls, served in the army. The daughters became secretaries and clerks. But her favourite was her son, Ya'akov.

Ya'akov was a bank clerk, a humorous, indulgent man who was very sensitive to his mother's moods, and to the fact that in Israel, Ben Gurion's 'human dust' didn't always receive the 'honour' the older generation of oriental Jews (like the Arabs) were used to. It was true that Tova didn't look a credit to the family. She was toothless and bandy-legged (from carrying children and heavy weights) and wore odd cast-offs. Not everyone saw the shining intelligence and the courage in her, but Ya'akov did. When I attended one of the family weddings, Tova thought herself insulted by the seating arrangements and made a fuss. It was Ya'akov, I noticed, who was not embarrassed, who soothed her diplomatically, and arranged for her to have the seat she wanted. The others were too busy.

For several months I studied Arabic with Fahmi El Ansari, a young teacher and scholar who lived in Bethany with his family. The traditional living arrangement was that father and mother occupied the main floor, with sons and daughters, according to seniority, in other parts of the building. Fahmi, who was unmarried, lived in the basement with his books; he was to accumulate a legendary Palestinian library. He had a devotion to learning and a disregard for worldly things that reminded me of Bezalel. He never failed to bring presents for my small son when he visited us, and the lessons always overran the hour. He was the only Palestinian with whom I did not discuss politics; we avoided the subject as if it were indecent, but it once surfaced inadvertently. Fahmi was trying to explain the meaning of a verb to me in a newspaper passage I was reading.

'It means "to get the factory".'

'The factory?' To industrialize didn't make sense.

'Yes, to get the factory, as the Israelis did in the war.'

'Oh, you mean to get the *victory*, to win?'

He nodded. We went on with averted eyes. When I gave birth to my daughter at the end of 1968 the lessons stopped temporarily, but were never resumed. Something happened in the summer of the following year which made relations with Palestinians very difficult, and made me hesitate to renew the tie with Fahmi, in particular. A mentally disturbed Christian Australian, having entered the Al Aqsa mosque at a time when the building was officially closed to visitors, set fire to the interior, permanently damaging the irreplaceable medieval *minbar*, or pulpit. The irony of what happened was that in order not to appear as an intruder in the Noble Sanctuary (what Jews and Christians call the Temple Mount), Israel had granted the Wakf, the Muslim trust, sole control of the area, and its fire-fighting measures were inadequate; by the time Israeli fire brigades arrived, the damage was done.

It was Fahmi's kinsman, Sheikh Judeh El Ansari, who was chief guardian at the mosque at the time, and he gave evidence in a stentorian, wonderfully irrelevant speech, stressing Muslim hospitality. What had happened was not Israel's fault, but it showed me what a terrifying responsibility Israel had taken on as the sovereign power in charge of Islam's major shrines.

The Palestinians I knew clearly felt that Israel was somehow behind the outrage. What I should have done was to go to Fahmi's house and express regret for the loss of the *minbar*; his family belonged to the clan which was the hereditary protector of the mosque. But at that time Israelis were smarting under accusations of deliberate negligence, and worse. I felt that my appearance might be interpreted as an apology. I think now that I was wrong, and that I was guilty of moral cowardice. Later, I learned that Fahmi had written a history of the *minbar*, whose charred remnants can be seen in the Islamic museum near the mosque, and that his relations with scholars at the Hebrew University continued until the Palestinian uprising.

The fire confirmed my feeling that the idea of a shared holy city was dubious and dangerous, particularly when all the shrines were jammed up against one another. So too did talks I had with two leading figures in the Jewish and Islamic religious communities, Rabbi Adin Steinsaltz and Sheikh Ikrema Sabri. Each believed that the other's religious community was in Jerusalem on sufferance, as a 'guest' or 'visitor' of his own community. (Christians, whose attachment to Jerusalem was symbolic, could not match the intensity of these two men's territorial feelings.)

Steinsaltz, famous Talmudic scholar and mathematician, was sensually aware of the city, sensitive to the light which 'appeared to radiate out of the stone' and to the wildness, the way outcrops of stone and scrub seemed to push their way between the buildings. He did not think it necessary to live in the old Jewish quarter, and insisted that when he visited the Wall it was for personal prayer, that it was not the place for public worship. (The ministry in charge would not have agreed.) But he had no doubt that the city was entirely Jewish. 'I'm not a religious chauvinist,' he said, 'but the feeling for Jerusalem is deep within some kind of Jewish collective unconscious.' The presence of Muslims or Christians was a reaffirmation of the city's history. 'They are visitors,' he said, 'like those who came to the outer court of the Temple in ancient times, who were not Jews.'

Unfortunately, Ikrema Sabri, preacher at the Al Aqsa mosque, was equally certain that the collective *Islamic* consciousness could claim Jerusalem as Muslim, and that the Jews' place there was dependent only on Muslim sufferance. 'The Koran', he insisted, 'tells us to take pity on the faithful of other religions.' With

Palestine an Islamic state, Jews would be allowed into Jerusalem to perform their rites. Islamic feeling, again strong in Muslim youth, should, he said, be the motivating force behind the campaign for the restoration of old Jerusalem to the Arabs to whom it belonged. But what struck me more than Sabri's words was the act of removing his Muslim robes (he had come straight from a sermon in the mosque) under which, a muscular young man, he wore a high-necked sweater and slacks. I suddenly saw this as a kind of battledress, and was not surprised to hear that he was frequently called into the Ministry of Police for 'friendly chats' with the Minister's aide.

Neither the Palestinians nor the Israelis, in that immediate post-war period, were living in the real world. The first explosions shook both sides out of their illusions.

In November of 1967, Yehuda and I went to see a film at the old Zion cinema in the commercial centre of West Jerusalem. We sat at the front of the balcony, and near the end of the film we noticed a disturbance just below us as someone got up and went out. On the screen, John Wayne, his gun hand paralysed, had been winning back Vietnam for Western democracy. Meanwhile, the first bomb to be planted in 'reunited' Jerusalem had been ticking away just beneath us. Someone had noticed the early departure of a couple of black girls (from the Nubian community in the Old City) and the parcel they had left behind. An alert usher had removed the bomb, and an amazingly brave policeman had run along Jaffa Road with the audibly ticking parcel, until he reached the Russian Compound, the police headquarters about two hundred yards away. There he placed the parcel on the ground and with other policemen kept away a curious crowd. The bomb exploded minutes later, leaving a small crater. In the cinema, the explosions in the last reel had been so deafening that we hardly noticed the thud of the real explosion just down the road.

Explosions in Jerusalem – and the first deaths, for few people who came so near a bomb were as lucky as we were – were followed by blasts in the West Bank as sappers demolished houses belonging to the families of suspected terrorists. Because several families could live under the same roof (as was the case with Fahmi's relatives), this was an act which penalized tens of innocent people. By March 1968, the frequency of sabotage and murder by Palestinians crossing from Jordan had led to the Karameh reprisal raid, when cars once more gave way to tanks rolling through the city on their way to and from the battleground.

We got used to looking out for unattended parcels and unexpected letters, and to opening handbags for inspection at cinemas and theatres. I even started doing it in London, rather to the amazement of ushers. Children were warned against picking up stray buttons, pencils, clocks and saucepans, and parents had to waste time doing guard-duty at schools – something which taught me how difficult it is to remain alert under the shade of an olive tree on a hot summer's day for four long hours. The system satisfied the public conscience, but was utterly pointless. The perimeter fence of one school I 'guarded' was breached in four places, three of them out of sight from the gate where I was posted. A small charge did once blow up near one of the children's schools, but the chances of anticipating or detecting where this would happen next were slight.

Much of the more daring activity ended with Hussein's massacre of the Fatah units in Jordan in September 1970 – what became known as 'Black September' – but before that the most ambitious attack ever launched from the West Bank took place, with rockets fired in broad daylight from the Judean desert towards Jerusalem. Entirely by chance, I learned almost immediately afterwards who had planned it.

I was writing a long feature article on the West Bank for the *Statesman* and travelled everywhere with Bashir, a young Israeli Arab from Nazareth, then living in East Jerusalem. Bashir was a drama student who had attended a school founded by Frank Sinatra, and he prided himself on being able to switch dialects and accents according to which part of the West Bank we visited, demonstrating to me the subtle differences between the Arabic of Hebron, Nablus and of the Bedouin Arabs in the villages.

But I sensed that behind this expertise he was uneasy with his disguises. The West Bankers had their own problems of identity at the time. One told me, 'The Jews don't trust us; in Amman they call us traitors, and the truth is that we scarcely know where we stand ourselves.' For Israeli Arabs, the psychological situation was even more complicated. Materially, many were better off than the Palestinians in the Territories. A few, like Bashir, thought that they could run rings round the peasants. But despite his smart sports clothes and chameleon style, Bashir felt himself to be in a false position and always described me as a foreign journalist, never as an Israeli, and not even as a Jew. The nationalist Palestinians I met were not taken in. It was they who always asked whether I was Jewish – a question I would not have admitted was relevant to an interview in Europe but which, here, had to be answered. There was no objectivity. Readers of the *New Statesman* might think me 'detached' and objective. The Palestinians knew better.

Friends of mine in a left-wing political party whose members had many contacts with the Palestinian elite had recommended that I should meet a young agronomist, Anwar, who was working with the Military Government. He had organized a mobile exhibition of Israeli irrigation equipment in the West Bank some months earlier. Israelis liked him because he was not a 'collaborator' but a man who could speak to Israeli officials on equal terms. He was working for his own people; pending a political solution, he wanted them to make progress. There were too many farmers still using old wooden ploughs and donkeys, and digging canals by hand.

I myself had soon realized that every time I met an outspoken independent-minded Palestinian in any public position, it was only a matter of time before he was deported. People like old Sheikh Ja'abari of Hebron, and Elias Freij of Bethlehem, supporters of Hussein and cautiously co-operative with Israel, were survivors. But frank nationalists like Saleh Abu Jaleh, the Mayor of El Bireh, Mohammed Milhem of Halhoul, and many others, found themselves, at that time, being expelled across the frontier.

(Jaleh told me angrily that the military administration had insisted that he could help control sabotage in the Ramallah area. 'With what force?' he asked sarcastically. 'Forty street-cleaners?') On the other hand, the much vaunted security services were not so efficient when it came to people whose loyalties were less obvious.

Anwar proved hard to trace. We looked for him first in Ramallah, where I had been told he was employed. But at the headquarters of the Military Government we got blank stares. An old watchman, who had been listening, took Bashir aside and said we might enquire in Bethlehem. There, after some hedging, they told us that Anwar had been arrested. It was no business of ours to ask why, they said.

Bashir did not want to enquire further, but I was curious. We drove to Anwar's family's village, Abu Dis, down in a cleft of the desert hills, to which the descent was so steep that we seemed to have entered a well of silence. Bethlehem and Jerusalem were near but quite invisible, and all around us was desert. The village itself was only partly visible from the road, as most of the houses clung like limpets to the steep slope below. I stopped near the mosque, which was on the road, so that Bashir could find out where the family lived. The only people there to ask were two old Bedouin sitting on the steps of the mosque, curved knives at their belt, who stared at us impassively.

Bashir told me to keep the engine running and was back in a moment. 'Let's go,' he said. 'The army was here last night and blew up the family's house – it must be serious.' He feared it would be logical for the Bedouin to revenge themselves on us. But, perhaps pig-headedly, I insisted on clambering down the hill to visit the ruins of Anwar's house. His old parents, sitting on stools in a neighbour's house, appeared stunned, but they allowed me to copy the name of their son's lawyer from a crumpled piece of paper (Bashir refused to write anything down, lest they think he could read Hebrew) before we headed back to Jerusalem.

The lawyer would say nothing, but it was already clear what had happened. Only someone of Anwar's intelligence could have organized the rocket attack (which caused some damage to the home of people we knew), and the facts came out at his trial some weeks later.

People went on visiting the occupied territories as if they were tourists. At first it was just the pleasure of not being fenced in, the removal of all those signs saying 'Danger! Frontier ahead.' In fact, they had crossed a much more dangerous frontier.

About six months after the war was over, I was visiting friends who had a patio with hanging plants in their house in Tel Aviv, and noticed a new garden chair. Not exactly new, perhaps, but weathered, with leather strung across a rough wood-frame in the style exported by Denmark, which was called safari. My friends were people of the same background as myself. Pleased that I had admired the chair, they told me they had 'picked it up' in a deserted village somewhere near Gaza; it was propping open a door and 'no one seemed to want it'.

I knew a number of people who employed Arabs – in workshops, in the kibbutzim, in factories. Some came through the labour exchanges and had trade union rights. Many did not. I knew people who employed Arab cleaning women for whom no one was paying National Insurance because the women hadn't actually got a work permit. If they'd had a permit, they would have had to pay tax, and they didn't want to pay tax, they wanted to pocket their salaries intact, so why make a fuss?

People were shocked at first at the sight of the refugee camps. Then they said, well, they weren't much worse than the villages after all. For years, Israel had been complaining that the Arab states had deliberately kept these people cooped up as a propaganda weapon and refused to resettle them. Now Israel was in charge and the people still remained cooped up in camps. Every time I talked to officials about this, I got the same answer, or rather too many answers. The refugees didn't want to move, they would lose their UNRWA flour ration, their displaced persons' status. Wasn't that what Israel wanted? Yes, but you couldn't take land away from Arabs and give it to other Arabs, they wouldn't take it, as a matter of pride. What about the land Israel was taking for Jewish settlements? The refugees didn't want to be farmers, they all wanted to work in towns. But if Jews were all commuters anyway, and weren't farming that land but just sitting on it . . . ? It was for security purposes.

Well, I said, if the aim of settling Jews in the West Bank was to protect Israel from armed incursions, why not establish military installations?

My question was really outrageous. Israel wouldn't put up military settlements because it wasn't a military regime.

These were not just the answers I got from officials, as a journalist. Many of my friends thought along similar lines. When right-wing settlers started defying the boundaries laid down for Israeli settlement in the Territories, going out with caravans and prefabricated houses, and staging pray-ins and demonstrations near some biblical or pseudo-religious site, people sighed nostalgically and said, ah, they were real pioneers, just like the old days, the old watchtower and stockade days, in hostile territory. Pioneers? With Volvos and air-conditioning units and bypass-highways and jobs in the towns in Israel?

Two friends of ours came up with ideas for resettling the refugees. One, an agronomist, suggested large-scale hydroponics, cultivating plants without water. This could be introduced, he said, in the more arid parts of the West Bank. I had accompanied Israeli water engineers on tours of duty in the Jordan valley, where the water resources were shared between the newly installed kibbutzim, in a defensive line along the river, and the Palestinian farmers. Israeli experts were teaching the farmers to use drip irrigation techniques. But growing crops without any water at all?

Another friend, an architect, suggested building 'refugee cities', using the same exciting and innovative designs which had won him international fame. It did not seem to occur to him that for as long as refugees were herded together, they would remain a disaffected and resentful group. From what I could see of Arab villages, the Palestinians wanted each to have his own little patch of ground, not our friend's hive-like complexes of walkways and balconies.

Eshkol turned down this proposal, saying that the refugees were not Israel's problem. But at this stage, the Labour Government was still disposed to listen to the country's intellectuals, many of whom were appealing to the politicians to come up with a political initiative that would get Israel out of the Territories altogether. So when an Israeli politician did advance a plan for partial withdrawal – the first and only such proposal over the next twenty years of occupation – he invited a small group of people – historians, philosophers and writers – as a sounding-board. By accident, I happened to be among them.

The politician was Yigal Allon, Dayan's rival for the Labour leadership, a hero of the War of Independence, and at the time Israel's Foreign Minister. His plan was that Israel should give back to Jordan most of the heavily populated West Bank, retaining a strip of land along the Jordan River, with radar posts on the spine of the hills, and a group of settlements near Hebron. The inclusion of that enclave puzzled me until I read up Allon's personal history. He had been involved in the loss of that area, settled by Jews, in 1948. Now he saw a chance to see his former errors corrected – something which happens to few generals turned politicians. The fact that it made the plan into even more of a jigsaw than it already was, was a minor issue.

At any rate, the assembled thinkers listened glumly to Allon outline his plan. One distinguished historian told the surprised politician that the plan was a recipe for war, not peace: Jordan would never accept it.

Worse still, it was never formally adopted by the Labour party. While Labour dithered, preoccupied as it had been during the Lavon Affair with rivalry over the succession and with internal quarrels, the nationalist right wing moved ahead. Fanatical rabbis and opportunists staked a claim in Hebron and around it. The Allon Plan floated ectoplasmically over Labour's head for years, too insubstantial even to be buried. Appeals for moderation and reason from Israel's intellectuals – Jacob Talmon foremost among them – were ignored. What disturbed me most was not the rampant nationalism of the right, the fanaticism of the religious politicians, but the confusion on the left of people like myself.

In March 1969 Levi Eshkol died suddenly in office. His heir should have been either Dayan or Allon. But the rivalry between them was so intense that the party compromised, appointing Golda Meir. The period of innovative ideas was over. Although popular with Diaspora Jewry, Meir was self-righteous, and incapable of taking the kind of initiative necessary to break the stalemate with Egypt. I called her 'Israel's Goalkeeper', defending what Israel already had but never venturing far from the baseline. Under her leadership, Israel moved ponderously towards the Yom Kippur War.

Between the birth of my second daughter in mid 1970 and the outbreak of the Yom Kippur War in 1973, my life was spent almost entirely at home or at the hospital in Ein Karem. Rachel was a frail child, born after a complicated pregnancy, and when she was eight months old she sickened with what, it was suggested but never proved, was a rare encephalitis virus. She lay in hospital in a state nearer death than life until she died in April 1972; Isaac, my youngest child, was born three months later. So until the outbreak of the war, when coincidentally I was scheduled to begin writing again, the outer world disappeared from my life altogether.

When I was later reproached by my children for not having been in the army, I retorted that my time was served in hospitals. Hospital was my army, my contact with the real Israel beyond the university, the Knesset, the world of writers and journalists: in hospital, I was given a uniform, confined to a limited space unless let out on leave (in Hebrew, the same terms are used), and had to obey orders; the intimacy that developed there was of the kind that ceases the moment you leave, and the casualties were mourned with soldiers' stoicism.

The hospital I knew best was Hadassah, in the hills above Ein Karem, an immense medical complex at the end of a winding mountain road. With its outbuildings, and its chimneys belching smoke, as Yehuda observed, it looked like a factory producing the sick. Equipped as it was with the finest medical technology, and with outstanding doctors in several fields, the hospital, like others in Israel, was bedlam. The doctors were at the mercy of the nurses, the nurses at that of the cleaners, and everyone at that of the clerks and doormen. Visiting hours were not observed; families and clans (and sometimes television crews) accompanied patients to the ante-room of operating theatres and visited their bedsides while they were still groggy from anaesthetics, discussing politics and cracking sesame seeds and pistachio nuts; some stayed on late into the night watching television in the wards. Talking, smoking, eating in the corridors and the wards, these crowds receded only when the doctors were making their rounds. The only way to obtain privacy was to retreat under the bedclothes. On Friday nights rabbis roamed the corridors chanting prayers. The exposed site on which Hadassah was built, beautiful though it was – Ben Gurion had chosen it – meant that the hospital was at the mercy of the melodramatic extremes of Jerusalem weather: howling gales in winter, while in summer the heat of the sun on the glass façades forced nurses in the children's ward to hang wet sheets over the windows.

The ward where Rachel was eventually placed was one of those allotted to very serious cases: babies with heart defects waiting for operations; babies who could not absorb their mother's milk or any substitutes; and babies so malformed that they resembled nothing so much as the babies born in the anxiety dreams of pregnancy, creatures which in mothers' imaginations become chickens, frogs or rag dolls, before disintegrating completely.

I learned how to recognize signs of trouble when I came along the corridor each morning. Curtains drawn over the windows separating the ward from the corridor, parents waiting outside, meant an emergency within, evidence that a child was trying to slip into death and the doctors were trying to hold him back. Annoyance and frustration were marked on their faces when they were losing. The curtain had shrunk in one place and did not quite cover the glass, so the child could be identified – something else I learned, as I learned the origins of various stains on the walls and the nurses' trick of burning surgical spirit, in a burst of flame, to sterilize the sink where they bathed the babies.

The parents' attitude to the doctors, like the behaviour of mothers in childbirth, reflected the culture they came from. The North African parents, like the Arabs from the West Bank, were stoical, unquestioning, respectful. The orthodox Jews had their own prayers and superstitions, and accepted what God had dealt them. Sabras of Western origin, and the few people of backgrounds like my own, were critical and inquisitive.

Greta had wealthy relations in Germany who sent her special brands of milk-powder that she brought along for inspection by the doctor. Her baby son rejected everything he was given, and though the doctors were continually trying to tempt him with different inducements to remain alive, he tired of new stimuli as fast as an ageing libertine. The doctors humoured Greta because they suspected that she might yet remove the child from their care and send him to other hospitals abroad, and they were reluctant to let him go till all their own virtuosi had taken turns at his little body.

Sami, an Arab father, always stood a little apart from the Jewish parents, and asked questions only timidly. He was the father of one of the two heart cases who might qualify for an operation if they put on sufficient weight to stand the strain. But no date had been set for his baby's operation, and the child grew no better, no worse, which was hard for everyone. Even the public relations people, who made much of their Arab patients, lost interest. Instead, they passed down the corridor to the Bedouin babies with tetanus of the umbilical cord (severed with rusty knives) – unusual cases, but interesting for the doctors.

Nira, of Moroccan Jewish birth, was, with her son Yossi, the ward's focus of hope. Yossi was a borderline case groomed patiently for his heart operation. Nira, neat and good-natured, never troubled the doctors, brought no books, never used words she didn't understand, never pestered the staff with awkward questions. The other parents encouraged her as best they could. We told her when Yossi had drunk half a cup of broth, when he laughed at the mobile suspended over his cot, when they had let him out of the oxygen tent for half an hour on a given day. Greta, with her air of financial authority and knowledgeable connections, would assure Nira that 'they had the best men here for Yossi', if not for her own son. Sami's glances of wistful envy and enquiries about operation dates were also, in their sad way, an encouragement.

I loved to watch Nira with her son because, unlike most of the babies in the ward, Yossi was well enough to respond to his mother's face. My own case was different. Rachel had been an exquisite child, with such huge dark eyes that people took her for a Yemenite, and a perfect, oval face. But people who paused to admire her by the cot soon realized that the eyes no longer saw and that her expression never changed. The spasms of unearthly joy that sometimes passed over her face were, I knew, no more than signs of a passing irritation in the brain; and if I sometimes fancied seeing a momentary contentment, a settling in her face when I picked her motionless body from the cot, it was a fancy I dared not encourage. So I watched Nira with something like jealousy when she bent to embrace Yossi, raising the oxygen tent over her head like a bridal veil, and when he raised his wasted arms in an unusual access of strength and pulled his mother's head down to his face.

One morning I arrived to find the curtains drawn and, peering through the exposed corner, saw the doctors gathered round Yossi's bed. Nira had not yet arrived, but all the other faithful of Ward One had gathered in the corridor. Sami, trying to encourage himself, knowing that if Yossi died the chances for his baby were even slighter, asked me whether it wasn't a routine examination. When Nira came, she was intercepted by the Matron, who was excellent at such moments.

I was asked to keep Nira company, and took her home to arrange for a neighbour to look after her elder child when he came back from kindergarten. Nira was clearly resigned to the possibility of Yossi's death, and all her concern was focused on his brother.

In the car Nira insisted on talking about Rachel. But I didn't want to talk about my child. She asked why I remained in the ward, why I hadn't gone back to work. I had to explain that it was because I could see that Rachel suffered pain, that the doctors didn't deny it – 'She suffers pain as an animal suffers pain,' one had said – and I felt I had to watch her constantly to prevent it and ask for the drugs to alleviate it.

Nira, who was warm-hearted and impulsive, was absorbed in her compassion for me, and it helped her through this difficult hour. But what I could not tell her was that I was pressing the doctors continually to increase the sedation, knowing quite well, from my observations, that Rachel was weakening and that the drug could tip her into the final coma. Nira was a religious woman, and she also had the fatalism that encourages endurance. My desire actually to hasten my child's inevitable death would have been incomprehensible and offensive to her. So I had to lie, and echo her optimism.

When we reached the children's ward again, the curtains had been drawn back, the doors stood open, Yossi's bed was empty, and a nurse was detaching his mobile and folding it into an untidy package of felt and wires. The Matron was furious with me for having allowed Nira to leave the hospital.

Nira was more puzzled than stricken at this stage. She said she was worried that Yossi would be cold in the mortuary, on the ice, though she knew it didn't make sense. Later she came back to ask me whether I thought she should give her consent to a post-mortem. Her people were orthodox and objected, but the doctors told her it would help other children if they could find out what had gone wrong. It was not, she said, that she herself objected. 'I keep thinking it will hurt him. That's stupid, isn't it? Should I agree?'

Perhaps I should have taken the doctors' part. They needed their post-mortem. But I told her I was sorry, I couldn't advise her. I was less rational than she imagined.

In the summer of 1972, a month before the birth of my lusty younger son, we moved from our tiny flat facing the Old City walls to a more spacious one in Caspi Street, overlooking the Judean desert and the Mount of Olives – a different angle on the same general prospect. Some twenty yards down the hill in front of our building was the old frontier; to the south the Farouk quarter, an Arab hamlet just beneath Government House (the old Mandate headquarters, now the UN), had housed one of the forward positions of the Arab Legion until 1967.

The house had quite a large back garden, something I had longed for, with my memories of England, for years. We laid a lawn of tough Kikuyu grass which could withstand the ferocious sun. But lawns are not suited to Jerusalem. The grass survived, but sent out tendrils that sabotaged the flower-beds and were as difficult to dislodge as Laocoön's snakes. It also broke the Qualcast lawnmower, and could only be kept under control if mowed every ten days. Where the lawn was shaded by the trees we planted, it promptly died off.

I did all the work myself, and dreamed of the children tending little patches of cress and parsley, but like most Israeli children they generally preferred playing in the road. When the cress and parsley weren't devoured by the Kikuyu grass, they were uprooted by the old Israeli Arab gardener to whom I resorted in despair every six months. Because he was an Arab, I overpaid him, and when the mower broke down terminally, could find nothing better for him to cut the grass with than a pair of nail-scissors. Mohammed spent happy days in the garden, paid by the hour, cutting Kikuyu grass with the nail-scissors and occasionally spreading his prayer-mat, no doubt thanking Muslim providence for having set him in my path. I learned too late that the right kind of garden for the climate was like those in Arab villages – with pots and hanging plants, and vine-covered terraces.

Caspi Street was not a homogeneous neighbourhood. I had not wanted to live in one of those well-established Jerusalem suburbs with house committees and ritual silence between two and four each afternoon. What I hadn't bargained for was the Shack people – our next-door neighbours: social welfare cases who hardly spoke Hebrew after twenty years or more in the country, who had never worn an army uniform and very few of whom had ever worked.

The shacks were what was left of a British Army camp which had become a transit camp for new immigrants; as with all such places, everyone who could, moved out within ten years. We had assumed they were due for demolition, and that the tenants who remained would receive compensation.

However, just after we moved to Caspi Street, the value of the land there suddenly climbed, and we found ourselves between the very wealthy and the very poor. Huge, fortress-villas went up on the side of the street nearest the view, with acres of plate-glass facing the hills and valleys, and only a few tiny, shuttered windows, like loopholes, facing the road itself. We were on the other side, next to the shacks.

At one end of the road stood a Carmelite convent (from which the sisters emerged only on rare occasions) and at the other, a cul-de-sac, some rickety old houses whose tenants were Hungarians who had fled the commissars in 1956. Caspi Street had been shelled heavily from the Farouk quarter in 1967 and these houses showed it. Even now the Hungarians kept guard-dogs, and it was natural that both they and the Shack people should feel that they were the real landowners, the veterans, who had stuck it out when things were dangerous and didn't like the newcomers.

The Shack people's resentment was obvious. The authorities had told them that they were due for rehousing, but they knew about land values and held out for high compensation. They settled in for a long siege. When it was cold they piled more asbestos sheeting on the roofs, and when it was hot they moved their mattresses out into the yard under the trees and turned the radio volume up.

So visitors to the villas in Caspi Street were surprised to see, on one side of the road, as they stepped from their station-wagons, families living in what might pass for any suburb between Florida and West Berlin, while a few feet away Mr and Mrs Ben Zouzou and their nine children, our immediate neighbours, lived in a miniature inner-city slum. Their shack was half-hidden by thorns and rubbish – empty cartons, plastic bags and the cardboard innards of toilet-paper rolls, strewn about like cartridge-cases on a battlefield. At night, the Shack people made forays to the new building sites to abstract a handful of bricks here, a few planks there (with the assistance of the Arab night-watchmen), and with this material they added another wing or two to their huts, repaired the roofs, reinforced the walls. Behind the Ben Zouzous' shack lived another neighbour, Mr Ohayon, who was fanatically clean and always hosing down his yard, or building trellises for his roses, a garage for his new car. No one quite understood why Ohayon, who had a steady job in town (he was said to run a garage) and, alone of the Shack people, a telephone, should remain in such wretched accommodation. Yehuda concluded that he was a divorcé whose wife was ruining him with the alimony. Beyond these two huts were another couple of dozen, divided by bushy paths. With washing hanging out on bushes and fences, and the elders parked by the prams on the doorsteps from dawn to dusk, it looked like an oriental set for Gorky's *Lower Depths*. But the actors looked incongruously well-fed, and there were large cars parked in the field, many of them stolen.

There were nightmares, too. One morning at dawn we heard anguished screams and rushed to the window. A red-haired woman was running up and down in the street, in dressing-gown and bare feet, screaming, 'No one can help any more! No one!' It was the wife of a policeman, one of the few salaried tenants of the shacks. Crossing the main road to come home that morning, he had been cut in half by a speeding taxi. His friends had come to wake her with the news.

Every few months the Ben Zouzous would spring-clean, bringing out the contents of their hut into the yard: pine-wood divans, foam-rubber mattresses, a mahogany lounge suite, refrigerator, two plastic bathtubs, a colour television, a stereo – a whole bargain basement of household goods emerged piece by piece, like a *trompe-l'œil* sequence from a Lumière film. When they celebrated, they brought in crates of beer and arak, put up coloured lights to decorate the yard, and the hostess wore blue satin.

The Hungarian grocer down the road, Bardosh, brought us monthly news from his brother in Siam and samples of new delicacies without our having to order; and a large cache of hash, so my elder son heard from a friend among the Shack children, had been unearthed under the floorboards of one of the vacated shacks.

The children had the adventure playground of the wadi across the road. Out of sight, after a few seconds' climb, were caves; paths only the Arab shepherds, with their hennaed goats, followed; wild flowers and purple thistles. There they crucified beetles on thorns, built bonfires, explored tunnels, collected worms and caterpillars, killed the odd viper, crawled under fences and through holes to inspect the Carmelite convent, and sharpened sticks with which to fight the Shack children, who were their nearest enemies.

In the village across the wadi, we had constant reminders of Palestinian hostility to the occupation: villagers defaced a memorial to the Munich athletes and burned down a forester's hut where tourists came to plant trees in what was called the Peace Forest.

At first we had nothing against the Ben Zouzous or Mr Ohayon. When their sewage leaked into our garden, we said it would be good for the roses. When we had a front-row view of their celebrations, it entertained our guests too. The trouble with the Shack people began gradually. Fraternization did not work. When we invited their children to play with ours, they handed over some worthless coins and walked off with the toys. They threw empty tins into our garden and several times a shower of stones landed round me when I was sitting there after a hard morning's work at the weeds. But open confrontation came with the dysentery scare and the rabies epidemic: the Ben Zouzous chose that summer to dig themselves a swimming-pool in their yard, and Mr Ohayon to adopt a six-year-old Alsatian.

Ben Zouzou dug himself a pool five metres by two, creosoted it, painted it sky-blue inside and orange and green round the edges, attached the end of a hose to the municipal main and led the water through a pipe purloined from the building site opposite, which also served as a balustrade, down the four steps into the pool. It was ingenious. My children, who jumped around in lawn sprinklers on hot summer days, were jealous. We waited to see how he would solve the problem of drainage. No problem: no drainage.

For the grand opening they invited all the children from the shacks, some of whom had bathing-costumes, and everyone, carried away with excitement, including the parents, jumped in wearing clothes. The water instantly turned grey and scummy. One boy surreptitiously urinated into a vacant patch.

When evening fell, a cloud of flies and mosquitoes settled round the pool, which could not be emptied. The next day we phoned the municipal authorities, but were told that nothing could be done. Ben Zouzou was not charging admission, and a man was free to do as he liked in his backyard. The Health Ministry advised him to use disinfectant, gave him a free bottle, and suggested that he bale out with buckets every few days. Now the water foamed like a giant bubble-bath.

Majestic flies invaded our kitchen windows, a couple of yards away. My younger son and I fell ill with shigella dysentery, but the Shack children remained healthy. We spent time and money consulting the law, but neither British common law, Talmudic precept, or Ottoman practice could suggest a way of closing the pool legally.

On the other hand, my complaints brought out the Shack mothers in force. How would I like to live in a shack? How were their children to tolerate the heat if not in the Ben Zouzous' pool? I had no fair answer to that.

The shrieks and splashing went on all day. Bluebottles skimmed the pool like kingfishers. The Ben Zouzous reclined on mattresses by the poolside, each propped on a pharaonic elbow, like a couple of human bookends, surveying their handiwork. They were impervious to my pleas for a little quiet, if only between two and four.

I suggested to Yehuda that we called the police. He looked at me coldly. 'They'll leave a stick of dynamite on the doorstep, or slash the car tyres,' he said. 'You don't speak their language.'

He proposed moving back to an ordinary Jerusalem neighbour-hood with people like ourselves. He had checked out the land situation and the Shack people were demanding so much in compensation now that they would never be moved. The hell with the romantic view, he said.

I said that it wasn't the view; I refused to be driven out of my own home. Why should I be bullied into submission?

'No confrontations,' Yehuda ordered.

Then came the rabies scare.

Caspi Street, like all outlying parts of the city facing east, was at the edge of the desert. At night, wild dogs, great yellow creatures with blank eyes, and sometimes jackals, wandered up from the wadi.

In the street itself there were two kinds of dog. There were the respectable, suburban dogs with collars and chains, that were vaccinated and exercised – the Hungarians' guard-dogs, the Dutch attaché's spaniel. The Shack people watched, and decided to keep dogs too. They would take any stray dog, put a rope round its neck, and tie it to a fence; when they remembered, they would throw it their leftovers.

I was responsible for calling in the municipal dog-catchers to take away one stray, a canine albino, that looked unwell to me. When the men came, they had no net or rope, so I took down a washing-line and led them to the dog, which promptly bit one of them on the leg. The Shack people asked why I should make trouble and take away their pet. I asked them if they knew about rabies and its effects. They looked at me as if I had invented rabies, but said nothing. As far as they were concerned, we were all enemies: the municipality, the police, the welfare and probation people, the Ashkenazi neighbours. I tried a new tack. Whose dog was it, then, exactly? They shook their heads; true, it was no one's dog. No one wanted to claim ownership because they might be taxed or charged for it.

Mr Ohayon's dog was not eligible for catching, because he knew all about licences and vaccinations. All the Shack people were in awe of him because he had told them how much it was worth to them to continue squatting in Caspi Street, and he had publicly announced that he would have to be carried out, feet first, before he would take less than a million. Ohayon frightened even my children. With his dark eyes in his bald head set on his squat white body – he sat out most evenings, in his spotless yard, dressed in singlet and shorts – he looked like a piece of tallow with two raisins in it.

The dog was kept chained next to a small wooden kennel in his yard, all day and all night. I asked a dog-owning neighbour whether this didn't constitute cruelty to animals. 'Not if it can get into the shade,' she said. The rest I knew for myself: what a man did in his backyard was his own business.

The dog reacted by barking and howling alternately, the mournful howl of a chained and desperate prisoner. It permeated all our conversations. At night it kicked around a tin bowl which held its food. When I complained to Ohayon, he said that the dog had previously lived on a farm and was getting acclimatized. He also said, with a meaningful look at our stout stone walls, that he needed protection against terrorists. His shack had a flimsy fence of wire-netting and asbestos walls. Again I had no answer, though foolishly I suggested consulting a vet for tranquillizers.

Like the Ben Zouzous, who could sleep at midday, in a yard full of screaming children, in open-mouthed slack-limbed abandon, Ohayon slept through everything, including my phone calls at one in the morning.

Yehuda kept a Beretta in the clothes cupboard (I had insisted that the bullets be kept elsewhere, for safety). At night, I would imagine loading it and shooting the animal. Like Lawrence in the poem about the snake, I cursed the education that would not let me kill the dog.

Then, after a rabid dog had run amok in town and bitten a score of people, the municipal authorities suddenly decided to take action against strays. One night they came down upon Caspi Street without warning, leaving poisoned pellets everywhere. The man next door lost his poodle, which gobbled up a pellet on its morning stroll on the lead, and the old Hungarian lady, a Holocaust survivor, who lived alone, lost her guard-dog. Mr Ohayon came home to find his Alsatian horribly stiff and silent in the yard. The squad had tossed a pellet right over the fence.

That was not what Mr Ohayon thought. I came home from a trip with the children and found him hosing down his yard and a huge crowd standing near him, just outside his gate. I hadn't realized how many people actually lived in the shacks. Mr Ohayon was making a speech. We gathered by my bedroom window and listened. He told them about his problems with me, and my complaints about the dog, and the Ben Zouzous chimed in with my official complaints about their swimming-pool. The crowd shuffled, muttered, and then shouted. I caught one phrase: 'The Ashkenazim are killing our dogs.'

It wasn't quite 'Let's get Whitey', but I wasn't going to let it pass. I took my daughter by the hand, and with the baby under my arm went to face the crowd over the nettle-field with the empty cartons. My knees were shaking and my daughter was pulling me back – the children had had stones thrown at them that week. I had never faced so many hostile people.

I said to Mr Ohayon, 'I'm sorry about your dog. It had nothing to do with me.'

Mr Ohayon looked at me with his currant eyes and said, 'It's a crime what you did. Killing a dog like that. I spent a fortune on his licence and food.'

'I didn't ask the men to come and I didn't kill your dog,' I said. That I had wanted to was of no importance at that moment.

The crowd gave a kind of collective sneer. I could see that no one believed me. I was suddenly determined to convince them. I put my hand on the baby's head.

'I swear,' I said as loudly and as solemnly as I could, 'I swear on the heads of my children that I did not kill that dog.'

The crowd was silent. Then they began to turn away. The Ben Zouzous shrugged their shoulders, people started arguing, Mr Ohayon gave me a last stare and went back to hosing down his yard.

'Why did you do that? What on earth were you talking about?' asked my son, who had been watching from the window. 'You were ridiculous. Swearing on our heads!'

I felt triumphant, though, and then a little ashamed, as if I had told a spectacular lie.

From the very end of Caspi Street, which was a dead end, you could see not only the cupolas of the mosques in the Old City but also the upper portion of the Western Wall. During those years, at Tabernacles, a bus full of ultra-orthodox Jewish boys from Mea Shearim would pass along the road – the boys shouting, laughing and scattering orange-peel – and pull up at the end. The boys and their escorts would then go down the hill and gaze silently at the Wall from a distance. (Orthodox Jews are prohibited from ascending the Temple Mount before the coming of the Messiah.)

I was moved by the romanticism of the boys who, I thought, were like medieval courtly lovers. They could so easily have approached the Wall and touched it, hand on stone, but they preferred to adore it from a distance.

One year, a small boy came running down the road after the bus had left. He must have been relieving himself behind a tree, and now he was sobbing, nose running and ear-locks fluttering. The bus was already out of sight. It was clear that he had been forgotten – orthodox Jews believe that counting brings misfortune, and even numbering houses attracts the angel of death, so they had not noticed that one child was missing. I called to him but he gave me an alarmed hostile glance and went on running and sobbing, sobbing and running, in alien territory.

We, too, walked across the wadi and the hills to look at the Old City from a distance. It was on one of those walks with the children, the baby in his push-chair, on the morning of the Day of Atonement, 1973, that we saw two jet planes cut above the city and heard that sound like scissors going through canvas above our heads.

'War,' said Yehuda. 'Let's hurry.'

The first morning of the Yom Kippur War, in my memory, means the sound and feeling of a child's push-chair bumping up the terraced hillside, before the first rains, where the earth is still baked hard by the summer's sun.

6

War

A S SOON AS the front door was open, Yehuda switched on the radio. Normally silent on the Day of Atonement, it was now broadcasting the code words for the various units to summon the reserves: Lightning, Summer's day, Heavyweight. Heavyweight, appropriately enough, was Yehuda's regiment; he had become portly.

The first thing he had to do was to round up the nine other men for whom he was responsible according to the relay system. As he still did not drive, we left the older children to their own devices, parked the baby with the elderly couple downstairs and went off together. We left till the last the two men who lived in the religious quarter of Givat Shaul. I was far more apprehensive of being stoned by religious Jews protesting against the desecration of Yom Kippur than I was of a possible bombing attack by the Jordanians, so I was annoyed when a soldier stationed near the Jaffa Gate stopped me and ordered me to switch off the sidelights. I switched them on again once I was out of sight.

In Givat Shaul, however, the word had gone round that Israel was at war again and the all-embracing dispensation of *pikuah nefesh*, the saving of Jewish lives, overrode the ban on driving, though it was not quite dark. Two fat little boys in prayer-shawls were keen to help us when we stopped to ask them if they knew where a certain Sergeant Schwartz lived. 'Schwartz the glazier or Schwartz the pickles?' We gambled on the pickles and won.

When we got back to Caspi Street, Yehuda had barely time to assemble his army gear before the officer in charge arrived; after a brief consultation in the living-room, they left together. I was absurdly annoyed that the officer and his men had neither greeted me, nor taken their leave, but had walked into our flat and out again as if they owned it. It was a grotesque reaction, but successfully blocked the emotions which might have accompanied a farewell to Yehuda. He was on his way, though I didn't know it, to the Golan Heights, and I wasn't to see him again until after the war was over.

Yom Kippur, then, was my first Israeli war. Just as I had questioned Eshkol's adviser weeks before the Six Day War and had been wrongly reassured, I'd had another misleading talk before this one. I was still training myself, after a two-year hiatus, to begin writing again about Israeli politics. A few days earlier, I had met, in Tel Aviv, the Israeli journalist Shabtai Teveth, who was now working on the authorized biography of Ben Gurion. Teveth had written a book on the occupation and was close to Moshe Dayan. I thought him an authority. I asked Teveth the same question I had asked others: what of Sadat's warning? What if the Egyptians did indeed try to cross the Suez Canal? It had been explained to me in great detail, with maps, that Israel's contingency plans would swiftly block any such attempt. But would they? Teveth smiled at me patronizingly. 'It's all bluff,' he said. Of course, he meant Sadat's threats.

Yehuda had told me, mendaciously, that he would be nowhere near the front, and knowing so little of the army (he was Education Officer, and I clung to the innocent sound of that) I decided to be stupid and believe him. In any case, I had little time to worry. Within days, I was writing weekly articles for several foreign papers and coping with an unruly boy of eight, a headstrong girl of five, and a one-year-old baby learning to walk. I was flattered when the municipality sent round a social worker, in the second week of the war, to know whether, as mother of a large family, I needed help.

Still, I had my minor problems. Chief of these was sources. The discomfited Arabists were nursing their pride in Army

Intelligence, and when I did locate them, argued that they were not allowed to speak (which was convenient; not one had predicted war). The politicians I knew were similarly on the defensive.

Front-line reporters also had their grievances. Terence Smith, the *New York Times* man, complained grumpily that the time was past when you could cover Israel's wars from your own Volvo (Nick Tomalin, driving a hired car to the Syrian front, had been killed by a Syrian shoulder-missile).

Another problem was domestic. The electricians and mechanics I needed for the car (a new one, which had sprung an oil leak) had disappeared to service tanks and planes, whilst the tankers that brought fuel for the central-heating in our building had all been conscripted.

In other ways, I did not feel much nearer the war, at first, than I had in 1967. Caspi Street, which had been on the front line then, was now serene, sunny and peaceful. There was one air-raid warning, during which I took the children down into our totally unequipped shelter. Joshua, my elder son, wanted to take the television down, and the neighbours wanted to keep the Shack people out. The alert was so brief that we were joined only by an old Hungarian couple from the end of the road who, remembering the shelling of Caspi Street in 1967, were visibly trembling.

Mira Hammermesh, a feminist film-maker and artist friend passing through Jerusalem on her way to Sinai, was irate that women were not more deeply involved in the war effort and that civilians were so disorganized. This was nothing new; in 1967, a dozen transport planes were all Israel had to defend its heartland, and now the entire civilian population of the Golan Heights settlements was swiftly evacuated, giving the lie to the argument that settlements meant security.

The war was a few hours' drive away, and soldiers at the front somehow maintained contact with their families. During the first week I must have had twenty calls from anonymous soldiers who had seen Yehuda somewhere and, over a mobile radio-telephone, assured me that he was well. On his way from the Golan Heights to the Sinai – for his unit fought on both fronts – he managed to write a few words on a standard army postcard (which was franked *Soldier! Write Home!*) and hand it to the man at an army filling-station.

After that, I didn't hear from him until the cease-fire, over two weeks later. It was lucky that I never glanced at the obituary columns of the papers, as a soldier with Yehuda's name (a very unusual one) was killed in the third and last week of the war. Families were notified by a grim trio of officer, doctor and social worker, or volunteer, appearing on the doorstep; but I, never having experienced an Israeli war, didn't know what to fear.

Like most people, I knew personally of soldiers who had been killed. One was a second cousin of mine, Jonathan Hyman, a lawyer and reserves officer killed on the Golan Heights. We scarcely knew each other, but had exchanged smiles at a traffic intersection in town the week before war broke out. It was the kind of chance meeting I would have forgotten had he survived, but on each anniversary of the war, ever since, I have remembered the characteristically gentle smile he gave me.

Another casualty was Ya'akov, the eldest son of Tova Touashi. Tova no longer worked for me; she was retired, living with her silent husband, and looked after a collection of cacti, which she liked because they didn't shed petals to be swept up. After a lifetime of cleaning, extra work was not welcome.

I knew she had four sons in the war and I kept in touch. It was hard to find her, as she walked the streets for most of the day during that war, covering miles. I recognized the same instinct that made me dash out, rather than wait for news, when a child was inexplicably late from school.

Ya'akov was first classified as 'Missing'. In Israel, there is no category of 'Missing presumed dead', since, according to Jewish law, there must either be a body, or witnesses to a death, before a person can be considered legally deceased and formally mourned. His body was returned weeks later. Even a year after the war, coffins were crossing the lines into Israel at the rate of seven a day.

At first Tova refused to accept that he was dead. When the family finally mourned, I went to sit with them. Tova and the elder relatives were sitting on the ground as custom demanded, the men unshaven. I sat down next to her and held her tight as she broke into heart-rending wails of grief. Her children, already stoical Israelis, tried to quieten her.

Petering out, she died a few years later. At her funeral, only the eldest daughter, the one who had never served in the army, who had married young, cried aloud, calling on her mother. The others looked embarrassed, especially in the presence of Josh and myself. Tova was about my age.

Mira told me of a woman she had met in Sinai, the mother of an only son. She had found her way to the front straight from the kitchen, in her apron and slippers; army vehicles gave her lifts, and she wandered from unit to unit looking for her boy. Officers repeatedly sent her back, dreading her reappearance. It was the only thing, they told Mira, that could shake their men's morale.

Lecturers sent to give pep talks during the fighting had some bizarre experiences. Our friend Kidan found himself shouting, above the scream and crash of Egyptian shells, 'And you must remember that ISRAEL IS THE ONLY PLACE WHERE JEWS CAN LIVE IN SAFETY!'

Unlike the Six Day War, the Yom Kippur War did not end with a dramatic finale, or surrender. When the first cease-fire was declared, Israel was holding the Egyptian Third Army in a pincer grip, and everyone I spoke to argued that it would have to be destroyed. But international pressure prevented a resumption of the fighting and led, eventually, to the 'disengagement of forces' on the Egyptian front, two months later. During this period, however, we all believed that war might begin again at any moment, and Yehuda was to remain in the army for four months in all.

He had a brief leave the day after the cease-fire. He was scarcely recognizable to the children, as he had grown a thick beard; the baby whimpered when he picked him up. Sand and dirt were deeply engrained in his skin, and he wore an unfamiliar padded uniform which was American standard issue – the winter had suddenly begun. One of the first things he did was to dismantle his sub-machine-gun. Josh, puzzled, asked 'Why are you breaking your gun?' Yehuda looked at me and said, in English, 'It was a bloody war; you should have stayed in Hampstead.' I said nothing. The irony was that it was during the war that I had begun to feel that for the first time I was a sharer, that perhaps after all I belonged.

We spoke little. He was unable to hear properly what I said, and a few days later a doctor told me that most of the men returning from the front had been temporarily deafened by the volume of noise, produced in Sinai by a concentration of artillery and armour greater than that of the fiercest desert battles of World War II.

Later, I reflected that wars separate men and women, perhaps, more than all else. Men do not speak much, I think, to women of their experiences in battle; there is a reticence, almost a prudery about sharing that knowledge, as private to men as childbirth is to women. The only evidence of what Yehuda had experienced in Sinai was his sudden deafness, which was gone by the next time I saw him, and something else which was to recur at intervals during the years that followed: it was the sound of an unfamiliar high-pitched voice in the bed next to me.

Yehuda's normal voice was deep and measured, but when he woke one night in terror, it was to scream in a whimper, kicking convulsively, trying to escape from some horror that pursued him. When I had woken him from this nightmare for the third or fourth time, he told me what it was. There was a young reservist with whom he had shared a tent in Sinai, a pleasant young man who had been married only a few days before the war. One day he had gone out and been blown to pieces by a shell. Yehuda, together with the unit's chaplain, had collected the remnants of the bridegroom's body and once more they shared a tent: the plastic body-bag lay under Yehuda's camp-bed for days, because the shelling was too heavy for it to be sent, with the unit's other corpses, to the rear.

While Yehuda was in the Golan and in Sinai, I was writing my usual little 'think pieces', analyses of Israel's problems and future 'war aims' now that Israel had, temporarily at least, lost its deterrent power. There was more despondency in Israel than was apparent to the outside world. While Kissinger still commuted between Jerusalem, Cairo and Damascus, Ben Gurion died. He lay in state outside the Knesset, and on a cold winter night I shuffled along with the tens of thousands who had come to file past the coffin. 'Ben Gurion founded the State, and now he's dead, it's dying,' I heard someone say. Only six years after the victory albums, the buying sprees in the Old City, and the near idolatry of Dayan, the mood was masochistic. Dayan was execrated. The country seethed, that cold damp winter, with an anger seeking a target.

My friend Mervyn Jones of the *Statesman* paid another visit to Israel and I took him to a protest meeting at the campus at Givat Ram, one of the first such gatherings after the war. I found myself unable to translate fast enough the outbursts of fury and bitterness at the lives lost because of the politicians' arrogance, their certainty that the Egyptians would not dare to attack. The most important of the speakers was Motti Ashkenazi, a brigade commander who had been in one of the positions overrun by the Egyptians at the beginning of the war. Ashkenazi had noticed the tracks of Egyptians, on reconnaissance missions on the Israeli side of the Canal a few days before the actual crossing; he had reported this to his superiors and been reprimanded for 'alarmism'. He was also critical of Dayan, who had neglected intelligence reports, failed to call up the reserves and, like the rest of Israel's leadership, had treated Sadat's warnings as so much bluff. Worse still, I thought, was the fact that Dayan had realized earlier than his colleagues that Israel should make some gesture, some initial pull-back, giving Sadat the opportunity to parley; too easily, he had allowed himself to be overruled. Now he was booed and cursed when he appeared at military cemeteries when casualties were buried; this was without precedent.

Until the third week of January 1974, when it became clear that the war was really over, Israel remained in a limbo of winter mists and political confusion. My children ran wild without their father's steady influence. Jerusalem in winter is a hard climate for small children, with a high incidence of streptococcal infections, which can lead to rheumatic fever. So we were constantly dashing off to laboratories for the taking of throat-swabs and blood-tests, and the administering of penicillin tablets that took my daughter's appetite away so that she would eat nothing but pickled cucumbers for breakfast. I was distracted and the children battled for my attention. Joshua and Sarah fought constantly, while the baby banged his new shoes on the floor to hear the noise, and tried to wreck the typewriter, his great rival. Josh brought home a squad of beetles and a story about a schoolfriend who had lost an eye in a schoolyard fight that morning; seeing that I reacted, Sarah competed with a sackful of caterpillars and a schoolfriend who had had her head chopped off in kindergarten.

Yehuda's army service went on and on. He missed Sarah's birthday, and Josh's birthday, and his own. After Sarah announced her intention of going off to visit him in Egypt, where he was stationed, I had to watch the front door carefully. He promised to arrive for the Chanuka party at the kindergarten Sarah attended, but missed that as well.

A mere war had not interrupted the teaching of the arts of ceramics, rhythmics according to Orff, and the recycling of yoghurt containers. The parents of the children deposited there belonged exclusively to the university and government circles of Jerusalem. The Children's World Kindergarten took war in its stride.

There were no guns among the toys there as a matter of principle, but as soon as the war broke out, mothers met with teachers to discuss the ethics of acting out war-games. The teachers were opposed to buying large authentic-looking weapons that made a loud noise. One father who was still at home (because of kidney trouble, he explained) but was in Civil Defence, had been round the toy shops and collected a sample of the available weaponry. Imitation machine-guns, a rifle without caps, and several small cowboy pistols were produced, as well as tiny tanks.

One teacher complained that the children would become rowdy if given these toys. The other argued that the children were in any case using their imaginations, building rocket-sites with the larger bricks and bombing airfields with marbles in the sandpit. She thought no new toys were necessary. 'We don't want to be left with an arsenal when the war is over. Anyway, the games make for sex distinctions, as it's only the boys who relieve their aggressions. I'm glad that some of the girls are already refusing stereotyped roles, like Ariela [she indicated one of Sarah's closest friends]. She takes messages from one unit to another; that's good.'

In the end the vote went against buying guns. But it was decided to make the Chanuka party more elaborate than usual, to compensate for skimped birthdays (always celebrated in grand style at the kindergarten, which was useful for working mothers) and the absence of so many fathers.

Then, just before Chanuka, came the news that Ariela's father was among the dead. Once again the parents were summoned to conference. The more intellectual of the two teachers insisted that everyone must make sure that Ariela did not feel different from the other children in the playgroup. She asked that fathers on leave should not come to the celebrations, and that only mothers should attend. It was the custom for men to light the first Chanuka candle; Ariela's eldest brother would be asked to do so. The option of asking a mother to light the candle was dismissed, not on anti-feminist grounds, but because Ariela would then feel that something was wrong, that something had changed.

At the Chanuka party, the children wore cardboard circlets on their heads, a yellow crayoned flame standing out over each of their foreheads like a miner's lamp. They were all given a candle to hold, stuck through a cardboard apron to catch the drips of hot tallow when the wicks were eventually lit.

The seven-branched candlesticks which the parents had brought blazed on the toy-shelves. To the accompaniment of a concertina the rhythmics teacher had brought along, the singing began: 'My father lit a candle for me/ The Watchman who keeps the flame./ Do you know for whom?/ In honour of Chanuka.' Fathers, I thought. It was impossible to keep them out. I glanced at Ariela, singing with the rest. She looked straight in front of her, holding her candle firmly.

The teachers circulated among the children and lit their candles. As usual, I was nervous. Despite the cardboard aprons, I was always afraid that the three- and four-year-olds would set themselves on fire. I restrained the impulse to stretch out my hand and tell Sarah to keep the thing level. And it occurred to me, quite suddenly, that while I was worried about the candle-flames, in a few years all these little boys might be hurled into an inferno like Sinai, in their turn. I saw the spoiling of little Israeli males, for the first time, in a totally different light.

Finally only the Shamash, the Watchman's candle, in the big candelabra standing on the table to one side remained to be lit. This was always the climax of the party, and the teachers called for silence. Ariela's brother stepped forward, put on a velvet skull-cap, struck a match and lit it. Holding it in his right hand, he began to intone the blessing. But he was interrupted by a terrible wail, rising in pitch. It was Ariela.

'I haven't got a father! I haven't got a father!'

No one moved except her mother, who got up, ran over to the little girl and put her arms round her. The children looked embarrassed, the teachers defeated; the parents were silent. Ariela broke away from her mother, who tried to remind her that she still had brothers to look after her, but that didn't help.

'I haven't got a father!' Ariela broke free, ran over to Sarah, who was sitting with her mouth open, staring at her.

'Sarah, I haven't got a father. Give me your father.'

Her mother again tried to interrupt, but Sarah was already on her feet, and she answered Ariela in an undertone but with great confidence. 'Yes, Ariela, I'll give you my father. Now be quiet.' And she was.

I was sending Yehuda socks, magazines and other luxuries. The army requested that wives and mothers send fewer cream cakes, which went bad on the way. I sent Yehuda cigars and a tiny jar of caviar. Embarrassed at the thought of eating this alone, he called in all his fellow soldiers in the unit and divided it up, which meant about one minute globule of Beluga per soldier.

For Yehuda, it was only a matter of time before he was sent home. But on the Syrian front, there was still great tension. Nearly four months after the outbreak of war, and three months after the cease-fire, there were some two hundred men missing on that front. Whether they were prisoners, or dead, no one knew but the Syrians, who refused to provide numbers and names of the Israeli prisoners in their custody. This was in flagrant defiance of the Geneva Convention.

In January, I was contacted by the Israeli Ministry of Foreign Affairs and asked whether I would write a pamphlet for distribution abroad about the suffering of the missing soldiers' parents. The next day I went down to Tel Aviv for my first briefing.

This took place in the basement of a news agency, where two army officers showed me the rough cut of a film made by foreign television reporters in Damascus. The film had not been shown in Israel, for obvious reasons. It showed about fifty Israeli soldiers sitting on the ground in what I was told was a fairground near Damascus. All but one or two were obviously young recruits just out of school, the boys who had borne the first brunt of the Arab attack in the Golan, where Israel was even more unprepared than in the south. Their hands were tied in front of them with headcloths; one had his hands chained with an ordinary padlock. Their heads were bowed, and as soon as a boy raised his head, it was cuffed down again. Their army boots, from which the laces had been removed, gaped open. Unshaven, sullen, defiant or afraid, they looked exactly like the Arab prisoners of war during Suez, or the Six Day War, whose photographs we had seen so often.

'The problem is that we can't identify them all,' said one of the officers. 'We have a rough idea, but the picture isn't complete. There are two or three in hospital, but the real trouble is that we have a number of unidentified bodies. Some of them were shot at point-blank range – their hands were bound, so it was after surrender – and the identification discs had been taken. So we don't know who's left. That's tough on the parents.' They re-ran the film for me several times. Some of the boys who were temporarily out of reach of the soldiers had raised their heads and their faces were clearly visible. But the faces of those sitting further back were obscured. This film had been shown to the parents of the missing soldiers and the few visible faces had been identified.

I asked what other information was available.

'Not much. A couple of foreign journalists visited them in jail and got a few names. We've used computers and identikit tests on the bodies we found, but now we're at the end of the road till we get lists. The parents are going through hell. Most just wait at home, but about fifty keep coming in to see us. We have a problem too: two couples recognized the same boy – in the corner there, just his cheek and ear are visible – but he can't belong to both.'

I asked when they expected to get the lists. The officers shrugged. Israel was holding nearly four hundred Syrian prisoners for an exchange, but the Syrians were clearly holding up the lists as a way of putting pressure on Israel during negotiations.

The army had opened an office in the General Headquarters in Tel Aviv, where parents could come for the latest information. The officers suggested that I interview as many parents as I could.

The collection of huts and cottages scattered beside gravel paths, in the shade of plane trees, did not look like the nerve-centre of one of the world's most modern armies. The big modern building at one side of the complex housed the bureaucrats of the Ministry of Defence. The GHQ looked more like a run-down sanatorium, especially when I caught sight of parents wandering about like walking wounded, avoided by the busy young soldiers hurrying from one cottage to another. Officially, the parents were supposed to stick to a big shed near the perimeter, but I saw them going into other buildings where they knew there were officers they could talk to.

The parents' committee (Israelis always formed committees) turned up promptly every morning to hear if there was fresh news. Others kept to their regular routine and dropped in after work. Most stayed at home. After a few days with the parents I began to wonder how I would have reacted in this situation. I had been raising my own children as if this was not going to happen, trying to pretend that by the time they were of army age the conflict would be settled and army service a boring routine. The Yom Kippur War ended that illusion.

Israeli children look tough and are physically very independent. But emotionally, I thought, they were coddled, because at the back of their parents' minds there was always the thought that they might not survive to maturity. Together with that, as a teacher, I had noticed they were incapable of comprehending the extent to which they were hated, as perhaps all young soldiers are. I thought often of Tolstoy's young soldier who during his first battle cannot believe that the enemy is really trying to kill him, as his family loves him so much. I hadn't liked those boys when, wheeling round a corner in a jeep, they laughed as they made old people jump for their lives. It was these same boys, half-arrogant, half-beaten, that I had seen on the ancient moviola. But I was more concerned now for the parents. Some had been taken to see the site of the battle, the burned-out tanks, and talked to their sons' commanders. One woman commuted to the office every day from her kibbutz. Her son was visible on the film but she was afraid of Syrian atrocities in jail.

Another couple had received messages in the wrong order: first that their son was wounded, then that he was not. He had been photographed in hospital. Which version was true? What could they believe? A Tel Aviv businessman visited the army morgue daily. His son did not appear on the film, so every time they found pieces of a body, a hand, or a foot, he went along to try and see if he could recognize it. There was one photograph of an Israeli prisoner in a Damascus hospital, who might have been his son, but the upper part of the boy's face was bandaged, so he couldn't be sure. Police experts told him that the lips and chin were similar to his own. He himself was more inclined to recognize a split seam in the boot the boy was wearing.

The most optimistic parent I spoke to, naturally enough, was an immigrant from Syria. To him, the Syrians were not the monsters the other parents supposed them to be. He thought that while they might have killed prisoners immediately after the battle, they would no longer do so, and that if his son was still alive, he would survive jail.

I wrote my report, and appended a request that all those who had read it and were concerned should write a letter of protest or approach the nearest Syrian Embassy, asking the Syrians to observe the conventions and make information on prisoners available to the Red Cross.

The man in charge of information at the ministry felt that my account of the facts and description of the families' state of mind was insufficient. I should, he said, attack the Syrians more directly, saying that their treatment of prisoners of war was worse than that of the Nazis.

I said that I thought the Syrians could easily disprove this and discredit the whole report. There was no parallel with the Nazis, who had used prisoners of war, particularly the Russians, for forced labour till death, and had shot English and American prisoners out of hand. But the official was not convinced. I had to go home, look up the historical facts and read them to him over the phone before he would concede the point.

In the end, the report was not distributed. The parents, worried that the publicity would so enrage the Syrians that they might maltreat their sons further, decided against it. A couple of months later, the prisoners were released, and I watched the boys, some of whose faces I now knew so well, coming off the plane at Lod Airport, on television. It was only then that I felt the war was really over.

7

Upheaval

CHILDBIRTH AND WARS had alternated in my life for a dozen years. Mothering imposes purdah, wars demand solidarity. There was no one moment when I realized that Israel was changing beyond recognition from the country I had come to nearly twenty years earlier. Despite, perhaps because of, its now distended frontiers, Israel now felt more constricted, a less exciting and also less confident place than it had been before.

The frontiers had receded, but I for one felt no safer. Perhaps because I had grown up in the Diaspora, perhaps because of my education, I was continually conscious of the barely hidden hostility of the people Israel was now ruling, shocked at the ease with which Israel had assumed its colonial role.

I'd liked the austerity of Israel in the early years – perhaps because it reminded me of childhood in the post-war world, in which shabbiness meant virtue, making things over had been a habit. For a time I'd also liked the feeling that everything was being created from scratch; whatever small part I played I felt was significant in a way it couldn't have been anywhere else. Now I was beginning to miss the density of a recent past.

Now that the country was more prosperous, the roughness and brashness of so many Israelis was more difficult to take in my stride. When I visited England, I realized that I myself had become more assertive, even aggressive. I didn't wait for people to finish sentences, and talked over them. I found I needed a conscious effort to listen, for I was used to 'discussions' in which people talked against one another, where conceding an argument was losing a battle. I had become impatient with stolid behaviour, hesitance, diffidence. When something I wanted wasn't immediately available, I wanted strings pulled. I was afraid that someone was stealing a march on me (no Israeli wanted to be, in the Yiddish term, a *'freier'*, someone easily fooled, outwitted). When I drove in England I cut in front of cars and overtook patient drivers. I jumped queues and hunted for bargains. I flipped through the daily papers looking for paragraphs on Israel.

For all the protestations that Israel had changed Jews entirely and made them like everyone else, Israel was, I now began to see, the place where Jewishness was most highly concentrated. It wasn't just that I had never understood what orthodoxy meant until I saw it in Israel. The dynamism which informed so much of Israeli life also looked increasingly like the old restlessness.

Perhaps because of the tensions of life in Israel, the Jewish wanderlust had not, in fact, been tamed; in some ways it was exacerbated.

When I first arrived in Israel, I met many people who didn't want to revisit Europe, the continent of their nightmares, or who had never been out of the country. Many, when they travelled, made for synagogues, 'Jewish quarters', kosher restaurants, anything for comfort and a sense of protection. Jews visiting Israel were asked whether they were staying, and if not, why not? This wasn't nationalism, but a justified fear of a world which had so recently proved murderous to Jews, incomprehension of those who didn't seek a refuge. When Israelis went abroad, in those years, they went as emissaries, to recruit immigrants or to represent the new country. The first real Israeli tourists, travelling for recreation, were faced with a reminder, painted in Hebrew on the walls of Naples harbour, in characters several feet high: 'Snob! Have you seen Eilat?'

Now half a million people left Israel on holiday every summer, an amazing exodus. The planes were packed with businessmen, contractors who had made money fortifying Sinai or building new settlements in the Territories. Parents of adolescents compared their own modest camping holidays in Israel with their children's demands for foreign travel before army service. Israelis I had met abroad in the late fifties had proudly brought back steam-irons and slim Italian umbrellas. Now they ransacked the bargain basements of Europe and America, congregating so densely in Oxford Street that during one Israeli election in the eighties, an Israeli newspaper took a straw poll in the heart of London.

The old pioneering image of the Israeli farmer was also proving misleading. The sophistication of Israeli farming, and a retreat from the open spaces of the Galilee and the Negev, meant that most Israelis lived in towns, like Jews in the Diaspora. The coastal strip had become an almost solid block of concrete. I was sad to see the wild, bushy coastline around Caesarea parcelled out in cottage condominiums and holiday villages, and the Roman aqueduct overshadowed by a giant, coal-fuelled power station. Tel Aviv, which Yehuda, one of its faithless children, had called the great idiot head of Israel, had lost its ramshackle charm. Among the skyscrapers it was hard, now, to find those arched and turreted villas built in the twenties and thirties, Viennese parodies of Ottoman style. Jaffa had become another Mont-martre, and 'pueblo Espagnol' cottages and mock Swiss chalets housed the wealthy commuters whose homes were guarded by intercoms and Dobermans.

Perhaps this was inevitable, mimicking what was happening all over Europe. But Israel had once been quite singular.

Beneath all the signs of growth, of prosperity, moreover, were anxieties scarcely voiced, which matched the old Jewish insecurities, or so I thought. All those new housing estates and factories and museums had been built with Palestinian labour, and in a country which had once prided itself on its independent and egalitarian ideals, this demanded a great deal of special pleading to defend.

The new working class was made up, after all, of those very same Palestinians who had fled or been driven out of the country thirty years earlier. People spoke of the 'greater injustice' of the Jews' persecution, the 'lesser injustice' of the Arabs' loss of land. The Arabs, or Palestinians (interchangeable in most Israelis' vocabularies), had failed to compromise, it was often repeated, had 'shown no political maturity', had refused partition. For nineteen years they had been out of sight, part of the greater enemy outside. Now, although they had not actually moved at all, they were perceived as having returned. Not as their leaders had promised them, or as they had hoped, to reclaim their lost land, but as Israel's new proletariat. By expanding its frontiers, Israel had reacquired precisely that hostile population it had lost, to everyone's relief, in 1948. It took a long time for Israelis to admit this, but it was just as that little boy had said in the Ashdod class on Homeland: the enemy was now within.

The waiters and the petrol pump attendants and the boys on the back of the garbage truck were Palestinians. Every building contractor and farmer, and many factory-owners, had 'their' Palestinians, people they could vouch for. Intellectuals and university professors and journalists and even a few politicians had 'their' Palestinians, too, in the West Bank universities and the newspapers in East Jerusalem. People had their favourite restaurant in East Jerusalem, or under the vines in Ramallah, or down in Jericho, where it was pleasant in the winter. Retailers from Tel Aviv and Haifa loaded up on spare parts, or vegetables, or building materials, in Gaza, or in Jenin, serviced their cars in Arab garages, which were much cheaper than those of the Israelis.

Most of the people in the circles I moved in argued that the Palestinians were 'doing well' and 'had never lived so comfortably'. There were few soldiers in sight on the roads. The Palestinians had Israeli refrigerators and solar-heaters, these last on the rooftops next to mats covered with drying carob-pods and *leder*, the flat dried apricot toffee. The hospital wards were crowded with Palestinians, many of them insured under Israeli insurance schemes, and Israeli doctors worked as volunteers in Palestinian clinics. Journalists who talked regularly with Palestinian sources knew of the growing nationalism and frustration, and above all, the envy of the Israelis, but noted their dependence and passive collaboration as well. A few researchers knew that Israel was profiting more from the Territories than the reverse, and that bitterness was growing; but most Israelis, seeing no alternative to the situation, preferred not to acknowledge this.

The novelty of visiting the Territories had long since worn off, but going through Arab areas to reach Jewish towns on the other side of Israel was usual: the quickest way from Jerusalem to the Galilee was through the Jordan valley; the quickest way to Beersheba was through Hebron. With Jewish villages and settlements dotted near the road on both routes, it was easy to forget that the countryside was 'occupied'. Occasionally a stone glanced off the chassis as we drove through Dahariya, the last village on the way to our friends in Omer, near Beersheba, a forty-five-minute drive rather than two and a half hours 'the other way'. One night we went by bus to a wedding in a Galilee kibbutz and back the same way a couple of hours later, through the Jordan valley. There was a line of Israeli kibbutzim (sole reminder of the Allon Plan) and a double line of electric fencing between the road and the Jordan River. 'Incidents' on that road were rare. Just north of Jericho were the hundreds of empty adobe huts which had housed the refugees of 1948, those who in 1967 had fled across the river into Jordan. Most of the huts were deserted, but occasionally a homeless family, or one banished by the military authorities from its village for recalcitrance, camped there. On our return journey we saw that the east bank of the Jordan valley, until quite recently empty darkness, was a solid band of villages with electric light. Hussein had settled 'his' refugees there. We hoped it was an indication that he anticipated no further wars.

My children, growing up in Caspi Street, had no chance of seeing the Palestinians as other than enemies or labourers. The children in the nearby village certainly did not want to fraternize, and every house in the street, including ours, was built by Palestinian workers. They sat under their little canopies chipping away at the limestone blocks that faced the houses; they stretched out to eat or pray on the unfinished roofs, and at night the watchmen huddled over charcoal braziers, or occasionally played *shesh besh* with men from the shacks.

Caspi Street, as Yehuda complained, had none of the feeling of an Israeli 'neighbourhood', or *shkuna*. Some of the villas housed UN personnel, some housed diplomats or others with no permanent ties to the country. Israeli children, from kindergarten age, wander in and out of neighbours' houses, play in the street, and only leave the immediate area to attend 'circles' for 'enrichment'. Sarah once asked Ariela whether she could come to tea that day. The child reflected solemnly for a moment and then said, reciting, 'Sunday I have piano lessons. Monday is museum. Tuesday is the ballet group. Wednesday I have Scouts. Thursday is my private English lesson. Friday is grandma. Saturday we're going on a hike. Sorry.'

My elder children, though they attended museum classes for a while and played the piano, were as unclubbable as their mother, and save for a taciturn grandfather and a voluble aunt in Tel Aviv, they had no family. They were all speaking English before Hebrew and were raised on English nursery rhymes. Concerned Israeli friends warned me that speaking two languages would make them stutter, but Joshua was skilled in simultaenous translation from the moment he could speak, and thought Yehuda and I could not converse at all without him. They thought it natural to read Beatrix Potter, though middle-class England was as remote from them as the forests of Grimms' fairy-tales, and were disinclined to read the wholesome prosaic stories of Israeli writers. Because I lived in two worlds, my children did too.

I wanted to transmit the certainties of my own childhood to them, and it was quite impossible for me to speak to them in Hebrew. Reliving my own very happy childhood through my children – the books I had read, the games I had played, and the things I had wanted to do but couldn't, like painting on an entire wall – I sometimes forgot that not all fairy-tales are international, and that nursery rhymes are never so. I dressed Sarah for a fancy-dress party as Little Bo Peep, complete with a shepherdess's crook, and she was mortified when not one child in the kindergarten knew who she was supposed to be.

There was a different problem with birthdays. All Jewish holidays, birthdays included, begin on the evening of the night before. This would have ruled out the surprise of the morning greeting, in bed, with presents. Yehuda deferred to me on this, but was never very comfortable with elaborate celebrations. He explained, too, that Israeli children celebrate birthdays at kindergarten or in school – at least they did in his ultra-socialist sharing childhood.

The children spent many of their summers in England, and their early years were in many ways replicas of mine. Unlike their Israeli friends, they had scrapbooks and doll's-houses, railway sets (there was only one one-track railway in Israel and it was not exciting to Israeli children), British medieval forts and soldiers, games of Happy Families and Scrabble, and a whole series of pets; hamsters, guinea-pigs, tortoises, goldfish, and finally a pair of kittens with the un-Israeli names of Ginger and Jenkins.

Sarah, with an American friend, fulfilled a fantasy of mine and went to get a Christmas tree. They cut down a pine sapling in a neighbour's garden and decorated it with silver stars before they were caught and I was reprimanded, on both ideological and environmental grounds, by the neighbour.

Joshua formed an Israeli branch of NATO with the sons of a neighbour who was a member of the Dutch legation; they devised elaborate ceremonies, including blowing a hole in the wall of the Carmelite convent with a chemistry set presented to Yehuda by the German Minister of Housing.

Isaac, with three little English-speaking friends, battled the Shack children and led football matches against teams which lined up on an ethnic basis.

All three of them read through my childhood library, from E. Nesbit to Ruskin's *King of the Golden River*, whereas Israeli children knew only of Winnie the Pooh and Enid Blyton – who, Joshua was disappointed to discover, was not buried in Westminster Abbey. The children hit one another with their croquet mallets (the Kikuyu grass raised tempers higher than English lawns ever did), ate cucumber sandwiches for tea in summer and scones in winter, and had edifying explorations of rather different private parts with their little UN friends. My students would have thought them thoroughly, deplorably, cosmopolitan. I didn't want them to see Gentiles as anti-Semites, or Diaspora Jews as strangers, but I couldn't stop them feeling the hostility of the Arab world around them. Joshua drew imaginary maps, pages of strange continents, like the medieval sailors' charts in which what is known grows and spreads, what is feared is pushed to the margin. The most striking feature of these maps of his was that Israel, as time passed, became detached from the Middle East and floated off towards Europe, first as an island in the Mediterranean, or a peninsula of Turkey, then part of Italy, and finally attached itself comfortably to the South of France.

But they were not English children. They went off to kindergarten during the Feast of Weeks with circlets of flowers round their heads (daisy-chains, my 'English' equivalent, did not qualify), sat around bonfires at Lag B'Omer, and observed other Jewish festivals in the open, which I knew from the synagogue. Nevertheless Joshua, whose knowledge of weddings, like his knowledge of railways, came only from books, asked of a marriage we were to attend : 'In which church?' Even this, however, did not budge Yehuda from his anti-clericalism, and the children grew up, like all their friends, as pagans, refusing even to go to a Reform synagogue, as I suggested. I failed to understand how they could manage without the pleasures of an early faith, and the still-greater excitement of breaking with it.

The odd dissonances continued when the children went to school. I grumbled intermittently about the excess of Bible study, but I did not consider myself qualified to criticize Israeli teaching practices; the bits and pieces of learning I had picked up in nine different schools in my own childhood scarcely rated the name of an education, and my children never got over the discovery that their mother actually thought the moon produced its own light.

It disturbed me, nonetheless, that well before they reached adolescence the schools were trying to teach them about the Holocaust. One educator I knew insisted that Israeli children should be constantly confronted with details. 'They have to live with the horror continually before their eyes.' I told him hotly that in my view this would produce paranoia. But I was confident that this would not happen, that the children would simply turn their eyes from the Medusa. Horror turned all too easily to farce. One Holocaust Day, an instructor in a youth movement shut his charges in a dark room and opened a canister of cooking-gas 'to give the kids the feeling of the Holocaust'. Those who stood it for a minute or two were rewarded with chocolate. He was reprimanded.

Yehuda complained of the decline of the youth movements, which had taught immigrants' children discipline and political education. But in the laxer atmosphere of the seventies, far fewer children now joined even a non-political club like the Scouts – which Sarah attended briefly until she became bored with tying knots and building fires. None of my children liked organized outings or dressing up in uniforms. But the school trips were different, and – but for Joshua, who always preferred his own company and avoided, wherever he could, school outings, particularly visits to monuments and war sites – they would go off very happily each summer to work as volunteers in a kibbutz, or for cadet corps activities. At the age of sixteen, Joshua and Sarah could handle guns. On one trip Joshua's class made to the Galilee, the parents who were supposed to stand guard fell asleep, and Joshua and a friend stood guard all night. When I went to collect him from the school bus the following day, he told me that his friend's rifle had jammed and that he alone had been responsible for the camp that night. I thought I recognized some of my own capacity for self-dramatization, so did not ask for more details.

Sarah brought home from her first rifle practice a piece of paper with a neat circle of charred holes ('Guess what?') and displayed a scar on her wrist from a cartridge that had fallen short, but was otherwise offhand about what it all meant. When she was in the cadet corps, she took part in a test intended to show the alertness of her class. She was told to get lost in the orange orchards and wait until she was found. Sarah hid so successfully that the class searched all day without finding her, and by nightfall the corps leader was hysterical. Sarah strolled back to base, bored and hungry, just in time to prevent her from calling in army helicopters.

When she was sixteen, her class went off to pick bananas in the Jordan valley. The children were housed in asbestos sheds (the settler kibbutzniks in air-conditioned bungalows), and treated dismissively. The bananas were over-ripe and seeped stickily over the pickers. The schoolchildren, in revenge, ignored the detailed instructions they had been given and hacked some plants to pieces. When Sarah's friends killed a viper that slid across her foot in the undergrowth, the kibbutz supervisor lost control completely. The kibbutz collected vipers, he shouted, and now they had killed a prize specimen.

I was very impressed by these adventures. Despite my World War II veteran status – which I made the most of – at Sarah's age, I had done nothing more daring than caddy on the local golf-course, expressly against my father's instructions, risking, at most, being hit on the head by a golf-ball.

In the spring of 1977 I went off to Iran and India to tramp through fields and ditches in dozens of villages. A Canadian research body had commissioned a film script on irrigation in Israel, India and Iran. India and Iran had two of the oldest irrigation histories in the world, Israel one of the newest, but the idea was to see where new technology went wrong when it reached the village; the way that small changes in local practice could be encouraged so that the new supplies of water from dams and reservoirs would not be wasted. We ought also to have taken in the problems caused by the Aswan Dam, but the relationship with Egypt was not yet established, and though I could have gone there wearing my English hat, it was doubtful whether they would co-operate once they knew Israel was in the picture.

Many Israelis I knew had gone as advisers and experts, in agronomy and medicine, to the African new states and non-Arab Asia. Iran in particular was full of Israelis, and I was curious to see how they were managing in a Muslim country, constructing a whole irrigation network of tunnels, reservoirs and canals in the north-west of the country. Driving to Qasvin, I passed the Iranian director of the project, whom I was supposed to meet, going in the opposite direction. But this, I found, was irrelevant. There was an Israeli in the director's chair, running his office. Israeli water engineers lent me a room in their flat, after warning me off the only inn in town. The Iranian housekeeper who cooked and cleaned for them clearly thought I had been brought there for a disreputable purpose (their families had stayed in Teheran) and banged down the evening meal in front of me with a look of contempt.

Without the Israelis, I wouldn't have seen how Iranian villages actually worked – villages still protected behind high mud walls, and gates that were closed at night against the wolves, where women still did their washing in the canal in the centre of the village street, and houses were heated by burning dried dung in the central well of the house. Iranian guides did not want me to see the interior, and in the south, without Israeli guides, I saw only what they thought I ought to see: private farms, whose owners had purchased Israeli drip irrigation systems; in fact it seemed to me these techniques had been taken up as a matter of prestige, as someone in the West might buy a computer to do the household accounts. I saw sprinklers used in flat windy areas where the water was carried away from the field, or evaporated before reaching the ground. I was driven hundreds of miles from Shiraz to see an 'experimental' crop grown by a wealthy landowner. His foreman, a smartly dressed young man, looked as if he had never picked up a spade in his life. Pointing out a field of tomatoes a couple of hundred yards away, he said this was the first crop grown with Israeli equipment. He opened the door of a new car standing on a gravel path leading to the fields and gestured me in.

'Surely we can walk,' I said.

'Why walk, when we can drive?'

In the nearby town, where my guide told me that 'the police had things well under control', the rebellion against the Shah was to break out a short time later.

It was only once, in the arid countryside near Shiraz, where the ground was dotted everywhere with the ancient *qanat* system, that I found the kind of inventive local project for which I was looking, a small-scale technique that would save water if adopted on a larger scale: in a greenhouse shaded by canvas, a country agronomist was using *kuze* pots, small earthenware containers produced on the spot. Minute quantities of rain water seeping through the inverted container could be regulated to irrigate the plant.

This was the one small dividend on my research in Iran which might have been of use, through the irrigation advisory service in Israel, to countries elsewhere in Africa and Asia. Three years later, when I was working on a book about Weimar Germany, I received a phone call. A Nigerian agronomist had seen mention of the *kuze*-pot technique in the service's bulletin and wanted more details. I looked up my notes and found that the director of the Soils Institute in Teheran had promised to send me a scientific abstract and had never done so. Khomeini and the Islamic revolution had intervened; part of the reason why the film was never made. Iranian–Israeli contacts had ceased save for the secret meetings of the arms dealers. It was chilling to reflect that my Shiraz guide and driver, who had planned to send his wife to Hadassah for fertility treatment, had probably long since been eliminated – not only from the agricultural service, for his former contacts with the Zionist enemy.

As for the local agronomist with the *kuze* pots, I felt sure that he must now be serving at the front in the Iran-Iraq war. All that was coming our way, in Jerusalem, from Iran, was a migration of marsh birds who, according to ornithologists, had fled the terrifying barrage of artillery fire in the marshes on the border with Iraq, and were roosting, among other places, in the pine trees of Caspi Street. To the distress of the official in the irrigation service office, and I suppose of the Nigerian agronomist, I was unable to pass on the secrets of the *kuze* pots.

It was in Shiraz, in April 1977, that I had caught a glimpse, on Iranian television, of the first ripples of the Israeli 'upheaval' – the victory of the right wing at the polls that spring. I was camping out in a deserted house because there wasn't a hotel room left in town. The Shah had decided, the week of my visit, to convene an atomic energy conference: partly in Shiraz, and partly in an ornate tent city just beneath the plateau of Persepolis, an extravaganza which looked like a National Theatre production of *Tamburlaine*.

I was watching the news in the house of a local Soils Institute official, whose house was packed with gadgets, but whose old peasant mother could not be got off the carpet to sit on a chair. Suddenly the familiar face of Yitzhak Rabin, the outgoing Labour Prime Minister, appeared over the Farsi commentary. My host told me that he had just resigned his candidacy at the elections, as his wife had been found to be holding an illegal foreign-currency account in Washington. There was much hilarity (even the old lady on the carpet rocked with laughter) when the Iranians discovered that a mere few thousand dollars was involved. 'And for that much they resign in Israel?'

What the Iranians did not know was that Mrs Rabin's peccadillo was only the latest in a long series of economic scandals associated with Labour hegemony and vested interests, the careless handling of national resources bred of too long a stay in power. When Menachem Begin's victory was announced, a hysterical Sephardi woman in the street outside his election headquarters screamed, 'Thirty years of corruption – all over now!'

The 'upheaval' at the elections, which were held a couple of weeks after I returned from India, coincided with the death of my father-in-law. For a veteran Israeli socialist like Shmuel Licht-blum, the victory of Menachem Begin was not just a change of government. It was a reversal of the natural order. In hospital, from his oxygen tent, he gazed at Yehuda with apprehension. 'What will become of you all?' he asked.

During the seven-day mourning period, the *shiva*, talk turned on nothing but the upheaval. Among the condolence visitors was Micha Shagrir, director of a documentary film company, who had spent years on a kibbutz. Looking at the photographs of the right-wing leaders in an evening paper, he said suddenly, 'Who *are* all these people frothing at the mouth?'

That remark, with its distaste for the newcomers, the fear that Labour's pragmatism had given way to fanaticism, military adventures, and the alienation of Israel's friends in the West, was typical. While Labour was in power, I had been in the Knesset press gallery many times when Begin, strutting to the podium in his lounge suit and tie, had lambasted Labour in his legally punctilious, old-fashioned Polish rhetoric. He was always received with gusts of appreciative, patronizing laughter from the Govern-ment benches, where Labour was so comfortably and, it seemed then, permanently ensconced. Now, no one was laughing.

However, Begin's policies, during that first right-wing term of office, were tempered by the presence in his coalition of Moshe Dayan (who had crossed the floor) as Foreign Minister, and by the Democratic Movement for Change, a liberal-centre party, headed by the archaeologist Yigael Yadin, which had siphoned off the crucial votes from Labour. The mood of shock and horror gave way to mutual reassurances, in our circle, that once Begin tasted power he would become more moderate, that he was a 'great parliamen-tarian' who was unlikely to be swept into rash adventures, and that his terrorist days were over. The Lebanon War was still five years away.

This view seemed to be confirmed when Sadat made his historic visit to Jerusalem at the end of the year. It was Begin, with Dayan as his guide, who signed the Camp David peace agreement with Egypt the following year.

It was not so much with emotion as with suspended disbelief that we watched Sadat emerge from his Egyptian jet at Ben Gurion Airport. It was a surrealist fantasy, to which no one had the right reaction. 'I don't know about peace,' said a bemused elderly workman interviewed by a television reporter, 'I only know about wars.'

The official welcome ceremony was attended by Egyptian security personnel dotted among the Israelis – undercover agents who were supposed to be incognito. They blew their cover by rising automatically to their feet when the Egyptian national anthem was played, seconds before the Israelis, who were unfamiliar with the tune.

Despite the fact that the Sadat visit represented the first breach in the wall of hostility surrounding Israel, that all my children were sent out of school into the streets to wave little Egyptian flags, and that tens of Israelis immediately applied for visas to visit Egypt, there was no great euphoria. Psychologists insisted that the dominant mood was caution, and that most Israelis were still bracing themselves for the next war. Various writers and political scientists whose opinions I canvassed were more optimistic, but were conditioned, it seemed to me, to expect catches. Would Israel now become 'Levantine'? Would socialism be still further threatened by cheap Egyptian labour? Would Tel Aviv become the brothel of the Fertile Crescent? When I raised what appeared to me a more pertinent worry, the possible solidarity of Israeli Arabs with the Palestinian cause, a famous writer said that on the contrary, Israeli Arabs would be more conscious than ever of the advantages they had over Arabs elsewhere. The same man thought that Israelis would now adopt 'oriental' accents when speaking Hebrew. Another argued that it was irrational for Sadat to expect to be given back all of Sinai, and that he would have to accept the principles of Zionism.

All these speculations were somewhat dampened by Sadat's actual speech in the Knesset. The man seemed not to have understood that Israel had won the Yom Kippur War. He was actually warning Israel that it would have to accept Arab terms for a settlement. Israelis who 'didn't know about peace' felt more comfortable with their worries; to be dependent on the Arabs' goodwill was more disturbing than to be threatened by their hostility.

When Israel agreed to vacate Sinai, including the port of Yamit and the flower and vegetable farms of Rafiah, I went down there to write a film script about the Israeli transfer. North Sinai was a huge market garden, the settlers' houses palatial by Israeli standards; but most of the workers in the fields and in the sorting sheds were Palestinians from Rafiah town and from Gaza. Yamit had been planned as a model town, where Israeli architects had clearly learned from the mistakes of the early development towns and, more important, had worked with no budgetary constraints. All but a hard core of settlers (who later had to be evicted with fire hoses after scuffles with soldiers) had left. The sparkling white beach was deserted, the flower-beds of the town were beginning to wither and the walkways became covered with sand. Outside the perimeter fence, I saw a Bedouin with a herd of goats, staring into the empty streets and gardens. But if he hoped one day to move into the town, his hopes were misplaced. On Begin's orders, the entire town was ploughed back into the sand.

The most noticeable result of the withdrawal from Sinai for us was the increasingly noisy sky. The jets which had exercised over the desert now confined their manoeuvres to Israel's limited airspace and, though this was forbidden, cracked the sound barrier frequently over Jerusalem, making our windows rattle in their frames and once more startling the migrating birds.

Shortly after the signing of the Camp David Accords in November 1978, we celebrated Joshua's bar mitzvah.

With my talent for missing key events, I managed to play no part whatever in the preparations. A maiden aunt who was our children's surrogate grandmother became ill with incurable cancer, and near the end I took her from a Tel Aviv hospital to London, where one of my doctor uncles took charge of her. We had been very close, and I arrived back in Jerusalem in a poor mood to load the tables for the one hundred and fifty guests Yehuda had invited, in relays, to celebrate Josh's passage to manhood.

The bar mitzvah boy had been ambivalent about this event all along. A born rationalist, he queried the sudden interest in a religious ceremony by a family which, in his experience, had never visited a synagogue. He suggested that the only reason we wanted him to go through the ceremony was as a matter of social conformism, of which he was scornful. We talked about it. Wouldn't it be awkward, we asked him, if he were the only uncircumcised boy in his class? He agreed that it would. Wouldn't it also be unacceptable if he, in his class, was the only boy whose parents did not invite his class friends and their parents to a celebration for his birthday? He concurred. Wouldn't it be hard to be the only boy not to receive a hundred and fifty presents? He conceded this point, only balking at going to a synagogue to recite his portion. He ended by doing something that conformed far more to recent Israeli fashion: having his bar mitzvah at the Western Wall.

Steinsaltz might have pointed out that the Wall was not a synagogue; but the orthodox had made it into a place where clans gathered; the secular, where demonstrations were held; and Yehuda, as a descendant of Hasidim, had no difficulty in arranging for Josh to sing at the Wall.

When Yehuda realized that I would return only within hours of the reception, he was inclined to cancel the social celebration. But this was too much for our friends, who stepped into the breach in a way that was very Israeli, and made it into something of a communal bar mitzvah. Each couple or family came bearing a tribute, each woman carrying a dish of savouries or cakes covered by a cloth or tin-foil; it looked a bit, I thought, like the procession of kings on the frieze at Persepolis.

Joshua's cantorial appearance at the Wall some days later (we had reversed the usual order) took place on an icy December day with rain pelting down on the huge outdoor plaza; so the bar mitzvah, one of a whole series taking place together and in competition, was held at the covered section of the Wall.

This was an area usually accessible only to men. As a special favour, because of Yehuda's pedigree, Sarah and I, as the only females present – we had no other family – were ushered down a narrow stone-flagged passage which led to the Wall, to sit behind a padlocked barred gate giving on to the prayer area, in the freezing damp and dark. Beyond the gate, we could see the Hasidim hurrying backwards and forwards with the green-baize-covered tables on which the heavy Torah scrolls were set out for the bar mitzvah boys.

It was difficult, in the dark and the confusion, to locate my first-born son, somewhere out there, singing inaudibly about Jacob's manservants and maidservants, goats and seed inheriting the earth. Under my breath I was humming the prisoners' chorus from *Fidelio*. Sarah complained audibly that her bottom was freezing, as Yehuda had insisted that in deference to his orthodox relatives she was not to wear trousers. Although she was allowed – another concession – to kiss the Torah scrolls through the bars of our prison, the only hand offered for me to shake (again, through the bars) was that of our villainous building contractor, who had bungled our heating pipes, and was there on a celebration of his own. Then just as I was about to take a swig from the bottle of brandy we had brought along, Yehuda snatched it away (through the bars), telling me that only men were allowed to drink to the boy's health.

I still felt that it was somehow more authentic than the Anglicized bar mitzvot I remembered from childhood, with toast-masters in red coats giving us the Queen in hotel ballrooms, and the boys making insincere speeches to their dear parents. Had Joshua made a speech at our home celebration, instead of circulating among the crowd, he would have explained no doubt that he was no longer a Buddhist Trotskyite, but a Trotskyite who currently believed in reincarnation.

Fears about the 'upheaval' had at first seemed exaggerated. But after the right wing's second victory at the polls in 1981, the real changes began. Crudely nationalist signs and symbols appeared; flags were hung behind each minister's chair; settlement of the West Bank became a priority; and the right acquired new coalition partners: the religious parties who until now had always sided with Labour. Israeli politicians now not only donned skullcaps to consult with Ashkenazi sages but made pilgrimages to oriental cult leaders, like the Moroccan Baba Sali. The gentle unassertive form of orthodoxy of Solomon Hirsch's generation gave way to that of Jacob: a new breed of nationalist orthodox Jews who took the Scriptures as their title deeds to the West Bank and Gaza.

This time, the 'upheaval' was genuine. Perhaps appropriately, it was prefaced by a ceremony which took place that year for the first time since I had been in Israel – the Blessing of the Sun. Every twenty-eight years since the creation of the world, according to orthodox calculations 5,472 years earlier, this ceremony had been performed (quietly, I assumed, since neither I nor our Diaspora Jewish friends had ever heard of it) among the orthodox the world over. Now it had become a state event. Thousands of orthodox Jews climbed on to rooftops and recited the blessing among the heaters, water tanks, television aerials and lines of washing, trying to get a first glimpse of the rising sun. The sun was now supposed to be in the exact spot in the heavens where God had first suspended it on the fourth day of creation. (How he had managed to work without light till then had never troubled me, but it was the subject of learned debate.)

This was not, religious scholars assured sceptics, a throw-back to ancient sun-worship. Nor was it a fringe event, like a hippy gathering at Stonehenge. The President of the State himself, who liked talking in folksy parables, attended early services. Physicians at Hadassah warned of the danger to the retina. The two chief rabbis issued conflicting rulings as to whether women and the blind (both handicapped, in tradition, where communal prayer was concerned) were allowed to pronounce the word God while reciting the blessing.

All this was interesting and harmless. It so happened that the Muslim Palestinians had celebrated the eclipse of the moon a few years earlier, banging on saucepan-lids to banish the 'monster' who had eaten it (the noise was faintly audible in Caspi Street). But biblical literalism was taking on an increasingly political tone. Right-wing movements, whose religious learning was often scant, were casting the Palestinians as 'sons of Amalek'. There were orthodox groups, I heard, planning the construction of the Third Temple on the site of the Dome of the Rock, and dress designers who were sketching the garments of the future High Priests. Those who spread this bunkum were a small group (they would have been surprised to know that the Evangelicals a century earlier would have sympathized) but they were useful to the right wing.

A strain of superstitious nonsense was even detectable in Israeli secular education. I was not surprised that the state religious schools found it hard to teach evolution; but I was amazed that in the University High School, secular and liberal (even 'leftist') as its atmosphere was, my daughter was taught, in a class on Oral Law, that a plague of locusts filtering that year into southern settlements from Sinai, had overflown the settlements of orthodox to attack the fields of the secular. Another subject which took up the time of fifteen-year-old boys and girls was whether opening and closing the adhesive fastenings of babies' plastic pants constituted inadmissible 'labour' on the Sabbath. Sarah thought this funny. I didn't.

When I first arrived in Israel, I had been disconcerted to hear the twenty-third psalm subjected to psychoanalytical treatment in a class in the very same school; and I wasn't sure I liked the Passover Seder at the kibbutz turned into a 'harvest festival', with loaves sharing the tables with matzot. But what bothered me now was that the chief rabbis of Israel, who preserved a total silence on anything resembling a moral issue, attributed all disasters, from wars to accidents at level crossings, to lapses in Sabbath observance, the recruitment of girls to the army, and Jewish consumption of pork.

Customs which, in the Diaspora, had seemed pleasantly archaic and innocent, part of religious myth and aesthetics, now buttressed political tribalism. A growing number of biblical shrines (according to my archaeologist friends, there was no scientific basis for most of them) were taken up by the right as settlement areas. 'Judea and Samaria', as the West Bank was also known, were declared non-negotiable, thus exacerbating the conflict. When Menachem Begin made his first speech after the victory of 1977, he took a skull-cap from his pocket and put it on to read a quotation from the Bible – something no secular politician had done before him. It was a gesture to the orthodox, and it worked. Backed by the religious parties, Begin now felt free to interpret the peace with Egypt as giving him a free hand slowly to annex the West Bank, Bible in hand. The future scummed over like a standing pool. I took refuge in the past.

During the three years that I worked on the biography of a man named Wilfrid Israel, a German Jew of British birth who had saved thousands of lives during the Nazi period, I returned many times to Kibbutz Hazorea – the place which this lonely, worldly man had imagined as a home, though he never lived there. To me, it meant sanity, a recognizable corner of the Israel I had come to so many years earlier. The founders, Wilfrid Israel's friends and protégés, were a little group of German intellectuals who had taught themselves to be farming pioneers. Now Hazorea had factories and a concert hall, as well as the little museum with the art collection Wilfrid Israel had left the kibbutz on his early death, but its founders were still there and had not changed. One had been a pupil of Einstein: he was chief electrician of the kibbutz; one was writing German Jewish history; the curator of the museum had worked on the famous Ullstein encyclopaedias of art. The little world of the kibbutz had enfolded the pearl of their talents, the inheritance of their pre-Nazi past. It was this that reassured me.

Wilfrid Israel's life had brushed my own: like my father, he had been a pacifist in the First World War; among his friends was my childhood mentor, Hans Feld, a Weimar cineaste who had taught me all I knew about the theatre. Wilfrid Israel, working for the Foreign Office at Balliol during the war, had been a wistful outsider in Oxford. He had imagined Israel not as what he called 'a dumping-ground for the dispossessed masses of Europe' but as a place of refuge for a select nucleus of pioneers.

On my last visit to Hazorea, my research completed, I realized that Hazorea had lost its spell for me. Wilfrid Israel had not lived to see the post-war world, the abandonment of the Jews of Palestine by Britain, the wars with the Arabs. He had never seen, could not have imagined, Kiryat Shmoneh, Ashdod and Yeruham. He had collected oriental sculpture, believing that he saw resemblances between Judaism and Buddhist worship. His only link with the kibbutz, beyond his friendships, was the legacy of those Khmer buddhas which had stood at his bedside in Berlin, and these odd remains of the life of a European Jewish intellectual now puzzled kibbutz children more familiar with the flints and shards of ancient Israel, upturned by kibbutz tractors, which were usually displayed in kibbutz museums or 'culture houses'.

Wilfrid Israel's ideal society, to which he had despatched so many refugees from Nazism, had been a mirage, precisely because he imagined it as the home of an elite. With all its contradictions, ugliness and conflicts, Israel, as it has come to be, represents the realities that persecutions, wars and the strains of an immigrant society have created. It was foolish to think that it could have been otherwise.

It was while I was completing my foreign research for the biography, in London and West Germany, in the summer of 1982, that Israel launched its 'limited' attack on Palestinian positions in southern Lebanon and broadened it into a full-scale war which reached its climax with the siege and bombardment of Beirut: the war which the Begin regime mendaciously called the 'Peace for the Galilee' campaign.

I was staying with friends in London when Yehuda rang and told me that the Israeli Army had gone forty kilometres into Lebanon on a search-and-destroy mission against Palestinian terrorists, following the assassination attempt the previous week on the life of the Israeli Ambassador to London, Shlomo Argov.

Ariel Sharon was Minister of Defence. Labour, now in opposition, had not opposed the raid, which had long been a military contingency plan, believing in the 'limited objective' story Sharon had spun to the Cabinet. In fact, Sharon was using the army to fight a war deep inside Lebanon, with the aim of establishing the Phalangist Christians as the dominant force there, dislodging the Palestinians. He had made no secret of his hope that the Palestinians would topple Hussein's regime and set up their own state in Jordan. But no one realized that he was dangerous and unscrupulous enough to use Israel's army, its young recruits and civilian reserves, as no other Israeli leader had done, in any but a war of survival.

The Lebanon War, on the contrary, was dubbed in Hebrew 'a war of choice', an elective war, unlike the others which, it was argued, had all been forced on Israel. It was the first war deeply to divide the Israeli public. For me, it was Israel's Theban war, in which young men were sacrificed almost as a ritual, without its leaders questioning whether their deaths were really necessary to the survival of the State.

The morning after Yehuda's call, I had an eerie experience. Waking in Notting Hill Gate, I heard the sound of cannon-fire.

That night, after a dinner party, I left the table and fiddled helplessly with a radio in the next room, trying to find a news broadcast which would tell me what, precisely, was happening in Lebanon and whether the Israeli Army had pulled back, as scheduled, after forty-eight hours. All I could get was the inane chatter of radio disc-jockeys.

The following day I went on to Berlin to continue my research. In my boarding-house in the Grunewald, I went every morning, before the staff, to pick the hotel newspapers off the doormat and try to get some picture of the Middle East news. About ten days later, in Munich, as the carnage went on and on, I decided to cut short my stay and took an almost empty Lufthansa plane back to Tel Aviv.

During the next two years I was to spend a great deal of time, like many of my friends, at protest demonstrations, at vigils outside Begin's house, and in the mass rallies against the Lebanon War in Tel Aviv's main square, Kikar Malchei Israel.

The most painful of these, in retrospect, was a demonstration of about ten people outside the Knesset. I had arrived early, with a friend, to hold up placards against the war, and found no one there at all. It was a chilly afternoon, and we stood rather forlornly with our placards while the Knesset members and Cabinet ministers drove past in their limousines, pretending to ignore us (only one left-wing member, Victor Shemtov, waved), and the big electronic gates opened to admit them and closed behind them.

After a few minutes we noticed a middle-aged woman standing on her own, not far away. She had no placard, but something about her suggested she was there for a purpose. We went up to her and asked whether she was part of the demonstration. She was, so there were three of us. We talked for a while about whether there was any point in remaining – we did, and were later joined by a few others and the inevitable police detachment.

Sharon's limousine went by. We held up our placard and, of course, he did not look at us. Then the woman said, very quietly, 'He killed my son. I want to see him in his grave.' Her son had been killed in an attack on the PLO position at the Crusader ruin, Beaufort, to the west of Mount Hermon – a battle after which Begin and Sharon had at first insisted that there were no Israeli casualties.

I had found the earliest demonstrations against right-wing

policies, in the late 1970s, disappointing and even embarrassing. The Israeli liberal middle class was not used to demonstrating. The unemployed demonstrated ('Bread and work!'); the immigrants in the slum districts demonstrated (as they had in the Haifa downtown area of Wadi Salib in the late 1950s); the settlers demonstrated, staging pray-ins at biblical sites on the West Bank. And they usually got what they wanted. People like us didn't demonstrate. For Yehuda's circle of friends, there was something disloyal, alien and amateurish about demonstrating for political reasons, especially with placards bearing English slogans for the foreign television crews.

At first, the people who turned up at 'Peace Now' demonstrations were either very young or elderly. The young kibbutzniks or secondary-school children might have enjoyed chanting 'One, two, three, four – we want, no more war', but I felt distinctly silly. Even the police smiled. Later, people turned up regularly at these demonstrations with babies in push-chairs and small children on their shoulders. It was all civilized and ineffectual. It was a social event; you saw people you hadn't seen for years, there were few hecklers, and the larger meetings, addressed by people like Amos Oz, ended with the singing of the national anthem.

It was difficult to whip up protest against the political deadlock when the Palestinians themselves seemed resigned to prolonged occupation and the surrounding Arab states made no noise on their behalf. Only terrorist activities drew attention to the Palestinians, and that did not incline Israelis to demonstrate for concessions. During the seventies and early eighties, several of our friends and acquaintances had been among the victims. In 1978, the Fatah planted a bomb on a Swissair flight to Israel. Among those killed were the parents of Yael Shalit, a Jerusalem social worker who had been in the next bed in my maternity ward in Hadassah, and whose son had attended the Children's World with my daughter. The brother and sister-in-law of Jeremy Isaacs, for whom I had once done research for a film on the Israeli Army, died, leaving two small children, one a nursing baby, when a refrigerator packed with explosives had blown up in a central square in Jerusalem. Finally Aliza, the wife of Micha Shagrir, on holiday in Paris, was killed by the blast of a bomb placed at the entrance of the Reform synagogue in the rue Copernic, as she was walking past on her way to dinner with friends. A few days earlier she had been at our house with other people, talking politics; she was among those Israelis openly sympathetic to the Palestinian cause. Micha was rightly enraged when the French Ambassador, before attending the funeral, enquired first whether it was to be held in the western or eastern part of Jerusalem.

As Israel's army went deeper and deeper into Lebanon and began to besiege and bomb Beirut, more people took to the streets to protest. As the war dragged on, and the casualty lists lengthened, there were reports that the numbers of volunteers for crack units and combat troops in general were dropping dramatically, notably among kibbutz youth. In the Public Record Office in London, I had discussed the war with a well-known Israeli historian of Zionism, an officer in the reserves. 'For this war', he told me firmly, 'I am not returning.'

But the younger generation was paying the price. Yehuda and his friends, this time, were either too old to serve or, as in Yehuda's case, no longer qualified for active service; he served in the military radio station in Tel Aviv. The Independence generation was uncertain how to relate to what was happening. One man kept saying, half-jokingly, that he wished he had the guts to assassinate Sharon. Others tried to rationalize the horror in strategic or ideological terms.

One evening, at the house of the poet Haim Guri, we met a Lebanese writer, one of a cultural delegation invited to Israel as part of the new Israeli-Christian Lebanese *entente cordiale*. This was the period when Israeli leaders were boasting of a new revolutionary alliance between Israel and the Christians who, together, would introduce a new order in the non-Muslim Middle East. There was more than an undertone of contempt, however, for Israel's new allies; I heard that when Israeli top brass met with Phalangist leaders on an Israeli torpedo-boat offshore, the Phalangists – the new Phoenicians – were seasick.

The Lebanese writer, a middle-aged man in a three-piece suit with soft, beringed hands spoke, in French, of the ancient friendship between Phoenicians and Jews now to be revived. To my astonishment, many of those present took this seriously. When another journalist friend of Yehuda's responded, we had a bitter quarrel; I thought all this vicious nonsense.

What shocked me more than the machinations of Sharon was the meek acquiescence of members of the left, who went on finding reasons to justify a criminal political involvement which was costing their own children's lives. I heard, through my teenage children, whose friends all had brothers in the army and air force, of signs of demoralization in the ranks – a fatal shooting accident involving a frightened soldier, a young pilot court-martialled when he returned from a bombing mission over Beirut with his lethal cargo intact. But most young men, schooled to believe that all Israel's campaigns were ultimately defensive, obeyed orders.

Then came the two events which polarized Israeli society: the Geva incident and the massacre at Sabra and Shatilla.

Eli Geva was a young career officer who saw children and old people through his binoculars as he gazed into besieged Beirut, and realized that they would be the first victims of an Israeli attack. He told his superior officers that he could not lead his men into the city, or console the families of men under his command who might die in the attack. He asked to be relieved of his command and to serve in another capacity; but he was dismissed from the army altogether. No other officer followed his example.

Eli Geva's father was a veteran of Israel's wars and a general in the reserves; his brother had been wounded in the Yom Kippur War. But many people I knew felt that Geva had broken the unwritten laws of the Israeli *chevra*, the group; this was more than disobeying orders during the war. He had deserted his men, they said, and put his own conscience before his duty to the men he led. Someone would have to do the 'dirty work' he had refused to do. The same argument was to be advanced later, during the uprising on the West Bank, against the tiny number of soldiers who refused to serve in the Territories.

The second event was the massacre, by the Phalangist Christians, of the Palestinian refugees in the Sabra and Shatilla camps near Beirut. The news came over the radio on the first day of the Jewish New Year. Only one instinctive reaction was possible: I went to Begin's house. Peace Now was slowly organizing a protest. The method of summoning supporters was like the reserves call-up system, by which each of us alerted ten others, but much more haphazard, of course, as every activist was a volunteer. No one had yet phoned me, and I found that most people present that morning had acted exactly as I had, from the feeling that they could not stay at home. As I came near the house, I passed a woman carrying a placard with a question mark she had hastily painted. We looked at one another. She said, 'I kept thinking of what they said then; they were just acting under orders.' The reports had said that Israeli soldiers had allowed the Phalangists passage into the camps, unaware of their intentions.

Begin was attending the New Year services in the Great Synagogue nearby. There was a small police detail near his house, quickly reinforced as the crowds gathered. When I arrived, there were barely a dozen people; within an hour there were hundreds. As usual, young couples had come with toddlers in push-chairs and babies and small children carried on their shoulders. No one expected violence.

A French television team arrived and I was asked why I was demonstrating. I said that I had heard of the massacre and felt that the Government had to provide an explanation of what had happened. Did I think that the Israeli army was responsible? The killing had been done, I said, according to the report, by the Christian Phalangists. It was too early to say how exactly they had been admitted to the camps, but one thing was obvious: Israel, as the occupying power in the area, was responsible for what happened there.

When Begin emerged from his prayers and was walking the

hundred yards or so back to his residence, the police asked the crowd to disperse. It was, of course, an 'illegal' gathering. There had been no time to request a permit – something Peace Now leaders always insisted on, believing their protesters should 'set an example of correct behaviour'. The small crowd began moving across the square, away from Begin's entourage, as requested. But then, inexplicably to me, the police officer in charge panicked and tear-gas canisters were fired at us, from close range. Elderly people, babies and toddlers wept, vomited and fainted.

A few days later, a huge rally was convened in Tel Aviv. We went down, taking with us two friends of Joshua's, who were in their last year of school. It is said that four hundred thousand people, or a tenth of Israel's entire population, were present that night. It was certainly the largest crowd I had ever seen in my life, in that vast square facing the Tel Aviv municipality; and it was in protest against the murder, by the Phalangists, of the refugees whom, officially at least, Israel regarded as its deadliest enemies. A close friend of mine, who attended every demonstration against the war, later said bitterly, 'It was wrong that the largest demo we ever staged was for the Palestinians; it ought to have been against the slaughter of our own soldiers.'

This protest was soon to be the theme of vigils. Meanwhile, in response to public feeling, the Government set up a judicial committee of enquiry into the circumstances of the massacre which found that Israeli officers, though not directly implicated, had not taken precautions to supervise the Phalangists' movements and prevent bloodshed. As a result, Ariel Sharon resigned as Minister of Defence.

From April 1983, as the Israeli casualties mounted, soldiers back from the front demonstrated continuously outside Begin's house, calling themselves 'Soldiers Against Silence', while a much smaller group, Yesh Gvul (There's a Limit) refused to serve in Lebanon at all. About one hundred of these were imprisoned. Peace Now organized vigils to help the Soldiers Against Silence, and each day, as Begin came out of his house, he saw, silently held up in front of him, a placard listing the number of Israelis killed to date in the war.

In May 1983, a tour guide who had lost his only son in the first week of the war, Zvi Ginsburg, set up a one-man pitch to implore Begin to withdraw the army at least to the 45-kilometre line which had been initially pronounced a 'defensive cordon for the Galilee', nearly a year earlier. The quiet, tree-lined avenue where Israeli prime ministers live, next to the city's music academy, became a forum for political argument and sometimes abuse hurled at the demonstrators by drivers and passers-by. Occasionally an old Yemenite blowing a ram's horn wandered between the two groups separated by the police – one attacking, one defending the war. The hostility to protesters against the war culminated in the murder of Emil Grunzweig, a leading Peace Now activist, at a rally outside the Prime Minister's Office building in the government campus later that year, when someone tossed a hand-grenade into the dispersing crowd.

Day after day, I watched Zvi Ginsburg appear outside Begin's house with a letter he wanted to hand to Menachem Begin in person. He was a robust, middle-aged man whose wife, his son's step-mother, tried to get him to rest and eat sandwiches, drink tea. Time after time, he tried to get near Begin or his aides, but was put off, promised a meeting 'soon'. It did not come. One day I spoke to him and suggested that I might approach a right-wing journalist I knew who was an intimate of Yehiel Kadishai, Begin's aide. After a slight hesitation, which I didn't understand at the time, he agreed.

It was late on a summer afternoon, not long before the Sabbath. Only a handful of people remained outside the Prime Minister's house with the placard listing the number of Israeli dead, which then stood at five hundred. I hurried to the journalist's house, five minutes away. After apologizing for the hour, for I knew he was observant, I explained the situation.

His first reaction was, 'Well, what's behind it?'

'Nothing. He's just a bereaved father who wants to prevent the deaths of other people's sons. He's been there for weeks, he just wants a word with Begin.'

The man narrowed his eyes. 'Come on, Naomi, don't be naive. Who's been putting him up to it?'

I refused to answer this. Would he, or wouldn't he get Kadishai to look at the letter? It would be, I said, as pointedly as I could, a *mitzvah* (a good deed, or commandment, synonyms in Hebrew) and after all, it was the Sabbath eve. That clinched it, and he rang Kadishai on the spot.

The next and the last time I saw Ginsburg, he was not standing, tense with expectation, waiting for Begin to leave the house; he was roaming the street distractedly, scarcely answering the questions of people who talked to him. I asked him whether the letter had been taken by Kadishai. He said that it had. I realized that he had now lost the very purpose that had brought him to Jerusalem, the purpose that had given some sort of meaning to his son's death. Now he was left with only the bereavement.

During the Lebanon War, the 'upheaval' finally overturned our own lives. In the second summer of the war, Joshua left Israel and did not return. He was seventeen, and due to begin his army service the following winter.

For four years, Yehuda would not communicate, by letter or by telephone, with his son. I mediated between the two as best I could.

I felt that what had happened was not only the impact of the war, but the result of having brought up my children, and in particular my elder son, in two worlds. I had thought the double background of my children's lives enriching; had assumed, perhaps too easily, that the experience of living and growing up in Israel would prove stronger than the magnetism of England, which I had taught the children to see as their other home. In any other country, possession of two languages, access to two different worlds, might have been an asset. In Israel, it was dangerous. Israel demands complete and total allegiance, over-riding all other ties, from its children, whatever their origins, as the very price of its survival.

When Joshua was three, a year after the Six Day War, Yehuda took him to salute the memorial raised to those of his unit who had died in the battle for Jerusalem. When the sirens sounded for a two-minute silence to those killed in Israel's wars, he had stood stiffly by his father's side as a small boy. At the time of the Yom Kippur War, aged eight, he had reacted with anger and distress to his father's absence, and like all children had drawn volumes of cartoons of Israeli tanks and planes. Each Remembrance Day, at school, he had dressed in blue and white, and stood through the ceremonies in the school grounds at which there was always one teacher or parent who would break down during the commemoration.

Israel did not indoctrinate its children. The army, in war or peace, was simply a part of their lives, as much as family and school; above all, it was a condition of belonging. It was typical of Israel that the very soldiers who, returning from the front, went straight to demonstrate in front of Begin's house, denied that anyone who had not served, in a war they condemned, had the right even to protest.

The upheaval had coincided with Joshua's bar mitzvah, and had made him fiercely politically-minded at an age when most children are more concerned with football scores than election results. Growing up in a household where six local papers were taken every day, where politics were fiercely argued over, and where the Diaspora was not 'exile' but another way of life, Joshua began secretly to nurse longings for a different future. During the 1981 election campaign, he had been the youngest, but one of the most active, workers in the local Labour branch; he took the defeat of Labour and its policies quietly, but more seriously than we guessed. He had always been a quiet, self-sufficient boy, and during the Lebanon War he withdrew to his room to prepare for his final school exams, with our female cat, Jenkins, pinioned to his side, planning his escape.

Like all Israeli fathers, Yehuda had assumed that when the time came, his support would help Joshua in the difficult transition from home to army, the abrupt termination of Israeli childhoods. He had talked to me often of his own emergence from the protection of a Diaspora-born mother to the coarseness of the army barracks. Fathers with army experience passed everything on to their sons, from the correct way to put up a tent to standing up to drill sergeants. But father and son did not talk of the Lebanon War, and when Joshua left that summer for a holiday alone in England, Yehuda had no inkling that he would not return.

In rejecting Israel, Joshua was himself rejected. Beyond the personal tragedy for his father was the fact that the doors were now shut against him. His own home was now out of bounds, his family inaccessible. We had to go to him. He could not come to us. Not only did the law isolate him, but a wall of enmity grew up behind him. Yehuda's friends never mentioned Joshua again by name, though some of the women were kinder. One of Yehuda's friends wrote a diatribe against the *yored* (he who 'goes down' from Israel), the 'cosmopolitan Jew living from his suitcases', which he told Yehuda was written with his son in mind. I understood the anger and I understood the resentment. To defend Joshua meant suggesting, to friends with sons in the army, that their lives were less valuable. But I was aghast when a friend to whom I appealed to try to soften the blow for Yehuda suggested that instead I should exert pressure on Joshua to return. I told him that neither Yehuda nor I wanted to force the boy to return by means of emotional blackmail. But he was unyielding.

I said hotly that I could not agree that Yehuda should be made to feel that his son was a criminal. It was not, I said, as if he were X (a public figure whose son had been convicted of drug-peddling).

'No,' said the friend. 'What your son has done is worse.'

I thought I could cope with the situation until one day, at an anti-war demonstration, I met a woman whose son had attended kindergarten with mine, and who herself had been a student of mine in my first year as a teacher. She spoke about her son, now in a tank regiment, and asked about Joshua. I told her. She looked at me for a moment or two in astonishment and then put her arms round me.

'How terrible for you,' she said. I was taken aback. I had been expecting hostility, and instead had been pitied.

8

The Children of the Intifada

WHEN THE TIME CAME for my younger son Isaac's bar mitzvah, none of us wanted to repeat the fiasco at the Wall. Isaac shared none of Joshua's reservations about the ceremony, and this time we chose a local synagogue, in a bramble-patch off a nearby side-street, a homely place. Though we were not of his congregation, the rabbi had agreed, insisting only that Yehuda and his son should put in an appearance for a few preceding Sabbaths.

The synagogue was so intimate that the forty-odd members of the congregation filled it to capacity, with only a thick muslin curtain separating men and women. This time, I was able to see and hear my son as his brand-new, clear tenor voice traced the vocal line of the biblical portion to be read that Sabbath, as well as the more taxing optional passage from the Prophets. When he had finished, there were murmurs of approval, the muslin curtain was drawn aside, and the women pelted Isaac with boiled sweets – a custom new to me.

It was an evocation of my childhood to see Isaac – named after my father – wearing my father's prayer-shawl. That shawl had gone with Josh to England, where for a few brief months, out of a sudden desire for Jewish company, he had for the first time in his life gone to synagogue. He could not attend Isaac's bar mitzvah, but I had brought the prayer-shawl back, and now it lay across Isaac's shoulders, worn thin more from age than use. The little congregation drank the sweet wine we had brought and shook our hands. But they knew as well as we did that they would not see us there again.

Three years later, at the height of the Palestinian uprising, the Intifada, there was an ugly echo of the sweet bombardment. A Jewish settlement in the West Bank was celebrating Chanuka, and the commander of the army unit patrolling nearby wanted to please the children. He emptied out his 'gravel cannon' – which fired stinging clouds of grit at the boys who threw stones and cinder-blocks at the soldiers – and filled it with boiled sweets. Like Isaac, the settlers' children were pelted with sweets, more sweets than they could ever eat.

Good children were pelted with sweets; bad children, the violent children of the Intifada, with gravel, steel marbles, rubber bullets (not innocent at all, some with a deadly core of steel), plastic bullets, tear gas, sticks designed for extra whack – some made by Arabs in a Tel Aviv carpenter's shop. At first, it was a boys' war. The Palestinians ambushed, stoned, cursed. This wasn't new: Isaac had been stoned in the Peace Forest down the wadi; the Shack people had stoned me in my garden; the orthodox Jews of Mea Shearim stoned motorists driving through their quarter on the Sabbath (stoning being 'the penalty inflicted by the law', which they would read out in synagogue on Yom Kippur).

Now the hills themselves with their ancient terraces were arsenals, and the stones were everywhere; piled at the entrances to villages like ammunition, arranged in barricades across the roads to slow down the patrolling jeeps in order to make them an easier target for bricks and petrol-soaked rags stuffed into bottles. So it was not long before the soldiers were using the 'real', high-velocity bullets; outnumbered, they fired into crowds, and the killing started.

I saw the instructions given to soldiers for when to open fire. It was a concertina-like print-out, containing row upon row of type: fire only when in danger, first in the air, then at their legs; only shoot to kill if you are in danger of your life; use this or that ammunition, depending on the kind of danger. What mortal danger did a crowd of boys with stones represent? Who measured how close the boy on the roof, or down the alley, was? Rubber bullets, 'steel marbles' – these made it all sound like a game, but they were lethal used at close range. High-velocity bullets caused more damage from a distance.

Grown men, the generals, the ministers, issued orders in the language of street gangs. Go for them, get them, show them, break their arms and legs: the arms that threw stones, the legs that carried the Palestinian boys away faster than the Israeli boys, in their clumping boots and clumsy riot-gear, could follow. Soldiers and rebels alike were boys barely out of school, some even younger – on the Palestinian side, sometimes as young as eight or nine – either playing truant or free to roam the streets after the army closed the schools. Any boy could use a slingshot. For Israel, it was absurd: men trained to use computerized artillery against massed armies, or to tackle an enemy armed with machine-guns and grenades, now patrolled bazaars watching for rocks pushed off roofs, petrol bombs thrown from side-alleys. Soldiers too, out of sheer frustration, sometimes threw stones back, or improvised slingshots.

Young soldiers told me of an incident in Gaza, in the second summer of the Intifada. An Israeli patrol came on a group of Palestinian boys playing football on a waste lot in the violent Sabra quarter. One pack of boys looked at another. The Israeli boys asked if they could join in. The Gaza boys nodded. The young soldiers piled up their guns in a corner and joined in the game: Israel versus Palestine, with corners, offsides, goals. Half an hour later, the game over, the boys suddenly remembered who and where they were. A Gaza boy reached down for a stone; the Israelis grabbed their guns.

As civil disobedience grew on the Palestinian side, and the Israelis responded with collective punishment, the Intifada became a conflict of wills between a subject population and those who tried to dominate it. But it began with the boys – those who, like Isaac, had been born after the Six Day War, and who, like Isaac, had now come of age.

Yeats's great lines kept thundering in my head:

> 'We had fed the heart on fantasies
> The heart's grown brutal from the fare.'

There was the fantasy of the 'benevolent occupation', and the fantasy of the Palestinians' departure – for the right wing, by means of 'persuasion', 'transfer', or force; for the left, of their own volition, for their own good. I kept hearing of the bright young Palestinians who, it was said, would 'rather live elsewhere'. Beneath the fantasies were the first signs of the brutality to come, when the fantasies proved empty. A distinguished judge recommended 'limited violence' against captured terrorists. When the Attorney-General, Yitzhak Zamir, insisted on the exposure of secret service agents who had beaten hijackers to death, he became unpopular and was later replaced.

'I wouldn't have them in the cadet corps,' an army officer had told me, with a smile of contempt, about the Palestinians he had dealt with, whose cells he had broken up so easily, fifteen years earlier. The Palestinians had no history; they hadn't fought for their independence. Wars had been fought over their heads, and they had trotted out white flags for generations of conquerors. Now suddenly, it seemed, they were throwing stones at soldiers armed with guns. Most Israelis were bewildered.

But there had been warning signs, hints and glimpses of what was to come: of brutality condoned, despair ignored.

In 1984, I attended the trial of the Jewish 'underground' – a grotesque term dating from the Mandate period, as if the Jews were still fighting a colonial power. The 'underground' was simply a Jewish terrorist group of West Bank settlers. They had blown the legs off two Palestinian mayors, killed and wounded students in Hebron, planted booby-trapped hand-grenades near mosques and schoolyards in the West Bank. They were rounded up by the security services after their attempt to explode bombs in five Arab-owned tourist buses failed. Some of them had planned to blow up the Dome of the Rock, the Muslim shrine on the Temple Mount – enough to set the entire Muslim world against Israel. It could so easily have happened, that every crack of thunder on a stormy night sent me racing across the road to see if the great Dome was still in place, winter mists scudding across it.

Yet few people were seriously alarmed. There were no crowds at the trial save for the defendants' families and friends, who crammed the corridors, lobbying journalists, pushing aside policemen, shoving their babies into people's faces and interrupting the conduct of the trial. The defence stressed their records as professionals, farmers, observant Jews.

At first I was reassured by the vigour of the prosecution; the murderers all received life sentences. But the campaign for their release began soon afterwards. Prime Minister Shamir called them 'misguided patriots'; the left wing dismissed them as madmen. They were anything but insane. Disciplined and orderly, they had carefully planned their brutal attacks, yet within a few years, their sentences were twice commuted, because they had 'expressed regret'.

Once more I took refuge in history, but this time it was to look further back, to Palestine before Zionism. I wanted to understand what had brought so many travellers, emissaries and adventurers to the country in the nineteenth century, after so long a period of neglect. I found more fantasies – intellectual, religious, political. It was as if this country had existed only to fulfil these fantasies, as if it were a country of the mind. The Arab peasantry was always described as 'obstinate, thieving and violent', even when it had 'an aboriginal attachment to the soil'. British soldiers digging for archaeological remains had been driven from the country by hails of stones. The Jewish minority was seen as the degenerate remnant of a once noble race, the subject of absurd experiments in conversion to Christianity, to hasten the Second Coming.

Long before the Zionists, Lord Shaftesbury had coined the phrase 'a people without a country for a country without a people'. The actual inhabitants, or 'tenants' as they were called, were seen as no more than part of the landscape, 'biblical illustrations', irrelevant to serious political or intellectual concerns. Their very existence was properly documented only in the archives of the Ottoman rulers, and in the rare Arabic books and documents which researchers like Fahmi El Ansari were only now beginning to assemble.

Behind the modern conflict was another problem waiting to be solved, and it wasn't that of Isaac and Ishmael. On what basis were the Palestinians to assert their separate political existence, save by creating their own history? This they could do – here was the irony – only with the help of the Jews, the example of the Jews, in their struggle against the Jews.

I had barely finished my book on nineteenth-century Palestine when I was asked to write a study of the Mayor of Jerusalem, Teddy Kollek, to be published on the twentieth anniversary of the Six Day War. I hesitated. I had no intention of writing a publicity brochure about the 'unification' of the city, which existed only in the physical sense, and there were libraries full of evocative and poetic descriptions of the Holy City. In any case, people who wrote books on Jerusalem usually had some religious affiliation; such books were not written by agnostics who didn't believe in the sanctity of stones. However, I had admired Kollek, at a distance, as a man with a difficult job, and wanted to see how he did it. I thought I would write a very prosaic account of how the Holy City was run, from the sewers up, taking in all the planning problems and horse-trading, Kollek's problems with the orthodox Jews, and the half-visible resentments of the city's Palestinians.

No one, naturally, wanted a book like this. Kollek, who had written one autobiography and was contemplating more, was a glutton for praise but had no wish for a frank portrait. The Jews did not want to hear about the problems of the Arabs, or indeed anything at all about them (at a launch party in London, I was surprised that not a single question I was asked referred to Arabs). The Palestinians did not want to acknowledge how far co-operation with 'the authorities' had gone.

Kollek hated the book when he finally read it, and tried to persuade me to rewrite it, accusing me, in a series of bitter private tirades, of lacking 'feeling for the city'. He refused to endorse the book, while literary editors, I heard, assumed it was a public relations exercise for Israel. The book fell flat on its face, no good as propaganda for either side, and the Intifada, which broke out when it had been on sale for only a few weeks, made it into instant history. But I was glad to have had a look into the city's works. Six months later, it might not have been possible.

From the outset, there was no personal chemistry between the famous Mayor and myself, unless I compare our rare barbed meetings to my own chemistry lessons at school, during which the teacher would bungle one experiment after another, ending up with a bench strewn with exploding test-tubes and broken glass.

Our first meeting was deceptively auspicious. Kollek was back from one of his fund-raising world tours, and our talk was punctuated by the mammoth yawns for which he was famous. I said that I wanted access to all the municipal departments, from finance to garbage; I wanted to go out with the various teams, follow him around a few times, and finally to have a couple of personal sessions to clarify outstanding questions. At first he was pleased, saying that this kind of detailed survey was what he had been trying to get people to write since 1967. But as time passed, my scrutiny began to annoy him.

There were many troubles in the city that year – between orthodox and secular Jews, Jews and Arabs, one Christian church and another – and I was there watching. I literally raced round Jerusalem in my little car, following the Mayor, and several times I turned up in places where I was not welcome, or expected. 'What, are you here again?' was the Mayor's unsmiling greeting.

Kollek (I refused to call him Teddy, which annoyed him) reminded me strongly of Otto Preminger, whom I had watched directing scenes from *Exodus* in 1958. He dwarfed the little men around him and I enjoyed his air of strolling on to the set of one of his productions in Jerusalem. Whether it was the première of an opera or a midnight mass, I always expected him suddenly to shout 'Cut!' for he treated Jerusalem as an elaborate set – and, with its echoes, natural floodlighting and dramatic backdrops, it served him well. Like all the great Viennese directors, Kollek had assembled a formidable array of 'angels' (patrons), and the beautiful, wicked old city acquired a whole new wardrobe of parks and facilities which rejuvenated it. But what interested me more were the endless deals going on backstage: from Israel's tacit consent to the suspension of many of its laws in Arab Jerusalem; to the arrangements for the Jewish Sabbatical year – saplings planted in plastic bags to prevent illicit contact with the soil; to the confabulations of priests who manoeuvred skilfully between their Jewish rulers and their Arab parishioners.

There was no reason to think that either Muslims or Christians liked having Jews running the Holy City, but nor was there any reason for them to complain about the way it was done. The most serious complaints I heard were about the status of a soap-dish on the roof of the Holy Sepulchre (with such things was the religious status quo concerned); Israeli customs duty on rosaries; and (from the rabbis) accusations of Hellenism and Bolshevism in City Hall. The apocalypse was held in abeyance. Kollek understood this very well, whether he was shouldering Torah scrolls on a public platform, pacifying the Mufti privately when Jewish rowdies ran wild, or doing business with the priests of the Eastern Churches, who had been at the Jerusalem game longer than anyone else.

But 'pluralism', Kollek's watchword, used as a blanket term, could not quite cover the naked hostility of Jerusalem Arabs to Israeli rule; here the accommodations were far more fragile. The Palestinians were not just another ethnic group, like the Armenians. Kollek knew this at heart, I think, perfectly well, and with the very limited powers he possessed (for much of his talent was sleight of hand) tried to ease the tensions. But the Arab actors, whether as 'residents' or 'tolerated guests' in what they considered their own city, walked on or off in the wrong places. The city was straining at what was called the 'seam' – the old scar of what had been the demarcation line before 1967. The Arab elite refused to recognize Israel's sovereignty. A strongly nationalist press functioned in East Jerusalem, and on its editors' walls there were maps of Palestine. Arabs refused to serve on Kollek's city council, which was convenient, as that cosy, bickering forum would never have accommodated a nationalist Arab.

Kollek's powerful charisma did not work the same way on the Arab merchants and mukhtars as it did on the Jews. For them, he was not the caring Mayor on twenty-four-hour call, but the chief, the *rais*, the man you curried favour with. If, as a one-time kibbutznik and official socialist, he was uneasy with this role, he concealed it under a blustering patronage. There was no nonsense, however, about sharing a pipe with a friendly chieftain. I only saw him twice in six months, walkabouts apart, in the company of Arabs: once, when he summoned the merchants to lecture them on violence in the wake of an Old City murder with which they could have had no connection; and once when he turned up two and a quarter hours late to a reception given by an Arab doctor who, to finance it, had gone deep into debt. He would protest, as no other politician would, against Jewish settlement in the Muslim quarter and the excesses of fanatics or hooligans. But he had no time for people he regarded as unimportant, and that included almost all the Arab elite, who either did not want to talk to the Mayor or never got the chance.

Kollek wanted to persuade the world that the way he ran the city justified Israel's political claim to its eastern half. But the Arabs went on protesting against Israeli rule. No sane person wanted the walls and barbed wire replaced, but soon after 1967 suggestions had been made for some kind of federal or administrative division of the city. If Kollek had ever supported such concessions, he did so no longer.

To the west, Jerusalem looked down, through pine forests, to the sea and towards Europe; to the east, towards the desert and Islam. Was there ever another city with two such faces? West Jerusalem, and the new suburbs to the east and south, were Jewish. East Jerusalem and the Old City were Muslim and Christian. Israel might have decided that Arab Jerusalem and the West Bank were separate, but this was a convenience of politics. The Arabs knew that they were not. So that when the Intifada started, Arab Jerusalem behaved no differently from any West Bank town. The stones and petrol bombs were hurled, whole areas of the city became risky for Jews to walk or travel in, and even the shopkeepers observed the strikes called by the rebels.

In order not to endanger Israel's claim to the city, firearms were scarcely used there against stone-throwers. The police and the Army kept order with tear gas and clubs, and occasional curfews in Arab districts, a military measure to which Kollek at first objected. But the truth was out. Jerusalem, 'united' by force, was kept together by force.

Outside police headquarters in the Russian Compound, Arab families squatted under the olive trees or on the steps of the Russian Church, waiting for the release or transfer of sons or husbands. All the police vans in town acquired wire netting across their windows against stones, and more people kept dogs for guarding or attacking. Jews stayed away now from the Old City bazaar, where Josh had bought rare stamps and I had wheeled Isaac as a baby. One night, while writing the book on Jerusalem, I had driven from a reception given by Jewish peace groups for Arab guests, straight to a 'security meeting' between the tenants of an outlying Jewish suburb, where the official 'absorption' office still had Russian placards, and the police. The talk among the intellectuals at the reception, over canapés and drinks in the suite of a smart hotel, was of 'co-existence'; in the bleak community centre, over tea-bags and dry biscuits, discussion focused on the absence of a local ambulance or fire brigade for emergencies, and the occasional stoning of buses from the centre of town. The second meeting had seemed to me then – it was, in fact – more real. Jerusalem was not Belfast or Beirut, but nor was it, alas, Kollek's 'pluralist' city.

It was during the year that I spent watching Jerusalem that Sarah ended her school career and joined the army. The very intelligent adolescents of the University High School knew exactly how shoddy were the myths of 'co-existence' with the Arabs and how incomplete the 'integration' of Sephardi Jews. In the satirical version of *Alice in Wonderland* which Sarah helped direct in her last term, the Old City was the local funfair where the spoiled children of Jerusalem's elite lived it up on Saturdays, shopping in the alleys and smoking narghiles. Sarah played Alice, a class-conscious Ashkenazi girl obsessed with status and academic success, patronizing Arabs, ill at ease with the working-class Sephardi Jews. In the last scene of the play, 'Alice' gets her come-uppance. Shorn of her airs and graces, she sits typing in an army office, snapping back coarsely at the arrogant officer who treats her like a waitress.

Sarah was more resourceful than her Alice, but her first weeks in the army, during basic training, sounded like English boarding-school life to me: ill-fitting uniforms, cold porridge for breakfast, square-bashing on the parade ground, bullying teachers, sanitary towels blocking the lavatories, and a snoring chorus in the dormitories. The only experience I could not parallel was her story of one of the few girls in her unit who was still a virgin; with her active consent, she was helped to puncture her hymen, using a brush used for cleaning rifles. For girls, serving in the army was, like boarding-school, 'character-forming'; you made friends, for however short a time, or perished of loneliness and misery.

At her first passing-out parade, I identified my daughter as the one girl among a thousand whose beret would not sit straight on her mass of curls, and who managed to march past with a look of resigned boredom.

Her second ceremony was more serious. Because of her perfect English, she was recruited to Intelligence, and sworn to secrecy 'even under torture'. Quite properly, my formerly talkative daughter, arriving home with her laundry and yet another bottled shade of hair-dye (a talisman against boredom, not part of her job), never breathed a word of what she was doing. Her commanding officer, fully one year older than she was, had been brought up in Hong Kong, and Sarah and he sang 'Rule Britannia' and English nursery rhymes between shifts, to the mystification of the Moroccan base-commander, who felt he was being teased. Sarah found her 'English' background a useful safety valve, and a defence. She tamed the young officer from the radio branch who courted her insistently by making him read Beatrix Potter, and solemnly recite 'This Little Piggy' and the dead-parrot sequence from Monty Python. Since she could manage a perfect cockney accent in English and a Moroccan one in Hebrew, it was perhaps a pity that she decided against a career either on the stage or in the Israeli secret service.

Whatever it was that she did in the recesses of her army base, she also had her stint of latrine-cleaning and guard-duty. There too, she would not be bullied. When a high-level contingent of officers arrived for a periodic inspection of the base without the usual permit, she refused to let them in until they had returned to their staff cars and radioed in to the base for clearance. 'If you think I'm going to risk seven years' jail for you,' Sarah informed the major-general, 'you're out of your mind.'

The Intifada began with a traffic accident in December 1987, when a Gaza car taking labourers to work in Israel collided with an army truck. The Palestinians thought it was deliberate on the soldiers' part; it was the labourers who died. But it did not matter, by now, how the violence started. The resentment and anger and frustration were too great.

About a week before that accident, I took an English visitor to Bethlehem to buy Christmas souvenirs: olive-wood animals from the manger scene. Bethlehem, with both Christian and Muslim Arabs, is only two miles south of Jerusalem. Just a few months earlier, I had heard the city's chief engineer tell Kollek that it was drawing customers away from the capital. Bethlehem was better appointed, he had said, the shopkeepers more courteous, the service better in the restaurants. The shops there imported goods the Israelis did not stock.

But now the shops were empty; the shopkeepers told us that business was bad. I felt, though my guest did not, that all our chance encounters were tinged with hostility. I had always found people there accommodating to the point of servility. If things had changed so much in Bethlehem, which was prosperous, where no violence had been reported, what was it like elsewhere? And so, with a revival of some of my old initiative, guiltily aware that I had shut myself away with books for too long, I joined the Israeli Association for Civil Rights as a volunteer. Within a few weeks the stone-throwing had become an epidemic, the military courts were bursting, the prisons were filling, and Palestinian deaths were rising day by day. No one was prepared.

The Association was a worthy, respectable, non-political organization with a distinguished roster of elderly judges at its head. It had over two thousand members, all but a dozen or so of whom contented themselves with paying their yearly dues. There were two full-time lawyers in the Jerusalem office, busy with monitoring censorship in the theatre, getting women on to religious municipal councils in the Negev, sponsoring secular burial, and a number of other creditable but scarcely urgent causes. It was about as ready for the uprising as a man with a bucket for a thunderstorm. Its spokesmen had made it clear that the Association was against deportations, administrative deten-tion, the demolition of the homes of security suspects, and other abuses of human rights. As the regulations in force in the Territories provided for all these things, this was whistling in the wind. The only weapon the Association possessed was that it could appeal to the Israeli Supreme Court, rather like running to the headmaster. This distinguished bench might have ruled itself incompetent to deal with matters of national security in the occupied territories, and stayed outside the human rights fray altogether. But it didn't. Almost inevitably, when appealed to during the Intifada, the Supreme Court had to weigh national security against the rights of individuals who were not even citizens of Israel. The outcome was predictable. But the queue outside the headmaster's office lengthened daily.

Soon the little office of the Association in Jerusalem was flooded with cases of the suspected abuse of firearms by soldiers, border police and settlers, and had become what was virtually a missing persons bureau for arrested men and boys, as the army pulled in hundreds of Palestinians. Within days, I could see that the political and legal obstacles to correcting abuses of human rights in the West Bank and Gaza were almost insuperable. Military rule of a subject population in revolt meant violence, and the end of human rights. The only solution was political. Everyone knew this. All the few volunteers could do was to witness some of what was happening, almost always after the event, and hope the lawyers could take action. Usually they couldn't. All I wanted to know, at first hand when I could, was what was being done in my name and my children's name – Sarah was in the army, Isaac was in his final years at school.

Having a daughter in the army during the Intifada meant that my perspective was slightly different from that of some of the other volunteers, and certainly from that of casual visitors or journalists. After a few weeks of the Intifada, many of Sarah's friends volunteered to serve in the security zone in Lebanon, where there was a very real danger of fighting heavily armed Palestinian or Shiite fighters, rather than put down civilian rioting. Palestinians attacked people in Sarah's unit, grenades were thrown and bombs left near her base – incidents never reported – and once, a petrol bomb was thrown at a soldier driving away from the base a few moments before her. I might be investigating a violent incident in a village from which men and boys had been stoning Sarah's friends.

I knew how resentful and furious she and her friends were with the politicians who had failed to find a way out of the conflict; with the settlers' provocations; with the soldiers brought to trial for the murder and beating of prisoners. But she defended the army as a whole. She saw my excursions in the Territories as a cause of amusement and concern. 'Don't think you can change anything,' she warned me. I didn't.

The most energetic volunteer in Jerusalem was Aharon Kempinski, an archaeologist who knew the West Bank well from his researches (he was debunking many of the myths settlers had attached to biblical sites), spoke Arabic, and was passionately convinced, as we all were, that the occupation was destroying the principles on which Israel had been founded. He had been trying to unmask abuses of civil rights for several years, and though he had been injured in a random stoning of his car a year earlier, on the main road near Hebron, this did not deter him.

When the Intifada had been in progress for a month, Aharon and I visited El Haq, a Palestinian civil rights organization which was keeping a record of every incident, in Ramallah. By this time, the rebels had ordered a general strike in protest against the occupation, and Israel's orders to the Army were to force the shops to open.

We took an Arab taxi from Jerusalem for the twenty-minute drive to Ramallah. Even Aharon now parked his car prudently in a side-street in West Jerusalem. All the way we could see the effectiveness of the strike from the shuttered shop-fronts both in East Jerusalem and on the main road. Save for one vendor of sesame rolls with his trolley, there wasn't a tradesman in sight. Arab drivers of cars with Israeli licence-plates took care to display red and white headcloths on the dashboard (when security agents began using this technique, it became scant protection; and when the Israeli police began entering villages in bread delivery vans, the bakers took cover).

In the centre of Ramallah, troops were forcing open the iron shutters over the shop-fronts with crowbars. Several shops had opened along the soldiers' route to prevent this happening. The main street was littered with rocks, glass, pieces of tin and roof tiles – evidence of a recent riot – and our Palestinian contacts kept tabs on our movements by telephone, warning us to keep out of one street, where a riot was in process, or to stay away from another, where soldiers were chasing demonstrators. Following the squads of soldiers breaking open the padlocks of the shutters, we saw, was a little Palestinian repair team, which removed broken padlocks and latches and replaced them as soon as the soldiers were round the corner. Once or twice they did so in full view of another squad of soldiers who looked on indifferently.

Months later, in Hebron, we witnessed the opposite procedure: soldiers welding shutters closed at hours when the rebels had ordered them to open.

We explained what we were trying to do, and asked for the co-operation of the El Haq lawyers. We needed affidavits from the victims of what looked like random or unprovoked shooting. But even on that first foray, I began to see how difficult it was going to be to bring anyone to account for the mounting death-toll. We wanted, that day, to find out more about the case of Kabil Hussein Musa, a sixteen-year-old shot in the back and killed by a local, very prominent Jewish settler, Pinhas Wallerstein, who maintained that he had acted in self-defence after his car was halted by a barrier of stones and he himself was stoned. Our enquiries, first from the lawyers and later the family, indicated that the boy had been running away when shot. But a year later, Wallerstein, though eventually charged with manslaughter, was still at liberty, while thousands of Palestinians, many of whom had never been tried, were in jail. By then, it was clear that settlers who argued that they were acting in self-defence were usually given the benefit of the doubt; any Palestinian caught up in a riot was not.

The Palestinian lawyers, from the outset, were sceptical about taking cases to the Israeli courts. Mona Rishmawi, our contact, was outspoken. She thought, wrongly, that the settlers were immune from prosecution. 'Cases like these may be useful in influencing Israeli public opinion,' she said, 'but I don't think they're any use to us.' She saw us as satisfying our own consciences, and obviously, although El Haq was sometimes helpful, the Palestinians had no interest in helping the Association present the 'human face' of Israel. They knew that as a respectable body headed by ex-Supreme Court judges and law professors, the Association had more chance of winning a case than radical lawyers like Felicia Langer. But their political interest was complex: while they wanted to influence public opinion in Israel, and the rest of the world, the worse Israeli behaviour was, the better for the Palestinian cause. The Palestinians were not concerned with Israel's conscience; they wanted them out of the Territories.

Doctors who came with us to the El Mukassad Hospital on the Mount of Olives agreed that the rioters had been shot at very close range by rubber and plastic bullets, or by ordinary bullets. At first the Palestinians insisted that they had been shot by 'dum-dums' – bullets whose casing had been deliberately cracked to fragment inside the body – but after we found doctors willing to examine the X-rays (which was not simple), that charge at least was retracted. But by that time, anyone who threw a stone did so at the risk of his life. It was difficult to see those damaged bodies, sometimes wrecked for life, and believe that this was the price of Israel's survival, as many people had convinced themselves.

Innocent people and children were wounded and killed because the riots almost always took place in alleys or winding narrow streets, or in densely built-up town areas where stray bullets could easily penetrate windows and doors. The instructions on when and how to open fire became increasingly detailed – and irrelevant. Even tear gas, and the canisters containing it, could be lethal to unborn children or old people, if fired at close range. In one village, I met two members of the same family, neither of whom, I was sure, had been rioting. One of them, a young man, was knocked down twice on his way to work as a waiter in a Jerusalem hotel by a Border Police jeep which had fractured his pelvis. The police involved insisted that the driver had lost control of the jeep on a slippery road during a stoning. When I visited the village, I recognized the waiter's mother; her daughter, a young married woman, had lost a kidney when a tear gas canister had hit her in the back. We tried to persuade the family to sue for damages; but nothing happened.

It was hard to get people to sue, often even to testify, because this was a form of collaboration with Israelis, recognition of their authority. The Palestinians were also afraid of retaliation. The Border Police, in particular, had a foul reputation. They were a paramilitary force recruited mainly from Jewish working-class families, and from the Druse minority traditionally hostile to Sunni Muslims.

One check of mine on the Border Police proved farcical. I was asked to go, on a Saturday morning, to Issawiya, a village to the east of Jerusalem, to look at damage the villagers claimed had been done the previous night by 'the army'.

Villagers from Issawiya, officially part of Israel, had been throwing stones since the beginning of the uprising, but they were unpopular with the police for other reasons. An illegal printing press had been found there, producing the rebels' leaflets, those instructions for the Intifada that Israel could not suppress. It was also the home of many members of Ahmed Jibril's Popular Front, one of the most extreme Palestinian groups, men liberated in an ill-judged swap of one thousand Palestinians for three Israeli soldiers some years back.

But I knew another side of life in Issawiya. Like every Arab village in the Jerusalem area, its roads and sewage system were primitive; so here, as elsewhere, the municipality had provided the mukhtar with pipes and building materials and had the villagers do the work themselves. A considerable number of the houses in the village, with its growing population, had been built without a permit, as the ministry involved had held up building plans for the Arab areas for years. Inspectors turned a blind eye to illegal structures, especially when they belonged to people who were not security suspects.

We entered the village by a narrow side-road. At the point where the road curved into the village, to where it ended in a field near the school, the damage was obvious. Windows of most of the houses on the street had been smashed. The ground-floor windows were protected by grilles, but individual panes had been smashed and upper windows shattered in what had clearly been a rampage. Something had been thrown through the window of one house which had set the curtains on fire; the tenants had extinguished the blaze but the curtains were charred. I noticed small pieces of plastic with Hebrew lettering on the floor and picked them up. I could see Israeli Army insignia and the words INFLAMMABLE MATERIAL. At the end of the road, near the school, a car belonging to one of the villagers had been vandalized.

The villagers did not deny that they had been demonstrating, and that the Border Police had ordered them, days earlier, to take down black flags flown in mourning for Abu Jihad, the PLO leader assassinated in Tunis some days earlier. They had also ordered them to clean the anti-Israel slogans off the walls with whitewash, a pantomime which went on steadily throughout the Intifada. But the slogans I saw on the village walls were all in Hebrew, obviously written by Israelis: *Zion Square* and *Arabs Out*.

I sent in a report next day. Foolishly, I enclosed the fragments of plastic which my daughter's army friends had identified as part of a flare. The police responded promptly – which was very unusual; investigations of beatings and killings could take months. We were, they said, the dupes of PLO propaganda. The damage we had seen had been caused by the villagers themselves, when stoning the army patrol. Some weeks later, municipal bulldozers, backed by a police detail, demolished several illegally built houses in that village.

At first, the army kept the roads open – where barricades and stones menaced the free passage of army patrols and settler commuters – but soon they moved into the villages. I heard of several cases in which the mukhtars told the army that they could keep order if the army stayed out. But that would have meant Israel 'losing control' of a village, admitting defeat. So that what followed were 'initiated actions', in which a village was selected for disciplining (for stone-throwing, slogan-painting, flag-flying) and a search for suspects. The result was always the same; the patrol was met with a hail of stones, often they opened fire, and injuries and deaths often followed. Whether or not the soldiers shot to kill depended on the officer in charge. At one notoriously rebellious village, a young man told me, 'Some of the soldiers come to do their job and don't shoot wildly. Others come just to kill, and the slightest provocation is enough.'

As the Intifada continued, our journeys developed their own bizarre rules. We travelled in Arab taxis between the towns; and to villages, in private Arab cars with Palestinians whom we knew. The ground-rule was not to travel on strike days (announced by the 'Leadership of the Uprising' – a faceless body which continued to function despite the imprisonment or deportation of suspected leaders) because then crowds of men normally employed in Israel would be on the streets. The rebels, dependent on the enemy for their living, went to work one day and rioted the next. Travelling through the West Bank with Palestinians was to feel almost invisible, whereas when, a couple of times, I drove in Israeli cars, I felt vulnerable. It was hard to believe that these were the same roads I had travelled in my own car, alone, a few years earlier. In Arab cars, I began to look fearfully at Israeli soldiers, with plastic visors and machine-guns, in their jeeps, and even more fearfully at the settlers, with their skull-caps and guns slung over their shoulders. But the same soldiers might be Sarah's friends, and the ragged boys who clustered round us in the villages were 'the enemy'.

You could see whether the army had been along the road recently from the flags and slogans on display. The signs of defiance reappeared within hours, even after confrontations which had ended with deaths. Villages declared their 'independence' by flying the Palestinian flag, high on an electric cable, or from lines strung across the village streets. Some were roughly patched together, mere rags; others were made of silk. In each village, its affiliation was clear from the graffiti on the walls, which had reappeared above the successive coats of whitewash. A glance told you whether the village was Fatah, or the Islamic Hamas movement, or both in rivalry. Stone barriers were cleared just enough to allow village cars to circulate, making it easier to replace the barrier if the army reappeared. There were the gaps where houses had been dynamited, little Red Cross tents sometimes replacing them. If the settlers had been through, there were Stars of David on the shuttered shop-fronts on the main roads, or *Arabs to Arabia*, or just *Transfer!* When the flags were gone, the colours could reappear anywhere: on a rock by the roadside, or on the palms of schoolchildren who flashed them mockingly at the Israelis. It was a battle of wills; and it was a macabre game.

The Association's lawyers visited the courts to observe the conveyor-belt system by which stone-throwers were tried. Pending these trials, rioters and sometimes 'administrative detainees' – people arrested for civil disobedience, banned political activity or other forms of rebellion – were held in detention camps. Five months after the Intifada started I went to Gaza to visit such a camp, nicknamed 'Ansar 2' (Ansar 1 had been a prison camp Israel set up in South Lebanon).

I hadn't been to Gaza for years. We had to leave our cars at the checkpoint at what used to be the Israeli frontier and go into town by an Arab taxi sent by a Palestinian activist. Five minutes out of Israel proper, with its cottages and fields, we drove into chaos. The area bordering the wide main road was covered with sand, stones, charred tyres and plain rubbish – municipal services were on strike. The buildings here were one solid wall of protest. What idiocy, I wondered, made Israeli generals think they could bury the uprising under layers and layers of whitewash?

Outside the military headquarters in Gaza, the British Taggart police fort, hundreds of people were waiting – standing, squatting, sitting – for the redistribution of identity cards: a new measure aimed at marking off the 'passive' Gazans from those with a record of disorderly conduct. The reissue also served to help check on the payment of taxes or customs duties. The 'tax revolt' was beginning (again, I remembered Ottoman rule) – in part a campaign of civil disobedience, in part the result of the poverty of people whom the repeated curfews had cut off from their main source of livelihood in Israel.

From the police fort we were taken by a soldier to the Ansar camp on the seashore. Here again, in the big open area near the entrance, hundreds of people, relatives of the prisoners, were gathered. They were waiting their turn for attention from half a dozen scribes sitting at tables with old-fashioned typewriters, filling in application forms for visits to relatives in the camp, or other official requests. I hadn't seen petition scenes like this since my visit to India.

I had read up the 'Standard Minimum Rules' for prisons, only to find them irrelevant. Ansar 2 looked like any other army camp, save that beyond the perimeter fence were other fenced-off enclosures, within which prisoners lived under canvas, about a score to a tent. When we came in they were chanting prayers. Gaza was heavily influenced by the Islamic movement, encouraged earlier by Israel as a counterweight to the PLO; ironically, it was to prove far more militant. The Koran was the only book I saw in the camp. Other prisoners were held in what were army storerooms, about ten feet square, windowless, with gates (no doors) the only source of air and light. There were other much smaller rooms, no more than cupboards with ventilation holes over iron doors: these were the *tsinuk*, or punishment cells, for solitary confinement, where prisoners causing trouble could be kept for up to a fortnight.

We were royally received with food and 'army whisky' – apple juice and tea – but treated as foolish civilians with no real idea of the army's tough assignment. Our briefing was terse: all the prisoners had been arrested for rioting and violence, detained for four days with the option of extending the period to eighteen days. Those charged were then tried in military courts; if they did not admit the charge, they would be held indefinitely until trial. Prisoners in 'administrative detention' (for which there was no need to bring them to trial) were transferred to a camp in the Negev. Minors and adults were held separately; copies of lists were sent to the Red Cross, which notified the families. Any questions?

We wanted to know precisely what we knew they would not tell us: how and where the preliminary interrogations were carried out, during which no lawyer (in cases where one had been enlisted) had access to the prisoner. This was not the job of soldiers, but of the Shin Bet, the security services, and all the complaints of brutality in prison that we had heard of related to what went on during those first hours and days. But no, we couldn't see the interrogation cells (save on the map on the office wall); no, we couldn't talk to the interrogators. Yes, the questioning could go on for days. At a stretch? No clear answer. What were conditions like in the interrogation cells? 'Different.'

We were allowed to visit the prisoners in the main camp, and to ask questions. The first man we spoke to, weary-looking and middle-aged, told us that he had been in Ansar for twenty-one days awaiting trial and had a family of seven dependent on him. The charge, to which he had not admitted, was flying the PLO flag and belonging to an organization hostile to the State. He said he had been taken to three separate army camps after his arrest, and beaten at each.

Here we had trouble. Among our group was an Israeli Arab lawyer and an Israeli accountant who was 'security-conscious'. They quarrelled over the nature and order of the questions. The two began shouting at one another as the prisoners looked impassively on. The army officers intervened. 'Hey, fellows, you can't do this! We don't argue in front of the prisoners! Think of the impression you're making!'

There were plenty of prisoners for everyone, but eventually the Arab lawyer left, incensed at his colleague's interference, and we went on to question the boys, the minors in the camp.

They were all in one big cell, twenty-three of them, eager to talk – though it was difficult to tell whether they were complaining or boasting of their ill-treatment during interrogation. Aged between twelve and eighteen, they had been held for periods up to five months without being put on trial; those who had finally come to court were left here to serve out their terms (none was longer than a few months) as it was presumably not worth transferring them to jail. Only one had seen a lawyer, and few had seen their parents since their arrest. Few denied that they had been throwing stones, and the most serious offender – who readily agreed that he had thrown a petrol bomb – was defiantly cheerful. You could tell that they were torn between pride at having attacked armed soldiers (one showed the scar from a bullet wound in his leg) and the hope of getting out earlier. Only one boy, who looked younger than his age (officially thirteen) and had arrived the day before, looked apprehensive. All said they had been ill-treated, though that ill-treatment ranged from slaps or blows with brooms to being made to stand in the sun all day.

The only boy who looked thoroughly unable to handle the role of freedom-fighter was a fifteen-year-old wandering freely about the camp. One of the Association's lawyers had told us she thought him mentally deficient, and asked us to see if he could be released. The soldiers were adamant that he had been medically examined and that there was nothing wrong with him.

Muhammad Naim refused to answer a single question, though he sometimes glanced at us obliquely. I could have sworn that he was just a desperate and wretched child in a child's pit of despair. When I questioned one of the officers further, he said that Muhammad had been turned in by his own father, who said that he had been throwing stones. I learned later that in large families, the father would sometimes bargain with the army to release a breadwinner in exchange for another son less important to the family. Poor Muhammad was such a boy.

I asked an officer on what evidence were the men arrested? Most were nabbed on the spot, others in their homes on the basis of 'prior information'. That left a wide margin for the settling of family and clan feuds to decide who went into Ansar and who stayed out. One of the officers assured me that 'every incident was filmed and the film examined'. He must have thought me a prize idiot. Every report I had read or heard indicated that the patrols ran into riots, very often, by accident. Or had the Israeli Army turned into a film company?

Finally we visited a cell full of adult prisoners, so crowded that there was no room to move between the mattresses. Only five of the thirty-three men there would speak at all, to ask for help, or legal aid. Some had been there for weeks, but not one had seen a lawyer. One said he would be released if he paid a fine of about a thousand pounds, but he could not afford it. We were again told what the boys had already made clear; those who confessed got lighter sentences.

In this cell, I saw for myself a young man who had been beaten after his capture, according to his account, by the Border Police. They had broken his right arm and left leg, and left him with massive subcutaneous haemorrhages over his left side and back. His limbs had been set and he had been sent straight to the camp, four days earlier. We asked the camp doctor why he had not been kept in hospital for further treatment, and he answered breezily, 'Oh, I always think patients are much better off at home.'

I wrote a report on Ansar, suggesting that since the Gaza lawyers were on strike, leaving such prisoners to their fate, Arabic-speaking lawyers in the army reserves might take on some of the cases, particularly those of the children. We had heard that a Druse lawyer, serving in the army, had released tens of prisoners in a matter of weeks, to the camp commander's relief. But the response was that the army had not the manpower, nor did the framework exist.

The defence of Palestinian clients who could pay high fees, unlike the prisoners we had seen in Gaza, proved a profitable source of income for a number of Israeli lawyers, both Jewish and Arab. A few radical left-wing lawyers did such work for political reasons.

When the Association circularized ten thousand Israeli lawyers, asking for their public condemnation of administrative arrests, the demolition of houses, deportations and other abuses of civil rights, one hundred and fifty responded. Whereas, after a year, doctors and teachers in Israeli unions came out in protest about Palestinian health conditions and the closure of schools during the Intifada, the Israeli Bar Association, those concerned with the rule of law, did not. Only a handful of lawyers, like our own volunteer Shlomo Lecker, took on Palestinian clients for nominal fees, despite all the obstacles and defeats, for the sake of the work itself. I thought they kept Israel's honour alive.

As we hadn't enough volunteers to chase after every incident, we had to find test cases. The most important opportunity came with the terrible Beita incident. A fanatical settler, leading children on a 'hike' near this West Bank village, took them into a crowd of stone-throwing villagers. He shot two Palestinians dead and then, by accident, one of his charges. This took time to establish, and during the hysterical aftermath of the event, the army, under pressure from the settlers, blew up fourteen houses in the village and planned to demolish more. It was Aharon who insisted that the Association – despite the fact that it was a Saturday – alert the Supreme Court, which ruled that no more houses in Beita should be destroyed without prior notice and the chance of a judicial appeal. But it took the Supreme Court a year more, by which time a total of over two hundred homes had been destroyed, finally to rule on the Association's further petition and agree that all demolitions should be subject to appeal. By this time, as we knew from our own observations, many of the houses that were being destroyed belonged to relations of the man or boy who had thrown the stone or bomb; it was not just the homes of the offenders. The politicians might think this was a 'deterrent'. The Palestinians believed that it was part of a concerted plan to make them homeless.

The Intifada, which had begun as a spontaneous outburst of despair, continued as a political rebellion. The Palestinians tried to cut themselves off from Israeli authority, even while many of them still commuted to work in Israel. They refused to pay taxes, tried to grow all their own food, and organized classes for their children (the schools, seen as 'focuses of unrest', were closed by the army for an entire year). Palestinian universities, which had been set up under Israeli rule, were also closed by the military government. Even the merchants, who had been the most cautious and complaisant of the Palestinians, obeyed the instructions on the rebels' leaflets, closed and opened their shops according to the instructions of the 'Leadership'. If they didn't, they risked finding the shops burned down the next morning.

In Jerusalem, the police threatened to arrest the shopkeepers and try them on charges carrying a penalty of up to two years' imprisonment. Kollek, to my amazement, took the police's part, in the interests of 'law and order'. The deadlock was neatly solved when the 'Leadership' changed the hours of mandatory opening to those recognized by Israel.

People said it was a war. And, in war, you couldn't sympathize with the enemy. But to me, it wasn't a war if one side had guns and the other knives, axes, stones, petrol bombs. There were even reports of confiscated swords; I hadn't seen men carrying swords since Bengal.

For ten months the civil administration held up permission for a clinic to be opened for the rehabilitation of men and boys paralysed as a result of being shot during rioting. It seemed a simple issue, but nothing was simple. The Palestinians did not expect Israel to help with the clinic; they appealed for funds and expert help abroad. When I started probing, I uncovered a morass of suspicion and fear. Israel was afraid that funds brought in for one purpose would be used for another. Israel did not want foreigners meddling in the West Bank and Gaza. Each side accused the other of playing politics with human lives.

For years, Israel had prided itself on the health care it had given the Palestinians, the specialized treatment for the chronically ill, the insurance schemes. Anyone who had spent time in an Israeli hospital knew that this was not an empty boast. But with the Intifada all this crumbled. Within less than six months from the beginning of the uprising, the intake of patients who could not be treated in Arab hospitals dropped by eighty per cent. In meetings with doctors, Palestinians and Israelis burning with outrage, we learned of children with leukaemia, heart complaints and other illnesses who were no longer being treated. 'You boasted of how well you treated us when we were passive,' said a Palestinian doctor. 'When we showed we wanted independence, it all vanished.' 'They were dying off like flies before we came,' said a Jewish specialist volunteer indignantly. 'Twenty years of work down the drain,' said an Israeli paediatrician.

Letters to the Minister of Defence from the Israeli National Council for the Child received the answer that treatment in

Israeli hospitals was 'a humanitarian gesture, not a right', and that the denial of services was the result of the tax revolt. One argument contradicted the other, but fortunately this was an issue on which the Israeli public, blind to so much else, was sensitive; rabbis, Knesset members and doctors complained and the treatment of the serious cases was resumed.

The Palestinians harangued the Israelis, the Israelis were angrily defensive. The Israelis preached to the Palestinians, the Palestinians reacted with accusations. These were the 'dialogues' I sometimes attended. Yet it was remarkable that these meetings took place at all, between two peoples struggling over the same land.

In Bet Sahour, a village south-east of Bethlehem, a young man had been killed in a confrontation with the army. Here there were many highly educated Palestinians, and the villagers were among the first to start self-help committees, an 'alternative economy'. One of the residents was the Dean of Bethlehem University, a Christian Palestinian, who had tried to organize his own market garden without a licence. He was sent to a detention camp in the Negev under 'administrative arrest' – six months' jail.

When we arrived, in two Israeli cars, we were ushered across the village street in groups of three. Any larger gathering, we were told, was illegal. The discussions, with doctors, accountants, teachers from Bir Zeit, were fruitless. Both sides repeated official arguments. End the violence, said the Israelis, you've made your point. Call off your soldiers, stop the shooting, said the Palestinians. One Israeli tried to explain that Israeli soldiers could not refuse to serve, that the army was the people. But the Palestinians, who had no army, were unmoved. A young Russian immigrant told the Palestinians that she knew what it was like to be a member of a minority, that she sympathized with their plight. The Palestinians were not impressed: they had seen many Russians among the settlers, and couldn't understand why a family from Leningrad should be given a home in the West

Bank while a Palestinian was imprisoned for growing his own tomatoes.

Later we went to visit the professor himself, just released from jail. His splendid villa, lights ablaze, was the scene of a reception: all detainees were visited in celebration when they were released. The ban on gatherings of more than three did not seem to be in effect on this side of the road, and a passing patrol showed only a routine interest in the party. Our host was passing round small pieces of olive wood patterned in black – made by detainees using their fingernails, he explained; it was their main form of recreation. Very few books were permitted in the camp, apart from the Koran. George Orwell, naturally, was banned.

Another time I joined a much larger group on a visit organized by Peace Now to the village of Nahalin. This was the scene of a recent incident, in which the Border Police had killed five men and injured forty-two. As a result, two officers were transferred and others reprimanded.

This time, too, we travelled in Israeli buses and cars, ambassadors of goodwill, or, in the eyes of the settlers who threatened reprisals, a bunch of traitors. Our number included left-wing Knesset members, philosophers and Arabists from the university, kibbutzniks, young American Jews studying conflict resolution. As we rushed past villages and refugee camps, the Peace Now signs taped to the doors of our cars, many Palestinians stared, smiled, made V signs and waved. Others scowled or looked puzzled. No wonder; one day the Israelis came through with jeeps and guns, the next with peace placards, in straw hats and sandals.

When the first cars reached the village, boys came out with stones, ready to attack the army escort; the village elders hurried after them, waving their arms to stop. As the army wouldn't let us into the village (the argument was that they couldn't let the settlers in either) we talked in the road, or in little groups under the olive trees.

The Border Police had provoked them, they said, had shouted obscenities; tens of villagers had been wounded; the police had stopped a car with a dying man inside. What did the Israelis want of them? What would the army do to them, one villager asked me, when we left?

Another young man was literally shaking with passion, tears of rage in his eyes. He couldn't move an inch outside the village, he complained, without being harassed, accused of stone- and bomb-throwing, even when with his children. Faced with so many silent listening Israelis, some uncomfortable, some sceptical, he ranged from grievance to grievance.

'Suppose,' he said, buttonholing one man, 'suppose your family is in Iran and you're here, wouldn't you worry? That's how we are, one in Jordan, one in Kuwait, one here, all split, all dislocated.' He pointed to the new settlements going up all round, prim little red-roofed chalets on the hills to every side. 'All land taken from us, from our fathers. What should I do, where should I go? To Jordan? I couldn't speak freely there,' he said, suddenly illogical. 'It's shit,' he said, 'shit living here, shit all the time.'

He patted the head of a small Israeli boy, standing near with his father, asked if he was happy. The boy, aware guiltily that this might be the wrong answer, glancing at his father, admitted that he was.

'I'm not,' said the Palestinian, 'I'm in shit.'

'But look, we're here, listening,' said the boy's father.

'Then something's wrong, isn't it?' said the villager.

Other Israelis were offering the Palestinians contradictory advice. Take what the Israelis are offering, limited autonomy, said one. Don't take it, it's just a trick to keep you quiet, said another. Don't confuse them, said a third. It was like the argument in the Ansar camp. One young Arabic-speaking Israeli was trying to get two blank-faced youngsters to tell him who the village leaders were, the Intifada heads. We don't know, and don't want to know, they said. I told the organizers I thought we had a provocateur among us. For God's sake, don't spread that around, they said, we'll all start suspecting one another.

A new immigrant from Odessa was explaining earnestly to a crowd of dumbfounded villagers, 'I've been here a year and a half, but I'm not staying; too many problems.'

A crowd of black-clad women came down the hill from the village – the mothers and widows of the dead men. One of the younger women took the megaphone. 'We feel we can negotiate with Israelis like you. The problem is your Government, the people who rule us all, they're killers and terrorists. We've made concessions, we're willing to live in our own state next to Israel. But if the Government refuses, there will be more Intifada until the whole country is liberated.' There were angry murmurs from the Israelis, which grew when she asked how people who had suffered from the Nazis could become oppressors themselves. At this point the organizer took her megaphone away. Such comparisons were not helpful, he said.

'You see, they really do want it all,' said someone near me.

'Let them want,' shrugged another, 'they won't get it.'

Suddenly one of the Palestinians spotted a tall grey-haired man among the Israelis. They embraced. The Palestinian was a building worker, the Israeli a contractor. What with curfews, and strikes, they had not met for months. Not even the news that the contractor was involved in building one of the nearby settlements discouraged the villager. 'If you're here,' he said, 'and you're in favour of compromise, then there's hope.'

Two days later the paratroopers staged a raid on Nahalin, crawling across the hills at dead of night. Later I went back with a few others to check on whether this had discredited our visit. The mukhtar's son, a teacher, laughed. 'They've released most of the men already,' he said. 'It was the taxes they were after.' His small daughter came in carrying tiny cups of tea with mint leaves, stared at us, whispered to her father. 'She asked if you were Jews,' he said pointedly. 'I said you were, but she said you couldn't be. Jews come with guns, in the night.'

The conflict between settlers and Palestinians worsened. In revenge for stoning incidents, and sometimes just to provoke, settlers stormed into villages shooting and vandalizing. In the

Hebron area, someone sprayed the Arab vineyards of two villages with poison.

Worst of all, the revolt turned in upon itself, the solidarity which had characterized the uprising began to collapse. Palestinians suspected of collaboration with Israel were murdered by their own people. Some were stripped and hanged; some axed or knifed to death, one teacher in front of his young pupils. Luckier victims, including one family I knew, had their houses or shops torched. Our informants told us that many such murders were old clan feuds, a settling of scores.

As fewer Palestinians were prepared to risk their lives in Israel's pay, the Shin Bet, the security service, changed its methods of recruitment. Students seeking permits to travel were told this was conditional on bringing back information. People whose papers were not in order were blackmailed, threatened with deportation if they didn't become informers. I helped deal with one such case. One abuse created another. The two peoples were locked in a cycle of violence and repression.

One of the most dangerous of the Palestinian 'punishment squads' against suspected collaborators came from Idna, a village to the west of Hebron. Hiding in the hills and in caves, they managed to elude the army for over a year, murdering and marauding, until a final shoot-out one morning in which an army officer was killed, as well as all of the three-man squad. The death of a soldier was rare and the whole village was punished. Curfews were imposed, electricity and water cut off, every car confiscated and returned only after the payment of the villagers' taxes. We heard that the killers' families were being victimized as well, and went to investigate.

A reliable escort was supposed to come to Hebron to accompany us, but he never appeared. Instead, the Hebron Graduates College provided us with a guide, a Muslim sheikh who was writing an account of the 'martyrs of the Uprising'.

Idna lay on a hillside approached through a long valley. At the entrance to the village was a heap of stones, and nearby a boy lounged at the roadside. One whistle from him, we learned, would have brought every boy in the village on to the road in a concerted attack. The boy had once demanded a shekel of every Arab driver, money which went to buy petrol for the bombs hurled at army patrols and settlers' cars.

The village was a huddle of winding streets, full of blind corners, sudden drops on to rock, and spaces where houses had been dynamited. There were few men about. Ironically, many still worked in the fields of Israeli farms just over the old border. But there were adolescent boys everywhere, and I was relieved that they seemed to recognize our driver.

The killers had belonged to the leading Tamisi clan, and we visited one of the widows and her mother-in-law. The widow had lost her home, dynamited by the army, and was living in a borrowed house. We were received in a room bare but for thin mattresses spread on the floor, bedding rolled on shelves. For months, the widow said, she had not seen her husband. After the shoot-out, the army had taken the bodies of her husband and his brother, and buried them somewhere in a 'closed military zone'. Funerals of men like this became occasions for demonstrations, so often were held at night, with only the family allowed to be present, but to remove the bodies to an unknown grave was the harshest punishment of all.

Unlike many homes of relatives of 'martyrs' that we visited, there were no photographs on display here. Our lawyer had an Israeli newspaper-cutting about the incident, and the widow spotted it. It carried a photograph of two bodies lying in the road, by a bullet-ridden car; to me they looked like two heaps of old clothes with shoes attached, but to the widow this was, apparently, the only surviving photograph of her husband. She asked for a copy, and proudly showed it to her children. That, she said, pointing to one heap of clothes, was your father, the hero.

Her mother-in-law, who had lost two sons, and whose husband was still in hiding, mimed her experiences for us with grim humour. She showed us her certificate of imprisonment for a month in Jerusalem, under interrogation; the well in the courtyard destroyed by grenades; and a cellar where she said she had been held for nights. But she would not testify to the harassment for fear of reprisals, and our lawyer said that the confiscation of the family orchards, and their destruction, was 'legal'.

In another village we visited, Tsurif, the mukhtar's son had been shot in a riot; his photograph, a certificate of martyrdom, hung in the reception room. All over the West Bank, such photographs were displayed like graduation documents.

On our way back to Jerusalem, we found ourselves behind two army jeeps carrying soldiers, baby-faced, with sub-machine-guns, helmets, plastic visors. Suddenly I realized that Isaac, in a year's time, might be serving here, looking just the same. If he travelled the route we had taken that day, crowds of boys like those we had seen earlier would taunt him and throw stones and petrol bombs. How would he react?

I remembered a young teacher, a company commander, who had claimed that on four successive terms of duty in the West Bank, his company had still not killed a single Palestinian. 'But I don't know about the fifth,' he had said. 'Not a day on service passes without our doing something which is against our conscience.'

When I told Sarah about Idna, and the widow, she responded sharply. 'What about those soldiers they kidnapped, whose bodies were never found? Their families have no graves to visit either.'

Two soldiers had indeed recently disappeared, of a dozen kidnapped on roads in Israel and the Territories. One body was found later in a shallow grave yards away. The other was never found.

One of our Palestinian contacts, Y, was a boy of Isaac's age. He was employed in an office in Israel and spoke fluent Hebrew, far better than many Israeli immigrants. His father, who had a shop in Hebron, also had Israeli friends, and when 'collaborators' began to be punished his shop was burned down. Y looked so much like an Israeli that he could travel on Israeli buses without arousing suspicion, listening calmly to settlers discussing the expulsion of the Palestinians. Rather like my escort during the seventies, Bashir, Y clearly took pleasure in playing the chameleon. In a sense, he was outwitting the enemy. But I worried about him. It would only take a challenge one day from a policeman for him to be in danger of a beating, or worse.

I asked Y what he would do when the conflict was settled – both of us pretending that this was indeed inevitable.

'Go back to school,' he said with a grin, reminding me of his age.

While Y was commuting between Jerusalem and Hebron, Isaac, in his last year at school, was off on a school visit to Poland, to the sites of the concentration camps and the Warsaw Ghetto. The message was, of course, that the Jews were only safe in Israel. The Arab states, and the Palestinians, it was implied, threatened that safety. But Isaac, when he heard of the settlers killing Palestinians, exploded angrily, 'Why don't they blow up *their* houses then?' How would he manage in the army, with sentiments like these?

In Caspi Street they were closing in our view: of Government House to the south; of the Mount of Olives to the east. No view is permanent. The houses opposite went up slowly. Each curfew, each fresh incident, meant that the Arab building workers failed to appear. The subcontractor, arriving in his Mercedes, went into hysterics, tearing at his sparse hair, screaming of the millions he was losing. A few young boys who did turn up clambered about with buckets, pasting stones crookedly on to the ill-finished concrete frame.

The new houses also blocked what had once been the children's free passage to the wadi and the young forest below – a forest exactly the same age as my Israeli-born children, who had been sent certificates of saplings planted in their names.

Now the wild hillside, with its rosemary and thistles, where the shepherds of the Farouk hamlet had pastured their goats, had been made into a public park with paved paths, pergolas, and public lavatories. Isaac, who had loved the wadi, its wildness and its silence and its caves, looked on sadly. It was no longer his private territory, but it drew crowds of strollers every Saturday: families with kites and dogs to exercise, and new immigrants – Ethiopians and, suddenly, almost as soon as they appeared on the newsreels, Russians in old-fashioned hats and mufflers. It was a reminder that Israel was still the only sanctuary for Jews, and a reminder on our doorstep.

The Shack people were long gone, rehoused, replaced by a small garden. Surprisingly, I almost missed them. They had been part of the temporary, improvised quality of our lives. I was afraid, above all, of permanence; of repression hardening into habit. An English friend who as a young serviceman had witnessed the turmoil of post-war Europe, wrote sympathetically of what he called 'the troubles of a time of transition'.

I hoped that he was right.

JERUSALEM, FEBRUARY 1990

Index

Abu Ghosh, 15
Abu Jaleh, Saleh, 110–11
Abu Jihad, assassination of, 197
Afula, Galilee, 57
Allon, Yigal (Allon Plan), 114–15, 149
Altman, Al, 16–17
Ansar 2 detention camp, Gaza, 199–203
Anwar, agronomist, 110, 111–12
Arbel Hills, 34
archaeology, 32–3, 34, 60
Argov, Shlomo, attempt on life of, 167
Ashdod, 49–62, 63, 65, 166
Ashkenazi, Motti, 136
Ashkenazi Jews, 55–6, 60, 65, 66, 126, 127, 188, 189
Aswan Dam, 154
Athens, 36, 37
Auschwitz, 37–8
Avdat, Negev, 65

bar mitzvah, 68, 73, 160–3, 176, 179
Bashir, Israeli Arab, 109–10, 111, 213
Bedouins, 14, 30, 109, 111, 117, 160
Beersheba, 43, 50, 149
Begin, Menachem, 62, 157, 158–9, 165, 168, 172–5, 176
Beita incident, 204
Beirut: Israeli siege and bombardment of, 167, 170, 171; Sabra and Shatilla camp massacres, 172–3
Ben Gurion, David, 21, 65, 86, 105, 116, 131, 136; and Lavon Affair, 87, 88, 89–90, 97
Ben Gurion Airport, 74, 94, 159
Ben Yehuda, Netiva, 28–9
Ben Zouzou family, 122, 123, 124, 125, 127, 128
Bene Israel (Indian Jews), 65, 66

Bet Sahour, 206–7
Bethlehem, 100, 110, 111, 190–1
Black September massacre (1970), 109
Blessing of the Sun ceremony, 163–4
Border Police, 195–6, 197, 203, 207, 208
Borges, Jorge Luis, 103
Buber, Martin, 20
Budapest, 41–2

Cairo, 'The Fiasco' in (1954), 87–8, 90
Camp David Accords (1978), 159–60, 165
Chanuka celebrations, 137, 138–9, 180
charity, 79–80
childbirth, 90–3, 115–20, 145
Children's World Kindergarten, 137–40, 169
circumcision, 54, 73
Confino, Michael, 38, 41
contraception, 29
Copts, 16, 17
Cranston, Helga, 45, 49, 46, 59–60

Dajani, Suleiman, 103–4
Davar (Labour newspaper), 88, 97
Day of Atonement, 4, 129, 130
Dayan, Moshe, 83, 90, 99, 102, 115, 131, 136–7, 158–9
Dead Sea, 27, 43
Dead Sea Scrolls, 85
death ceremonies, 73, 74, 93–4, 158
Democratic Movement for Change, 158
development towns, 44, 45, 46–9
Diaspora Jews, 25–7, 68, 80, 83, 115, 145, 152, 163, 165
divorce and separation, 77–9
dogs, stray, 125–8

Dolci, Danilo, 18
Dome of the Rock, 182
dugri relations, 28–9

Eden, Sir Anthony, 10
education, 19–20, 21, 24, 58–9, 60–1, 83, 137–8, 152–4, 164
Egypt, 87, 88, 115, 154–5; Camp David Accords, 158–60, 165; Six Days War, 96–9; Yom Kippur War, 131, 134, 136–7
Eichmann trial, 26
El Ansari, Fahmi, 105–7, 184
El Ansari, Sheikh Judah, 106
El Haq organization, 193, 194
El Mukassad Hospital, 195
Eleazer, 27
elections, Israeli, (1977) 157–8, 165; (1981) 163, 176
Eliash, Pnina, 20
Elkins, Mike, 98
employment, 51–2, 55–6, 61–2
Eshed, Haggai, 97
Eshkol, Levi, 86, 88, 96, 99, 114, 115, 131
Evenari, Michael, 65
Exodus (film), 17, 185

Farouz, Lebanese singer, 102
Fatah, 169, 198
Feast of Weeks, 152
Feld, Hans, 166
'The Flower of Cities' (song), 102
Freeman, John, 81
Friej, Elias, 110
Fuld, Bracha, death of, 25

Galilee, 22, 23, 29, 46, 48, 57, 63, 94, 95, 96, 147, 149, 153
Gardner, Helen, 8
Gaza, 148, 160, 181; Ansar 2 camp, 199–203; Intifada, 190, 192, 199, 205; orthodox Jewish settlement, 163; Palestinian refugee camps, 103
Geva incident (Eli Geva), 171–2
Ginsburg, Zvi, 174–5
Givat Ram campus, 136
Givat Shaul, 130

Golan Heights, 30, 47, 131, 132, 133, 136, 140
Great Crater sculpture garden, 65
'Greta', 117
Grunzweig, Emil, murder of, 174
Guri, Haim, 170
Guy, Philip, 132

Habima, national theatre, 43
Hadassah Hospital, 90, 91, 92–3, 115, 116–20, 164, 169
Haifa, 50, 87, 148, 169
Hammermesh, Mira, 132, 134
Hartman, Geoffrey, 34
Hasidism, 16, 17, 59, 63, 64–5, 68, 162
Hebrew language, 4–5, 19, 27, 46, 53, 59, 69, 84, 111, 121, 150, 159
Hebrew University *see* Jerusalem
Hebron, 102, 109, 114, 149, 182, 194, 210, 212
Hefer, Haim, 60
Henly, Nurse, 92
Herzl, Theodore, 3
Hirbet Minye, 33, 34, 35
Hirsch, Jacob, 75, 79, 80, 163
Hirsch, Solomon, 75–7, 79–80, 163
hitch-hiking, 43–4
Holocaust, 26, 79, 94, 153
Horns of Hittim, 34
hospitals and health care, 90–3, 115–20, 195, 205–6; religious, 76–7
Huleh valley, 30, 45–6
Hungarian Jews, 121, 123, 125, 127, 132
Hungarian Crisis (1956), 10
Hussein, King of Jordan, 14, 96, 109, 110, 149
Hyman, Jonathan, 133

Idna village, 210–12
immigrant absorption, 46
India, trip to (1977), 154, 158
Indian Jews, 65, 66
Intifada (Palestinian uprising), 180–2, 187, 190–213
Iran, trip to (1977), 154–7
irrigation/water conservation, 65, 71, 113, 154–7; *kuze* pot technique, 156, 157; *qanat* system, 156

Index

Isaac, (Naomi's son), 115, 120, 124, 128, 137, 151, 179, 180, 192, 213
Isaacs, Jeremy, 169
Islamic Hamas movement, 198
Israel, Wilfrid, 165, 166
Israel Bonds, 16
Israel Electricity Company, 55
Israel Museum, Jerusalem, 84–6
Israel Philharmonic Orchestra, 100
Israeli Air Force, 96, 98, 171
Israeli Army, 17, 33, 61, 95, 105, 130, 132–6, 137, 140, 172, 176–7; casualties, 133–4, 140, 170, 173–4; Geva incident, 171–2; Intifada, 180–2, 190–212 passim; Lebanon War, 167, 170–1; PoWs, 140–4; women recruits, 84, 165, 188, 189–90, 192
Israeli Association for Civil Rights, 191–212 passim
Israeli Bar Association, 203
Israeli-Christian Lebanese entente cordiale, 170–1
Israeli Supreme Court, 191, 194, 204
Issawiya village, 196

Ja'abari of Hebron, Sheikh, 110
Jaffa, 147
Japanese, 16–17
Jenin, 148
Jericho, 102, 148
Jerusalem, 12–17, 28, 44, 45, 48, 65, 76, 84–6, 100–9, 111–29, 137, 148, 149–52; Abbysinian St, 16, 17, 18, 28, 35; Al Aqsa Mosque fire, 106–7; bazaar, 101–2; bomb explosions, 108, 169–70; Caspi St, 120–8, 130, 132, 149–52, 157, 164, 213–14; Grete Asche Pension, 16; Hadassah Hospital, 90–3, 115, 116–20, 164, 169; Hebrew University, 12–13, 19, 24, 43, 82, 107; Imperial Hotel, 103, 104; Israel Museum opening, 84–6; Israeli Annexation, 103–9; Jaffa Rd, 14, 70, 76, 96, 108; Kollek's administration, 184–8, 205; Mahane Yehuda street market, 72; Mea Shearim quarter, 16, 17, 76, 128, 180; Moghrabi quarter torn down, 101; Old City, 13, 15, 86, 94, 101–2, 128, 129, 187, 188,
189; Sadat's visit to, 158–60; shelling of (1967), 98; Arabs in, 15, 184, 187–8, 189, 193, 204–5; Wailing/Western Wall, 101, 107, 128, 161, 162, 179; West, 15, 102, 108, 193
'Jerusalem of Gold' (song), 101, 102
Jewish Agency, 44, 45, 47, 51, 54, 104
Jewish New Year, 3, 73, 172
Jewish Sabbath, 14, 15, 68, 74, 77, 165, 179, 180
Jewish 'underground' trial (1984), 182–3
Jibril, Ahmed, 196
Johnson, Paul, 98
Jones, Mervyn, 103, 136
Jordan, 14, 21, 88, 94, 114, 167; Black September massacre (1970), 109
Jordan river/valley, 35, 113, 114, 149, 154
Josephtal, Giora, 68
Josephus, historian, 27
Joshua (Naomi's son), 90–1, 92, 104, 106, 132, 134, 135, 137, 150, 151, 152, 153, 160–3, 176–8, 179, 188
Judaism, 21, 72–5, 76–80

Kadishai, Yehiel, 174–5
kappara ceremony, 72
Karameh reprisal raid, 109
Kassit, Tel Aviv, 30
Katowice, 36, 37
Katsav, Moshe, 47–8
Kempinski, Aharon, 192–4
ketuba (marriage contract), 70
Khomeini, Ayatollah, 156
Kibbutz Ginossar, 30, 31, 35–6
Kibbutz Hazorea, 165–6
kibbutzim, 21–3, 32, 33, 46, 47, 48, 57, 61, 65, 75, 81, 83, 86, 112, 113, 149, 164
Kidan, Aharon, 96, 134
Kidron, Mickey, 50, 95
Kinneret cemetery, 23
Kiryat Shmoneh, 45, 46–9, 57, 166
Kissinger, Henry, 136
Knesset, 75, 82, 136, 158, 160, 168, 206, 207
Kollek, Teddy, Mayor of Jerusalem, 85, 101, 184–8, 190, 205

Kransdorf, Moshe, 75

Labour Party, Israeli, 24, 40, 47, 62, 74–5, 83, 86–90, 97, 114, 167; election defeats, 157–8, 163, 176; 10th Congress (1965), 88–90
Lake Galilee, 23, 29, 30, 31, 35–6
Langer, Felicia, 194
Lascelles, Mary, 7–8, 9, 20
Lavon, Pinhas, 88, 89
Lavon Affair (1965), 87–90, 97, 114
Layish, Yehuda (Naomi's husband), 67–72, 73, 77–8, 80–1, 86, 95, 96, 97, 98–9, 108, 116, 122, 125, 127, 130–1, 132–3, 134–6, 137, 140, 150, 151, 153, 158, 161, 162, 167, 169, 170, 175–7, 179
'Leadership of the Uprising', Palestinian, 198, 204, 205
Lebanon War (1982), 158, 166–8, 170–7
Lecker, Shlomo, 203
Leibowitz, Yeshayahu, 20–1
Lenin, V. I., 29, 36
Levenberg, Alisa, 46, 48
Lichtblum, Shmuel, 158

Malkin, Sarah, 40
Mapam Party, 36
marriage, 70–2, 74, 77–9, 80–1
Masada, 27–8
'Maurice', Casablancan Jew, 57–8, 60, 61, 62
Mehta, Zubin, 100
Meir, Mrs Golda, 90, 115
Mendilow, Adam, 21, 101
Meron, spring pilgrimage to, 63–4
Milhem, Mohammed, 110
'Miriam', Moroccan, 56
Mitnagdim, 59
Mixed Armistice Commission, 94
Moore, Foot, 74
Moroccan Jews, 52–3, 55–6, 57–8, 60–1, 62, 63, 64, 65, 66, 91, 118
'Motti' (sabra technician), 55
Mount Carmel, 2
Mount of the Beatitudes, 30
Mount Scopus, 20
mukhtars (Arab clan leaders), 23–4

Musa, Kabil Hussein, murder of, 194

Nablus, 103, 109
Nahal Oz farming settlement, 95
Nahalin, 207–9
Naim, Muhammad, 202
Nasser, President Abdel Gamal, 87, 88, 96, 97, 98, 99
Nathan, Shuly, 101
National Water Carrier, 35
Negev, 65–6, 86, 95, 147, 191, 200, 206
Nes Ziona, 57
New Statesman, 81, 82, 97–8, 103, 109, 110, 136
'Nira' and 'Yossi', 118–20
Noguchi, Isamu, 85, 86
North African Jews, 12, 15, 46, 50–61, 62, 63, 65, 91, 117

Ohayon, Mr, 122, 123, 124, 126–8
Orthodox Jews, 16, 17, 75–80, 117, 128–9, 163, 164, 180, 184, 185
Oxford University, 5–9, 19, 69, 166

Palestinian Arabs, 14, 15, 23–4, 75, 79, 83, 100–15, 117, 123, 147–51, 159, 164, 169; Beita incident, 204; health care, 205–6; informers, 210; in Jerusalem, 184, 185, 186, 187–8, 193; Lebanon War, 166–7; punishment squads against collaborators, 210; refugees, 103, 112–14, 149; Sabra and Shatilla camp massacres, 172–3; tax revolt, 199, 204, 206; uprising (Intifada), 107, 172, 180–2, 187–8, 190–213
Palmach, 15, 17, 28, 60
Paris, 10, 18, 19, 81, 170
Passover, 75, 76, 77, 94, 164
'Peace for Galilee' campaign *see* Lebanon War
'Peace Now', 207; demonstrations, 169, 172–4
Peres, Shimon, 90
Perrot, Jean, 34
Phalangist Christians, 167, 170–1; Sabra and Shatilla camp massacres, 172–3
pikuah nefesh (saving of lives), 74, 130

Index

Pins, Jacob, 17
Pliny, 27
PLO, 168, 197, 200, 201
Poland, 37, 38, 213
Polish Jews, 38, 50, 65, 68–9
Popular Front, Palestinian, 196
pork, consumption of, 75, 165
Preminger, Otto, 17, 185
'primitives', 52–4, 62

Rabani, Bezalel, 30–5, 44, 50
Rabani, Tirza, 31, 32, 34, 35
rabbinical courts, 77–9
Rabin, Yitzhak, 157
Rachel (Naomi's daughter), 115, 116, 118, 119
Ramallah, 111, 148, 193–4
Robertson, Bryan, 85
Romanian Jews, 50, 54, 60
Rome, 10, 18, 81
Rose, Billy, 84, 85
Rothschild, Dave, 15
Russell, Bertrand, 3
Russell, John, 85

Sabra and Shatilla camp massacres, 172–3
sabras (Israelis born in Israel), 24–5, 26, 28, 55, 68, 75, 117
Sabri, Sheikh Ikrema, 107–8
Sachs, Arieh, 19–20, 102–3
Sadat, President Anwar, 131, 136; Jerusalem visit of (1977), 158–60
St Mary's Paddington, Lindo Wing, 90–1, 92–3
Sali, Baba, 163
'Sami', Palestinian Arab, 117, 118
Scholem, Gershom, 20
Safed, 65
Sarah (Naomi's daughter), 137, 138, 139–40, 150–1, 153–4, 162, 188–90, 192, 212
Sde Boker Kibbutz, 65
Sephardi Jews, 56, 60, 62, 63, 64–5, 79, 157, 188
sexual relations, 28–9
Shack people, 121–8, 132, 150, 151, 180, 214
Shaftesbury, Lord, 183

Shagrir, Aliza, 170
Shagrir, Micha, 158
Shalit, Yael, 169
Sharett, Moshe, 89–90
Sharon, Ariel, 167, 168, 170, 171, 173
Shemtov, Victor, 168
Shenson, Lennie, 18
Shin Bet, security services, 200, 210
Shitrit, Meir, Mayor of Yavne, 62
Shmuel, Polish Jew, 56
Shukeiry, Ahmed, 89
Sinai, 133, 134, 135, 136, 164; Israeli withdrawal from, 159, 160
Sinai Campaign (1956), 33, 95, 98
Six Days War (1967), 89, 96–9, 103, 104, 106, 131, 134, 141, 176, 181, 184
Smith, Terence, 132
Sokolow, Nahum, 3
'Soldiers Against Silence', 173
Somerville College, 6–9
Soviet Jews, 32, 38, 39
Soviet Union, trip to (1960), 36–41
Stalin, Josef, 36
Steinsaltz, Rabbi Adin, 107, 161
Suez crisis (1956), 10, 141
suicide, 27–8
Syria, 30, 81, 88–9, 96, 132; Israeli PoWs held by, 140–4

Tabgha hospice, 30–5
Talmon, Jacob, 20, 115
Talmud, 27, 76
Tel Aviv, 15, 25, 30, 36, 43, 48, 49, 57, 62, 67, 68, 86, 87, 112, 131, 140, 147, 148, 159, 168; mass rallies in, 168, 173; Quarter of Hope, 77
Territories, occupied, 103, 113, 114–15, 146, 148–9, 172, 191, 192, 194, 212; see also Gaza; West Bank
Teveth, Shabtai, 131
Thody, Philip, 19
Tiberias, 32, 33, 35, 44, 82
Tomalin, Nick, 132
Topol, Haim, 95
Torah, 79, 162
Touashi, Tova, 71, 104–5, 133–4
transit camps, 44, 46, 77
Tsurif village, 212

U Thant, UN Secretary-General, 96
University *see Jerusalem*
University High School, 164, 188

Vietnam War, 82, 83

Wadi Ara, 48
Wallerstein, Pinhas, 194
War of Independence (1947–9), 15–16, 94–5, 114
Warsaw, 36, 38
Weizmann, Chaim, 3
West Bank, 102, 103, 109–12, 113, 117, 148, 163, 165; Beita incident, 204; orthodox Jewish settlements, 80, 113, 163, 165, 169, 180; Palestinian uprising (Intifada), 172, 180–2, 187, 190–213; trial of Jewish terrorists (1984), 182–3

Ya'akov (Tova's son), 105, 133–4
Yadin, Yigael, 158
Yamit, 160
Yavne, 27, 28, 62
Yehoshua, A. B., 25–6
Yehuda (Naomi's husband) *see* Layish, Yehuda
Yeruham, Negev, 65–6, 166
Yesh Gvul (There's a Limit), 173
Yiddish, 56, 68
Yochai, Simeon Bar, 63, 64
Yom Kippur, 4, 72, 73, 180
Yom Kippur War (1973), 115, 129, 130–44, 160, 171, 176

Zamir, Yitzhak, 182
Zinder, Heizi, 60
Zionism, 2, 3, 21, 26, 38, 83, 159, 170, 183